IMAGES
of America

BEAR CREEK VALLEY

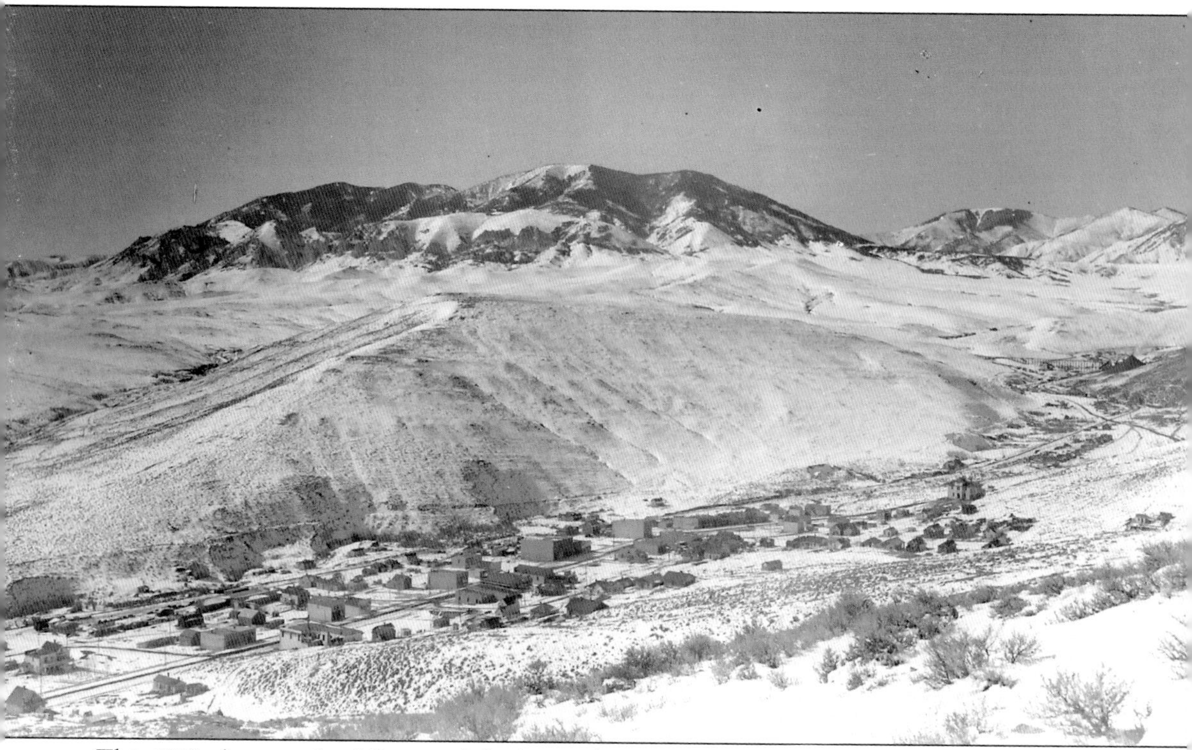

This 1917 photograph of Bearcreek looks south toward the western city limit. Mount Maurice dominates the background. Foster Gulch (left) joins Bear Creek Valley at the eastern edge of town, just out of frame. The white, two-story Bearcreek Elementary School marks the town's western city limit (lower right). Farther west, the slack piles of the Bear Creek Coal Company Mine are evident in the distance. The mine's trestle extends across the valley toward the mountains. Near this trestle, Scotch Coulee joins the valley from the base of Mount Maurice. The valley winds westward for several more miles before reaching the town of Washoe and the high ridge separating it from Red Lodge. Virtue Gulch (not shown) joins the valley from the north, roughly halfway between the city limits of Bearcreek and the Bear Creek Coal Company Mine. (Planichek.)

ON THE COVER: Mary Mourich, like so many others in Bear Creek Valley, dedicated herself to preserving and sharing its history. Mary and her extended family were longtime residents of Scotch Coulee. She displayed her photographs and historical documents each year at Red Lodge's annual Festival of Nations celebration. Her notes on the original version of this photograph read, "Yugoslavian tradition included a Bearcreek-Scotch Coulee tree party. This party was held in the fall of the year at harvest time. Starting with bunches of wrapped grapes as ornaments, other items such as money, embroidery work, and other items of value were added as decorations. These items were then sold at the end of the festival and the proceeds given to charity." (Mourich.)

IMAGES
of America

BEAR CREEK VALLEY

Jeff McNeish and the
Carbon County Historical Society

ARCADIA
PUBLISHING

ISBN 978-0-7385-7041-9

Published by Arcadia Publishing
Charleston, South Carolina

Printed in the United States of America

Library of Congress Control Number: 2009921919

For all general information contact Arcadia Publishing at:
Telephone 843-853-2070
Fax 843-853-0044
E-mail sales@arcadiapublishing.com
For customer service and orders:
Toll-Free 1-888-313-2665

Visit us on the Internet at www.arcadiapublishing.com

To the people of Bear Creek Valley—past, present, and future—and to all those working to revitalize it today.

Contents

Acknowledgments

I remain humbled by, and grateful for, the generosity and support of the many people whose assistance, historic preservation efforts, and donations of photographs made this book possible. I would like to thank Donna Madson, Carbon County Historical Society executive director, and the good people of Arcadia Publishing, particularly my editor John Poultney, for providing me the opportunity to tell this story. For sharing not only their photographs and memories of this wonderful place, but also their friendship, I thank Sam and Jessie Mourich (Mourich); Bob and Jeanne Wakenshaw (Wakenshaw); Frank and Linda Planichek (Planichek); Shirley and Dick Garcia (Garcia); the John Indreland family (Indreland); Pearl DeVille (DeVille); Cy and Beverly Murfitt (Murfitt); Dick and LuDon DeVille; Dennis Burns (Burns); Mitzi Fredlund Vorachek (Vorachek); Clement, Terry, and Randy Lodge (Lodge); Art Kidwell (Kidwell); Betty Waters; the Carbon County Historical Society (CCHS); and the Montana Historical Society. A special thank-you to Tom Egenes (Flash's Photography) for his donation of photographs and for continuing his parents' work by preserving a lifetime of Carbon County photographs through his family-owned business, Flash's Photography (www.flashs.com). To Debra Hronek, Carbon County Historic Preservation officer, and historians Jon Axline and Joan Brownell, my eternal thanks for supporting this project and making my dream of placing the Smith Mine on the National Register of Historic Places a reality. I am forever indebted to Steve Robbins—friend, author, and all-around good guy—for his patient assistance and hours of proofreading. In teaching this mathematician the finer points of grammar, Steve proved true the words of Henry Ward Beecher: "Good-humor makes all things tolerable." For their constant support I owe an immeasurable debt to my family and friends: Stephanie, Duane, Kayli, and Collyn Hons; Jason McNeish and Kim Arnold; Jon, Christy, Justeen, and Aurora McNeish; Alex Hamman; Bill Cenis; Bob Webber; Cathy and Dan Wiltgen; Galen Hronek; Susie Robbins; Penny Redli; and Tressa McGregor. For instilling in me a love of family and place, I thank my parents, Jack and Barbara McNeish. For her unwavering support and love, I thank my wife, Tami McNeish.

INTRODUCTION

The foothills of Bear Creek Valley roll out of the Beartooth Mountains and into the high prairie of southern Montana east of a steep ridge separating the valley from the town of Red Lodge, Montana.

The valley encompasses four large, converging gulches and one creek with a smaller tributary stream. On the valley's southwest side, Scotch Coulee runs in a northeasterly direction for 3 miles before turning directly east. Bear Creek, namesake of the valley and its only surviving town, begins in the Beartooth Mountains and flows along Scotch Coulee, through the town of Bearcreek, and joins the Clarks Fork River near the town of Belfry, Montana.

The Keucking Creek (pronounced "Kicking") Drainage starts near the top of the steep ridge at the valley's western border. It runs directly east for 2 miles before merging with Scotch Coulee at the point where the coulee turns sharply east. Keucking Creek flows past the old town of Washoe and empties into Bear Creek. Over the decades, the name Keucking Creek slowly fell out of use, and this small stream now goes nameless, or is referred to as Bear Creek as well.

On the valley's northwest side, Virtue Gulch runs in a southeasterly direction for 2 miles before uniting with the valley a half mile east of where Keucking Creek merges with Bear Creek. Another one-half mile east of this point sits the town of Bearcreek, the smallest incorporated town in Montana.

Foster Gulch, the valley's fourth large geographic feature, runs parallel to the northeasterly portion of Scotch Coulee and completes Bear Creek Valley by joining with it at the eastern end of the town of Bearcreek.

Apart from the ruins of the Montana Coal and Iron Company's Smith Mine along Keucking Creek, Bear Creek Valley offers only fleeting and easily overlooked hints that, for six decades, this now-rural terrain sheltered Montana's largest industrial coal-producing area. Few clues remain to indicate the hundreds of miles of abandoned tunnels that lie beneath its hills and valleys.

Reclamation efforts and time have erased the slack piles and coal-processing plants of six corporate mining companies and more than a dozen privately held or "wagon" mines. The tracks, water towers, and turntables of the Montana, Wyoming, and Southern Railroad have been removed. Old roads connecting mines and communities now only remain as faint scars on open cattle ranges.

Hundreds of local houses, once home to more than 3,000 residents, have been moved to neighboring towns or destroyed. In its heyday, the valley housed immigrants from Scotland, England, Ireland, Wales, France, Belgium, Germany, Czechoslovakia, Austria, Slovenia, Serbia, Croatia, Montenegro, Finland, Norway, and Sweden, but local traces of these settlers' transplanted traditions, cultures, foods, and languages have almost disappeared.

The once thriving company town of Washoe has been reduced to roughly a dozen homes and one new commercial establishment, the Washoe Quilt Shoppe, which occupies the original Washoe Coal Company Mine office building. The shop proudly displays a sign in front reading, *Washoe Business Loop*. The town's school, post office, general store, pool hall, baseball field, and doctor's office have been all but erased.

Two mine complexes owned by the Washoe Coal Company, a subsidiary of Marcus Daly's Anaconda Copper Company, have vanished. Its Company Row neighborhood remains as only a memory. Neighboring enclaves between Washoe and Bearcreek, bearing such colorful names as Caledonia, Cousin Row, Scotch Coulee, Horseshoe Bend, Chickentown, and Stringtown, have also faded away.

West of Keucking Creek's intersection with Bear Creek sits the most complete group of industrial ruins in Bear Creek Valley. This assortment of buildings, named the Smith Mine, were once owned and operated by the Montana Coal and Iron Company. In 1943, this mine claimed the lives of 75 men in Montana's deadliest coal mining accident in history. Of all the mining operations once housed in this valley, the Smith Mine is the one surviving coal mine in the region; perhaps this is fitting.

When the coal mines shut down, so did much of Bearcreek. Missing from Main Street are the mercantile and dry good stores, union hall and banks, bars and bakeries, a co-op store, a furniture store, and butcher shops of the past. Lost to time are such icons as the Lamport Hotel; the Happy Hour Theatre, where silent movies were shown; Little Joe's confectionery; and Dr. John Carl Frederick Siegfriedt's home and hospital. The old community swimming pool now serves as a residential basement. The twin baseball fields anchoring the east and west ends of town have both disappeared. The elementary school has been torn down, as has the high school and its gymnasium, the home court of Montana's state basketball champions. The terms *Hi-Bug* and *Uptown*, once the recognized names of distinct Bearcreek districts, are today used by only a few longtime residents.

Today, though coal mining has largely left the area, efforts are underway by concerned citizens and institutions to revitalize this valley. Agriculture and spillover tourism from neighboring Red Lodge drive the economy of today's Bear Creek Valley. New businesses and homeowners are rediscovering the area. After years of decline, the town of Bearcreek is active and growing again. Two businesses and the post office remain in the once-booming business district along Main Street. The popular Bear Creek Saloon and Steakhouse occupies two original town buildings (formerly the homes of the Union Market store and the Bearcreek Bar). Just down the road, the Hungry Bear Café occupies one former site of the Bearcreek Post Office. The town's original sandstone bank building still stands, and it now serves as city hall.

With this welcome new growth has come the risk of losing the area's unique past. Fortunately, thanks to the work of local citizens, work is underway to prevent this from happening. Already, the Smith Mine complex has been placed on the National Register of Historic Places, and Bearcreek's original bank building, now housing city hall, has been renovated and restored to its original condition.

It is hoped that by illustrating the history of Bear Creek Valley—the coal mines, the people and their immigrant cultures and neighborhoods, the businesses, and the community builders—this book will play some small role in its revitalization.

One

Beginnings

Coal made Bear Creek Valley possible. It was first discovered locally in 1866 on the Red Lodge side of the steep, narrow ridge dividing the Bear Creek and Red Lodge Valleys.

By 1888, the Rocky Fork and Cooke City Railroad completed installation of a spur line from the Northern Pacific tracks in Laurel to Red Lodge, and the development of the Red Lodge coal field began in earnest. The Bear Creek Valley remained largely untouched, though prospect entries driven in the valley had proved extremely promising. In 1892, the Geological Society of America pointed to the lack of transportation into the valley as the only obstacle to the area's rapid development.

In 1905, the Montana, Wyoming, and Southern Railroad (MW&S), a privately owned short line, overcame this barrier by constructing tracks from the Northern Pacific Railroad in Bridger, through the town of Belfry, and on to the end of Bear Creek Valley.

Constructed incrementally beginning in 1905, the MW&S reached the Washoe Coal Company Mines in 1909. During these four years, a flurry of large-scale coal development began in anticipation of the coming transportation.

With the arrival of the coal mines came miners and their families, all of whom needed places to live. This need led to the incorporation of the town of Bearcreek by surveyor George T. Lamport and his son-in-law Robert Leavens in 1906. The company town of Washoe was established by the Anaconda Copper Company's Washoe Coal Company subsidiary a year later.

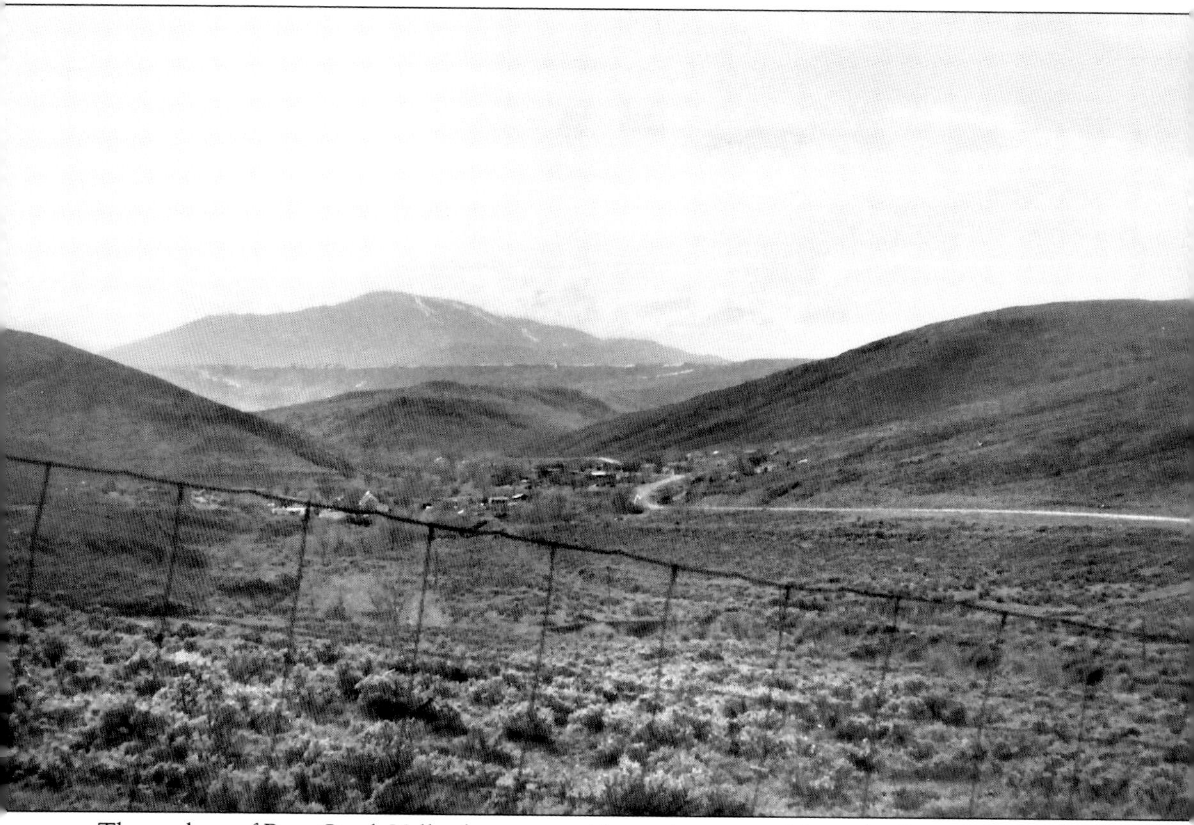

The geology of Bear Creek Valley becomes evident when viewed from the Bearcreek Cemetery. From behind two hills flanking the town of Bearcreek (center), the valley is comprised of the Keucking Creek, Scotch Coulee, and Foster Gulch drainages (left) and Virtue Gulch (right). Scotch Coulee, not visible here, joins Bear Creek Valley from the south several miles west of the town. Foster Gulch is also out of frame, to the left, in this photograph. The Keucking Creek and Scotch Coulee drainages form the southern half of a distinctive "V" shape, while the Virtue Gulch drainage forms the northern half. At the end of the Keucking Creek Drainage sits the town of Washoe. In the far distance, the high ridge separating Bear Creek Valley from Red Lodge is visible as is the Red Lodge Mountain Ski Resort on the distant mountain peak. (CCHS.)

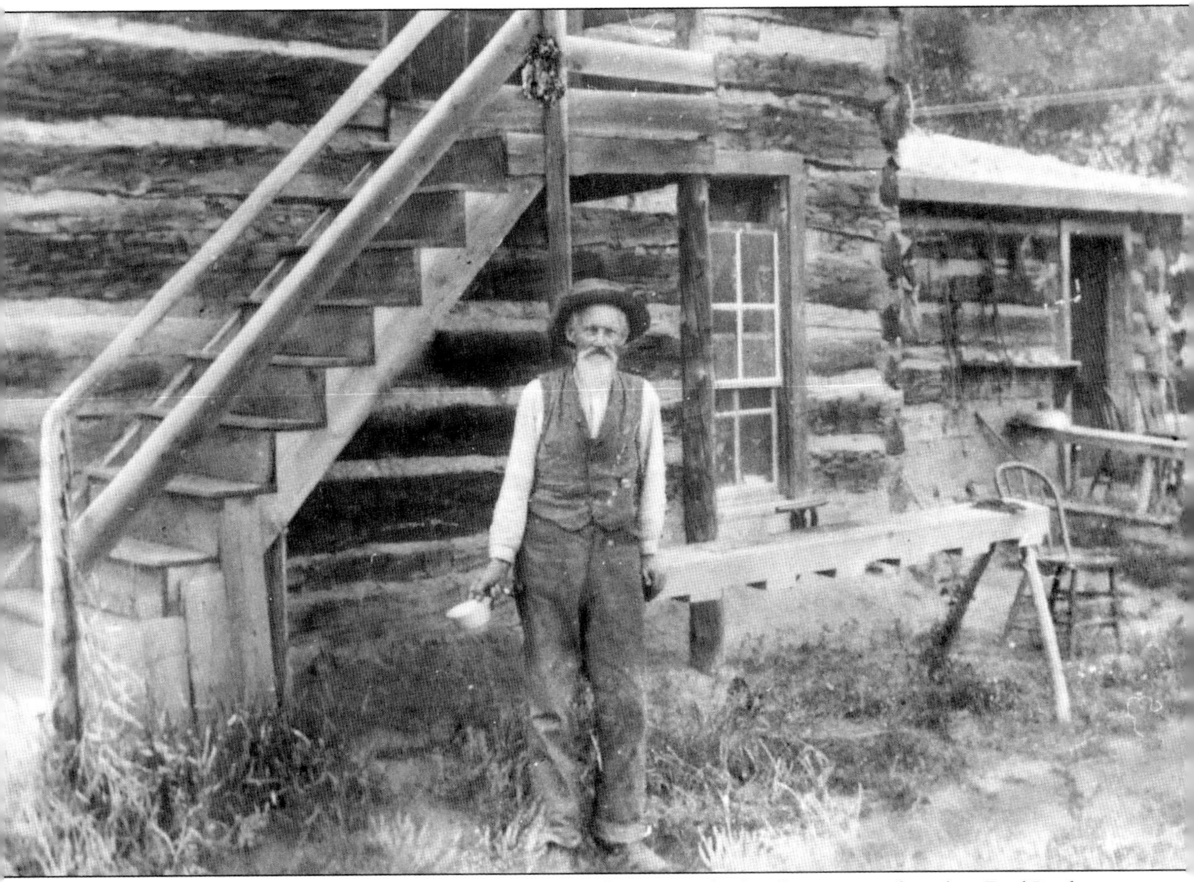

The history of coal production in Carbon County began with the discovery of coal in Red Lodge Valley, over a ridge and to the west of Bear Creek Valley. Gold miner James "Yankee Jim" George (above), born in 1835, discovered coal in Red Lodge Valley sometime in the 1860s. Active coal mining in this valley began in the late 1880s, and production in Bear Creek Valley followed a little more than a decade later. The famous author Rudyard Kipling wrote of George, "Yankee Jim saw every one of my tales and went fifty better on the spot. He dealt in bears and Indians, never less than twenty of each; had known the Yellowstone country for years, and bore upon his body marks of Indian arrows; and his eyes had seen a squaw of the Crow Indians burned alive at the stake." (CCHS.)

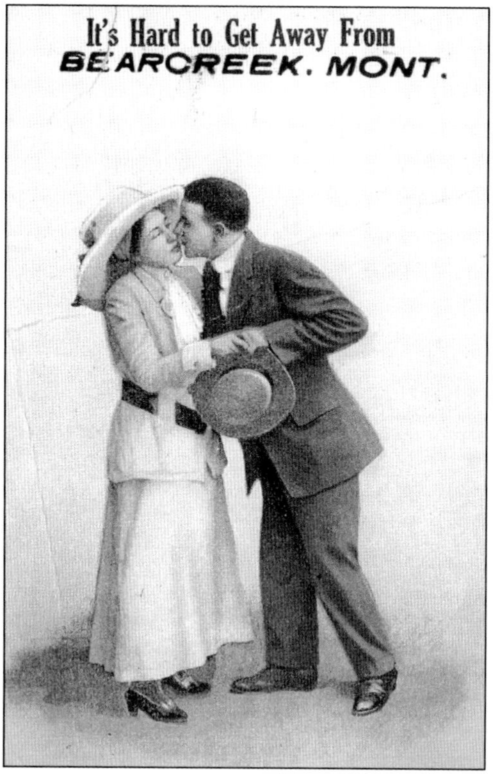

The sentiments expressed on this 1912 postcard from Adam Wakenshaw to his wife, Mag, are felt by Carbon County residents today. It is difficult to go anywhere in Carbon or the neighboring Montana counties without meeting someone who grew up in, or has direct ties to, Bear Creek Valley. (Wakenshaw.)

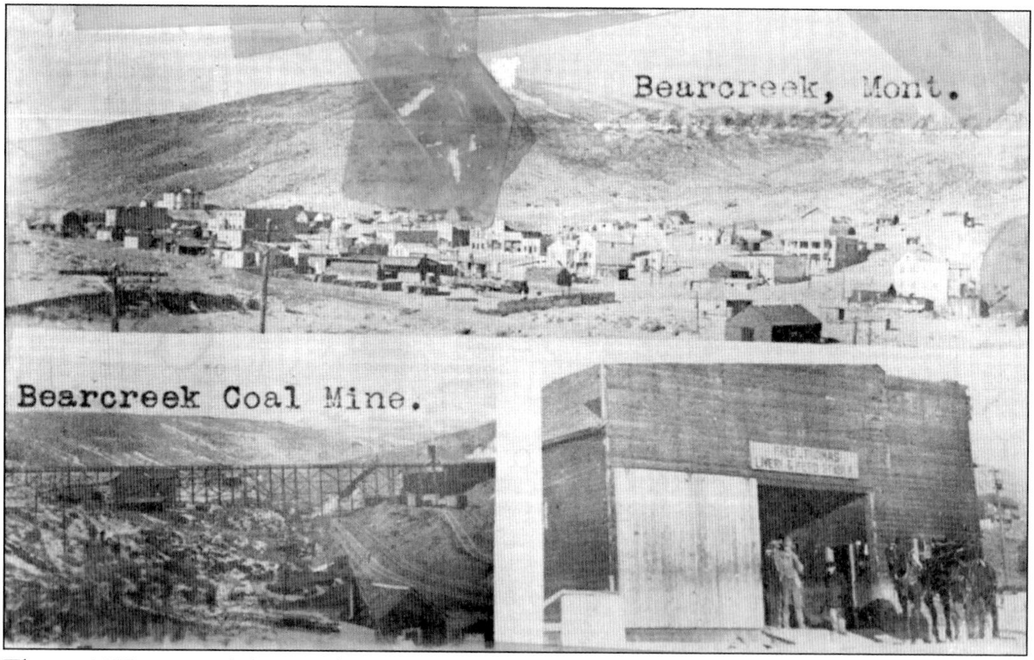

This *c.* 1915 postcard depicts three early Bear Creek Valley scenes. At the top is the western half of Bearcreek, viewed from the south. The Bear Creek Coal Company Mine is shown on the lower left. The Fred Thomas Livery and Feed Stables complete the collage in the lower right corner. (Murfitt.)

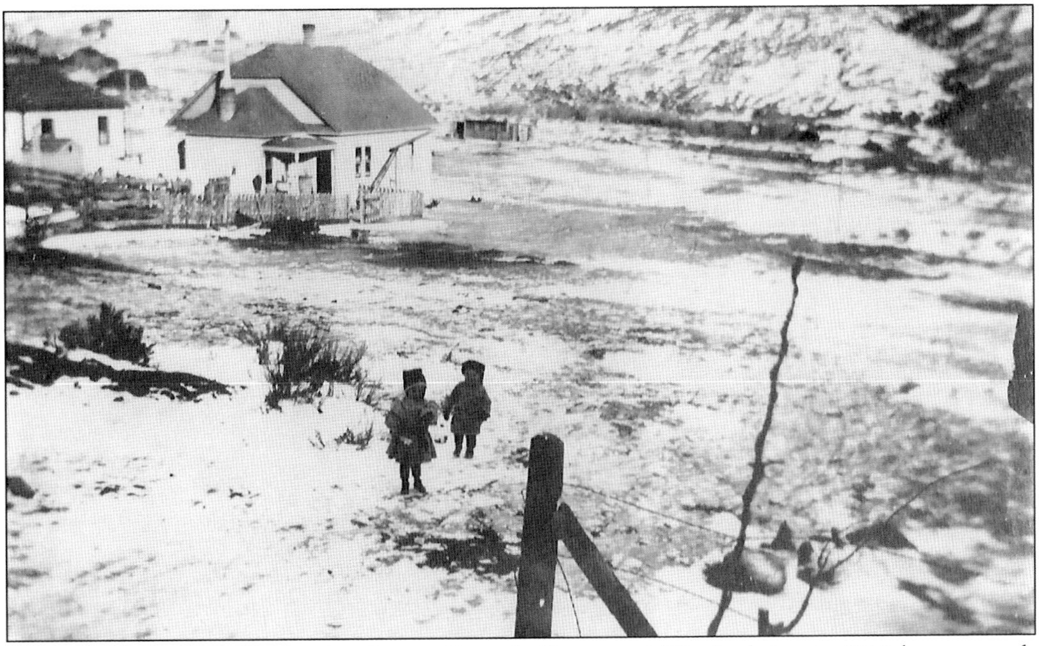

Mamie and Pen Wright, the daughters of Joseph Henry and Elizabeth Louise Wright, approach their home in 1907. The girls' father, known as "J. Harry," co-owned the Clark-Wright Company Bank, served as vice president of the Bear Creek Coal Company, and acted as treasurer for the International Coal Company. (CCHS.)

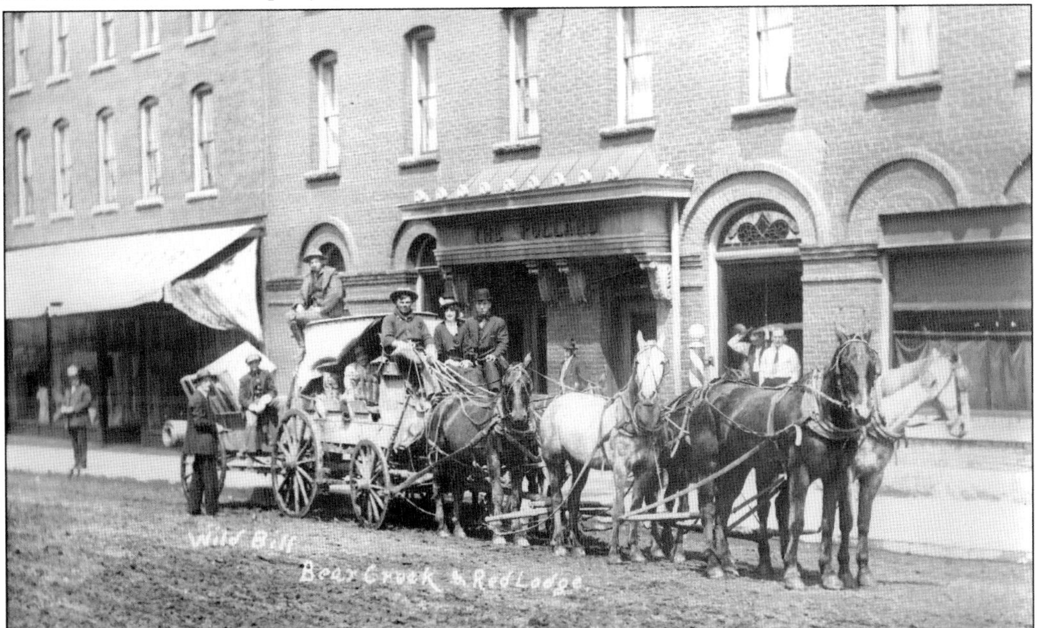

In the early 1900s, the local stage provided the most comfortable form of travel between Bear Creek Valley and Red Lodge. Charles D. "Wild Bill" Revelle, shown holding the reins, made this trip daily. Though wet conditions and unimproved roads often caused the coach to sink to its hubs in mud, the undeterred Revelle's advertisements touted his dependability with the slogan: "Rain or Shine Wild Bill for Mine." (CCHS.)

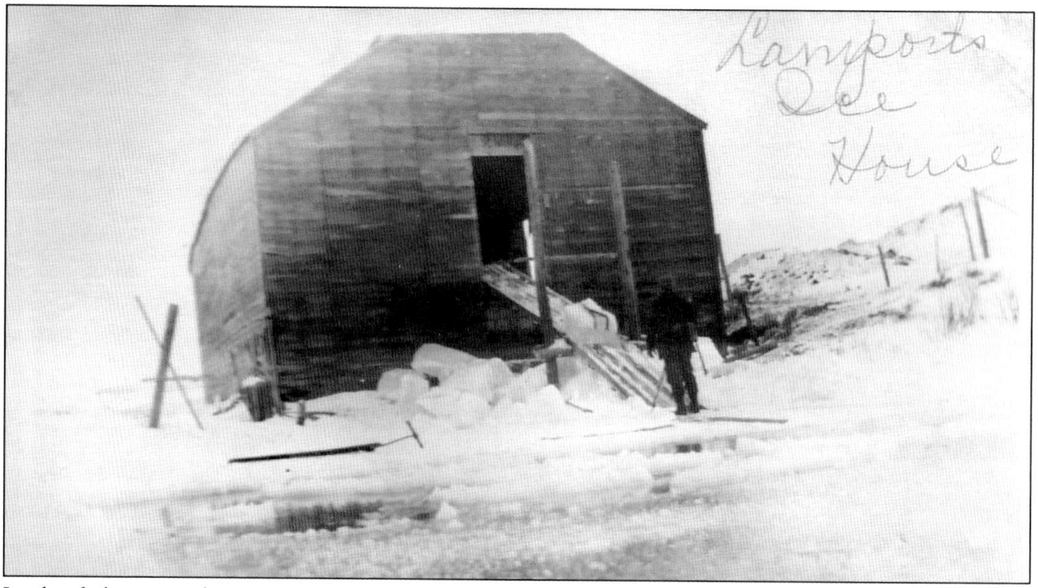

Lack of electric refrigeration required the harvesting of ice during winter months. The George T. Lamport family operated an ice business in the early days of Bear Creek Valley. The icehouse and harvesting pond (above) used Bear Creek water and sat several miles up Scotch Coulee from the main valley road. (DeVille.)

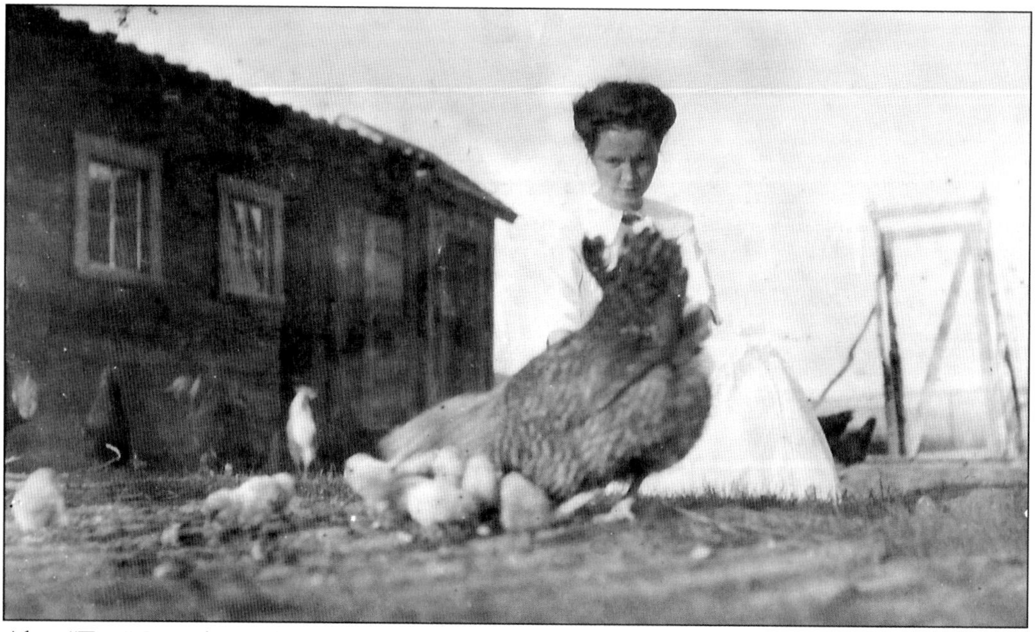

Alice "Tate" Straight tends chickens in this 1910 photograph. Alice's husband, Cleve, operated a local lumberyard, a hardware store, and a mortuary. Valley families produced much of their own food by growing large vegetable gardens and by raising chickens, goats, and milk cows. Many immigrant families also brewed their own wine and spirits. (CCHS.)

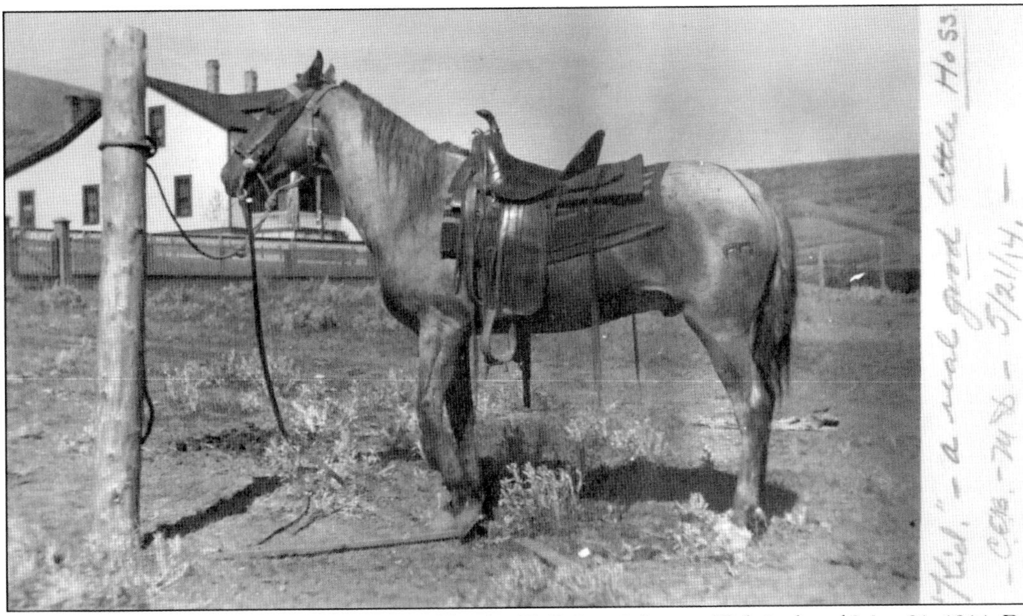

This postcard of Washoe physician Dr. Charles E. Beltzer's horse, Kid, is dated May 21, 1914. Dr. Beltzer's home in Washoe stands in the background. With deep snow in the winters and muddy, unpaved roads in the spring and summer, horses provided a more reliable form of transportation than automobiles. (CCHS.)

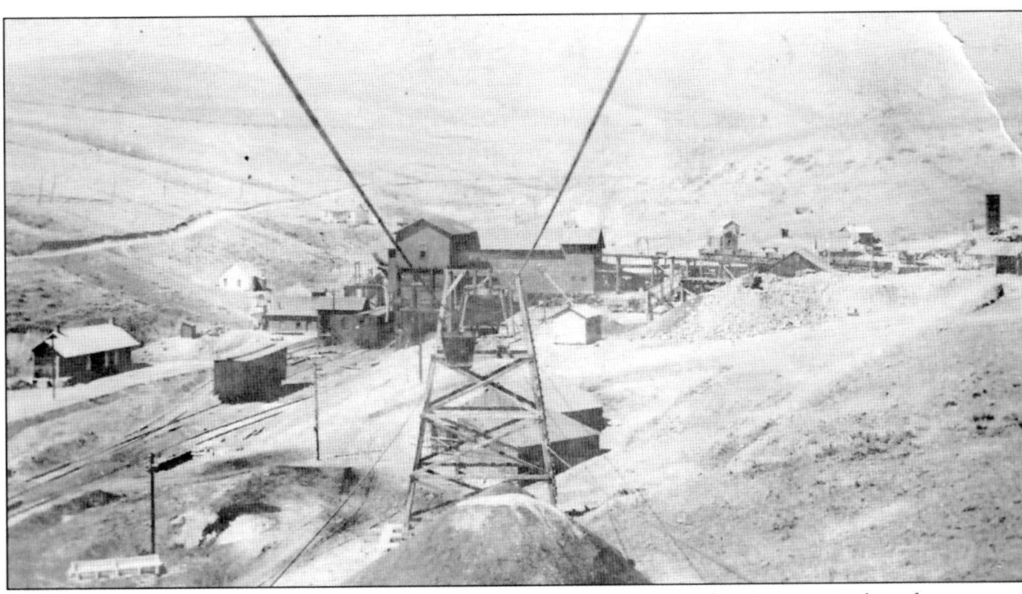

This unique view of the Montana Coal and Iron Company's Smith Mine was taken from on top of a tower that facilitated the removal of waste products, or slack, from the coal-processing plant. Slack was composed of small bits of unusable coal, shale, and dirt associated with the mining process. (CCHS.)

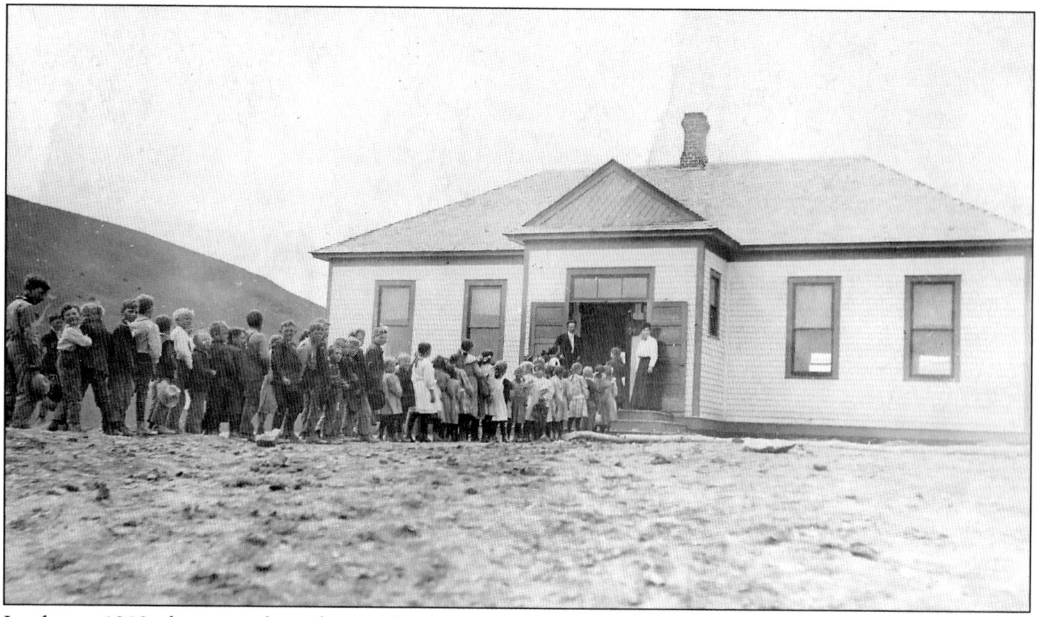

In this c. 1910 photograph, at least 40 students line up to return to class in the original one-story Bearcreek Elementary School (above). A second story and an addition were eventually added to accommodate the large number of students pouring into the valley. A two-story elementary school in neighboring Washoe also operated at maximum capacity during this time. Many foreign-born students came to class with only a rudimentary grasp of English. According to many oral histories, it did not take them long to master English, nor did it take their English-speaking friends long to learn some of the more colorful non-English phrases. A formal class photograph of grades one through three (below) shows 30 students dressed in their best clothes. (Both, Mourich.)

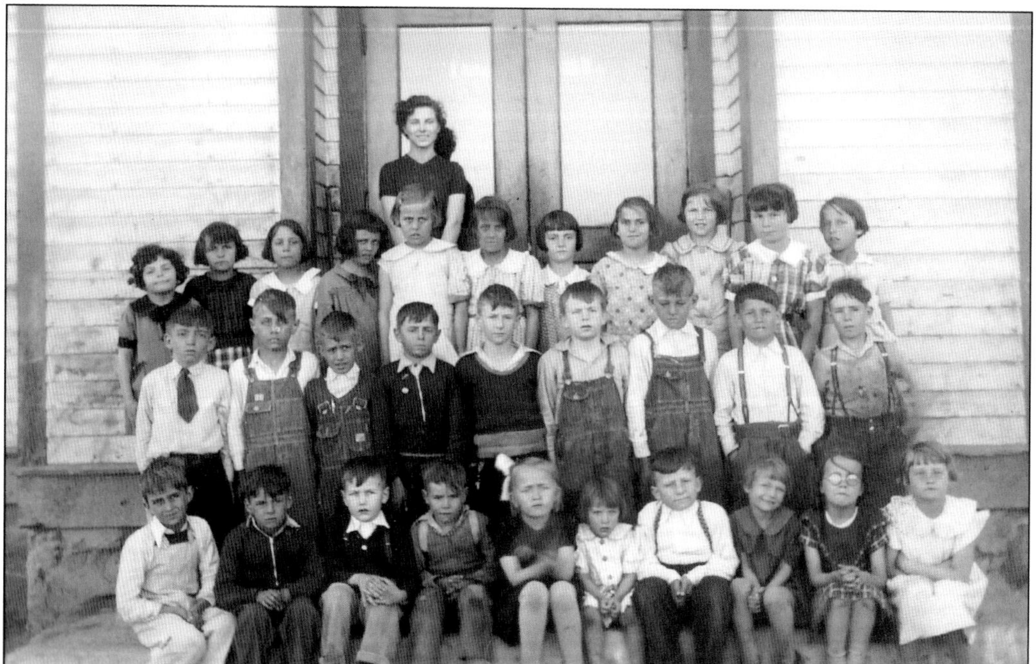

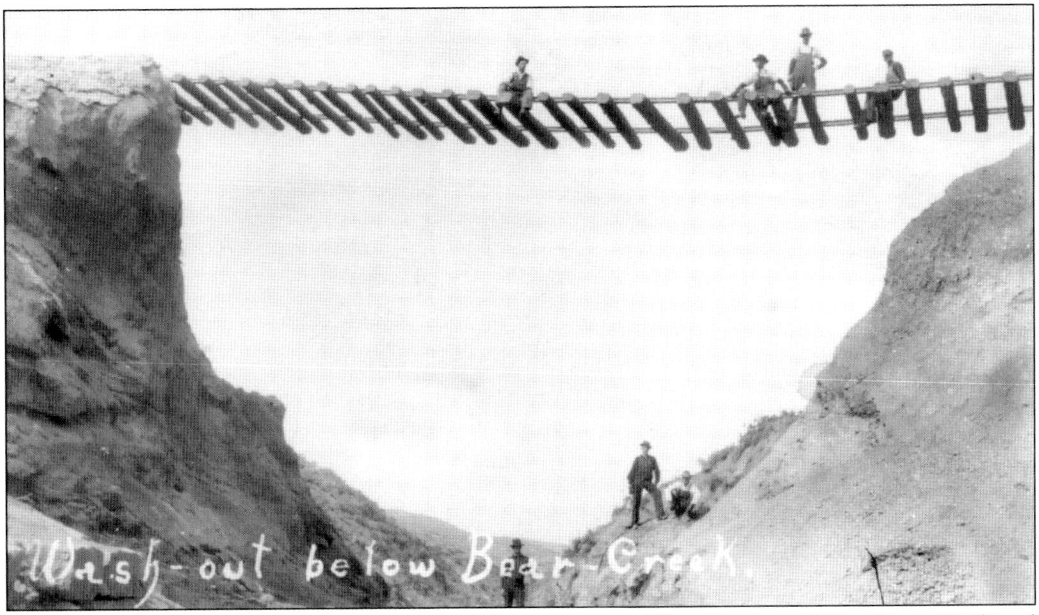

This 1912 photograph shows a section of the Montana, Wyoming, and Southern Railroad (MW&S) suspended above a washed-out gully between Bearcreek and Belfry. Severe rainstorms and flooding affected the town of Bearcreek more than other parts of the valley. During the Great Depression, the Works Progress Administration built flood ditches around the perimeter of Bearcreek to protect the town from flooding. (Kidwell.)

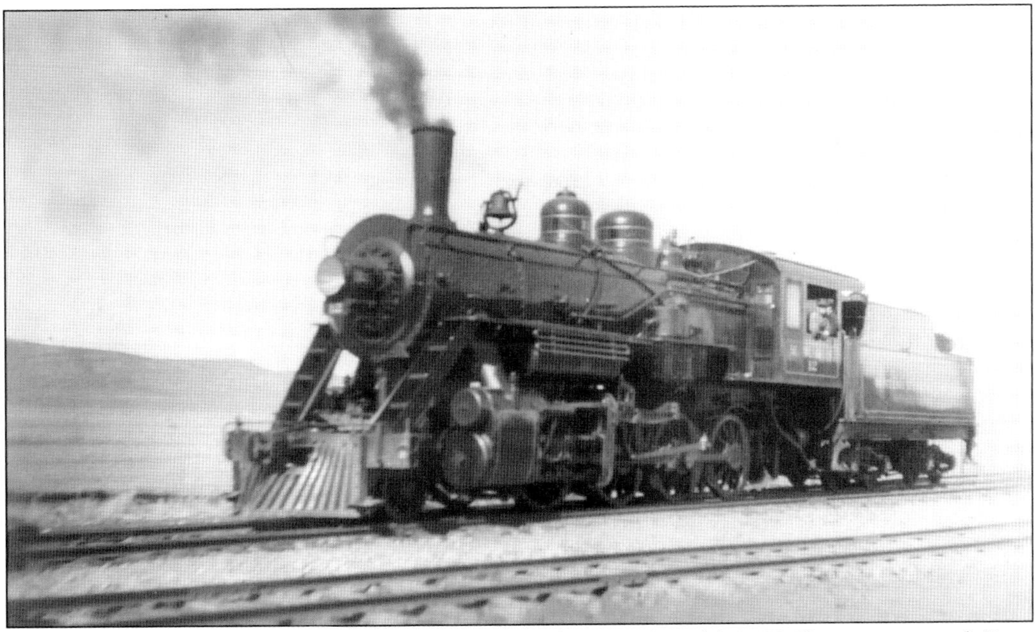

Engine No. 12 of the Montana, Wyoming, and Southern Railroad (MW&S) steams towards Bear Creek Valley from Belfry. The MW&S was not limited to industrial traffic; a McKeen motor coach ferried passengers between Bridger and Bearcreek six times a week. Local residents quickly nicknamed the motor coach "The Sub" due to its distinctive, submarine-like appearance. (Kidwell.)

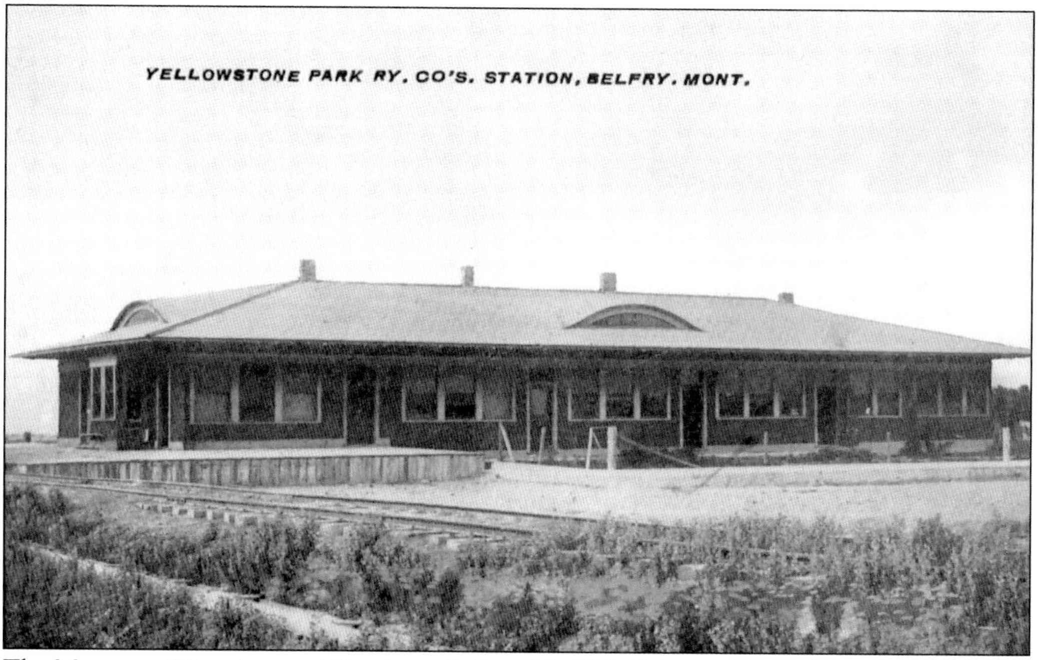

The Montana, Wyoming, and Southern Railroad (MW&S) began life as the Yellowstone Park Railroad. This early-1900s postcard shows the Belfry, Montana, station house in Clarks Fork Valley. From this station, the MW&S line turned west toward Bear Creek Valley and its many coal mines. (Author's collection.)

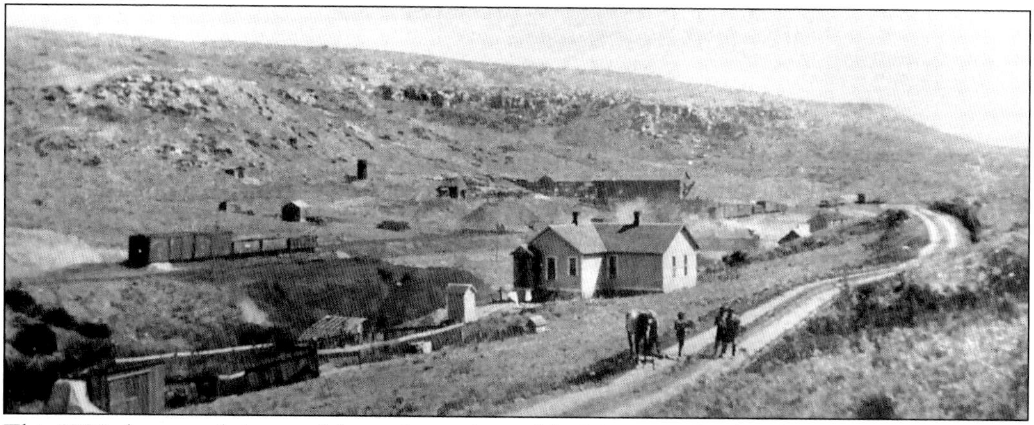

This 1909 photograph is one of the earliest taken of the Montana Coal and Iron Company's Smith Mine. The company initially focused its mining endeavors to the north, in the hills behind these buildings, via two separate entrances. To illustrate the rapid development of the Smith Mine, in 1909 it employed 115 men, was active for 179 days, and produced 57,000 tons of coal—up from 22,000 the year before. (CCHS.)

Two

Coal Mines

Beneath the hills and gulches of Bear Creek Valley lie seven seams of subbituminous coal varying in thickness from 4 to 33 feet. The majority of mining activity in the valley occurred in the second and third seams from the surface. The thickness of these seams (8 and 9 feet, respectively), the quality of the coal in them, and their relative proximity to the surface, made mining them lucrative. This drew a wide assortment of mining interests to the valley, resulting in the highest concentration of coal mines in Montana.

An inventory of Bear Creek Valley mines operating from 1888 to 1970 shows that Virtue Gulch was home to the Smokeless and Sootless Coal Company Mine (later the Brophy Coal Company Mine), the International Coal Company Mine, the North and South Side Mine, the New Mine, the Danichek Mine, the Kolarich Mine, the Ron Mine, and the McCarthy Prospect.

The Keucking Creek Drainage contained the Simms Mine, Northwest Improvement Company Mine, the DeVille Mine, the Roadside Mine (also called the Janskovitch Mine), the Coulee Mine, the Flockhart Mine, the Bear Creek Coal Company Mine, the Montana Coal and Iron Company's Smith Mine, and the Washoe Coal Company's two mines.

Scotch Coulee held the Burns Mine, the Lamport Mine, the Cestnik Mine, and the Montana Coal and Iron Company's second of three mines in the valley.

Foster Gulch contained the Montana Coal and Iron Company's Foster Gulch Mine and the Eagle Coal Company Mine, previously called the Flaherty Mine.

The Montana Coal and Iron Company operated strip mines in the hills to the west of Foster Gulch and to the west of Scotch Coulee.

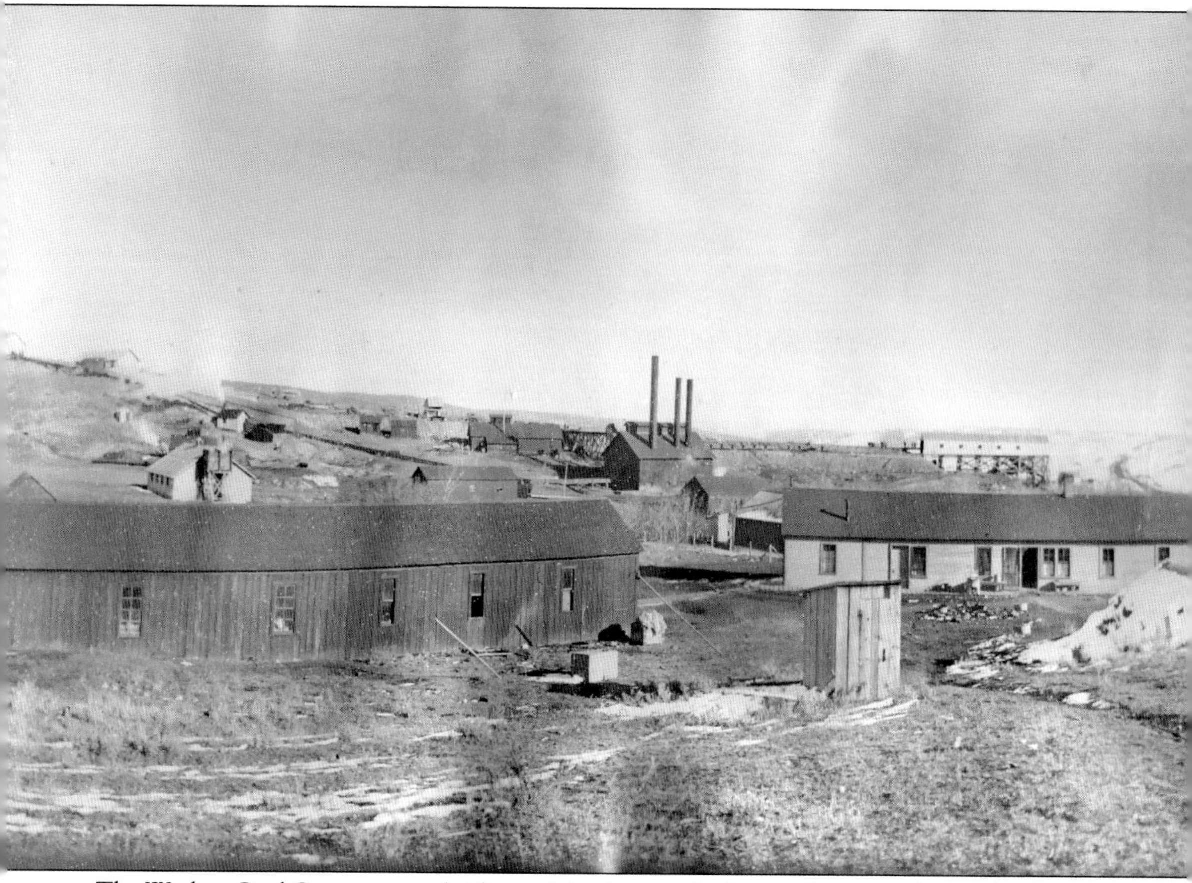

The Washoe Coal Company, a subsidiary of the Anaconda Copper Company, began development of its property at the western end of Bear Creek Valley in 1892 by opening the first of two mines designed to fuel its Butte, Montana, copper smelters. The company closed the 1892 opening after a year due to high transportation costs. Mining activities resumed in 1907 with the arrival of the railroad and continued until 1938. After 1912, the mine operated intermittently due to competition from its sister coal mine in Belt, Montana, and persistent problems with weak roofs and flooding. The foreground of this 1904 photograph shows the mine's washhouse (left), an outhouse (center), and a bunkhouse (right). In the background, starting at the top of the hill (left), lie the Washoe Coal Company Mine No. 2 entrance, a white boardinghouse (to its immediate right), a power plant (with three chimneys), and the tipple building on a raised platform above the railroad tracks. To the far right stands the original Washoe Elementary School. (Mourich.)

This photograph shows the Washoe Coal Company Mine's processing plant. Coal-processing plants of this era separated the coal into sizes suitable for different applications, such as fueling industrial power plants, powering railroad locomotives, and heating homes. They also cleaned the coal of dirt and shale debris. (CCHS.)

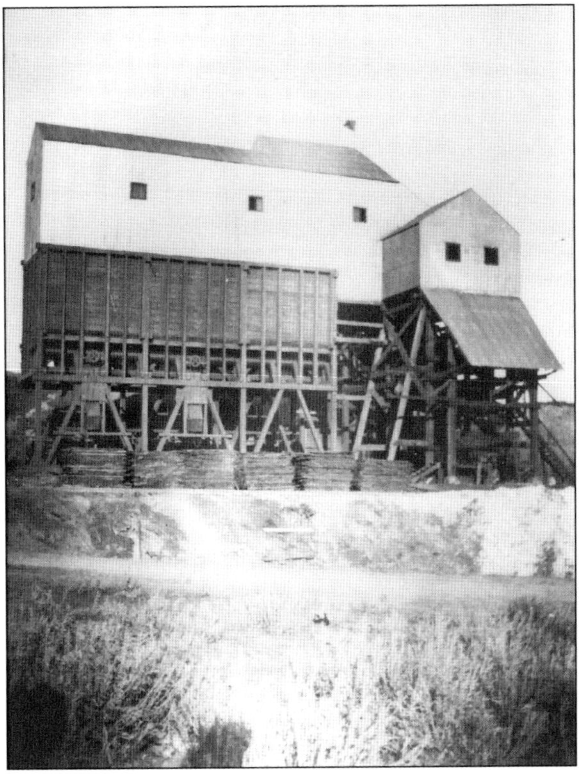

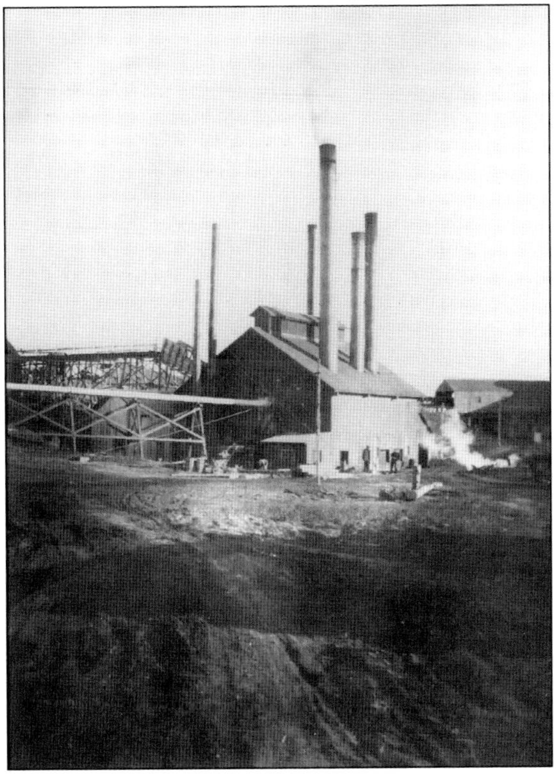

This photograph shows the Washoe Coal Company Mine's power plant. Industrial-scale mines in Bear Creek Valley initially needed to build their own power plants to provide steam-generated electricity for their operations. Around 1920, electricity became available in the valley and within several years was at a rate competitive with self-production, and these power plants fell out of use. (CCHS.)

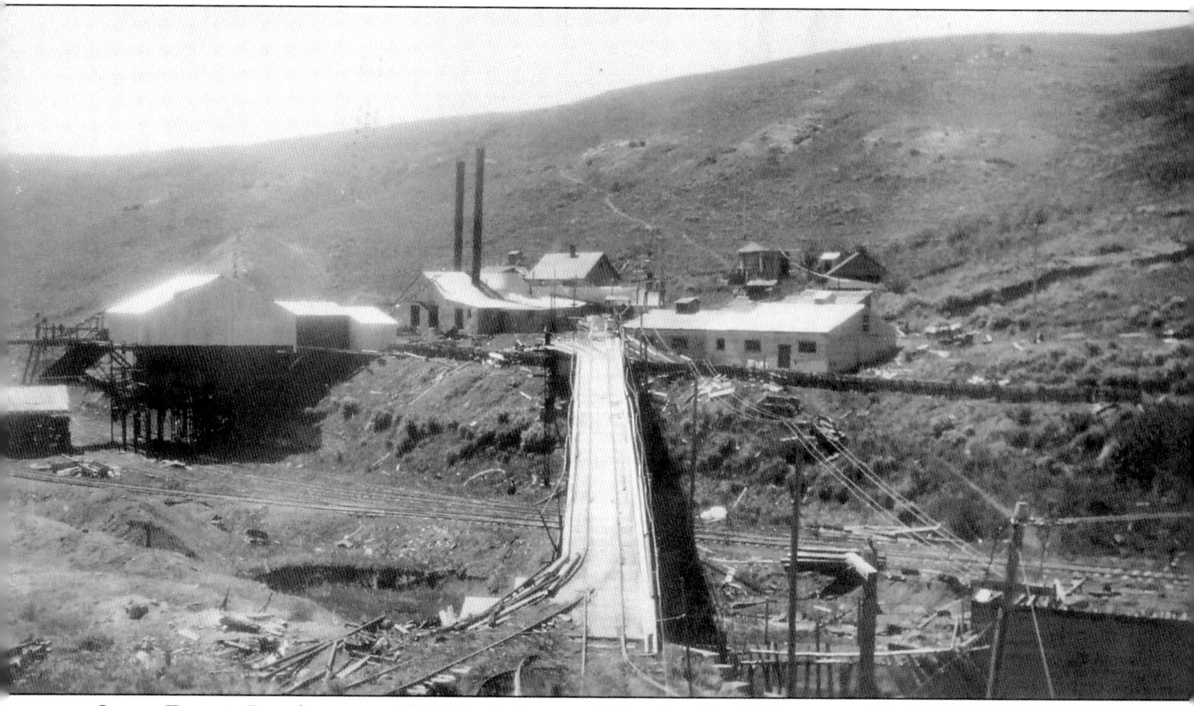

James Francis Brophy opened his Smokeless and Sootless Coal Company Mine at the western end of Virtue Gulch in 1908. It proved to be the longest lived of the valley's corporate mines, closing in 1967. In the interim, the corporation saw several major changes. The Great Depression forced Brophy to lease the mine to the Hansen Coal Company from 1932 to 1940. In 1940, James Francis's son, James R. Brophy, leased the mine and renamed it the Brophy Coal Company Mine. Later the younger Brophy changed the name to the Clean Coal Company Mine. This 1920s photograph, taken from the hillside above the mine entrance, shows a trestle crossing Virtue Gulch to the processing plant. The buildings shown include (from left to right) the coal processing plant, the power plant (with two chimneys), the mine office building (behind the power plant), a repair shop, and—behind that, on the hill—a water tower. (CCHS.)

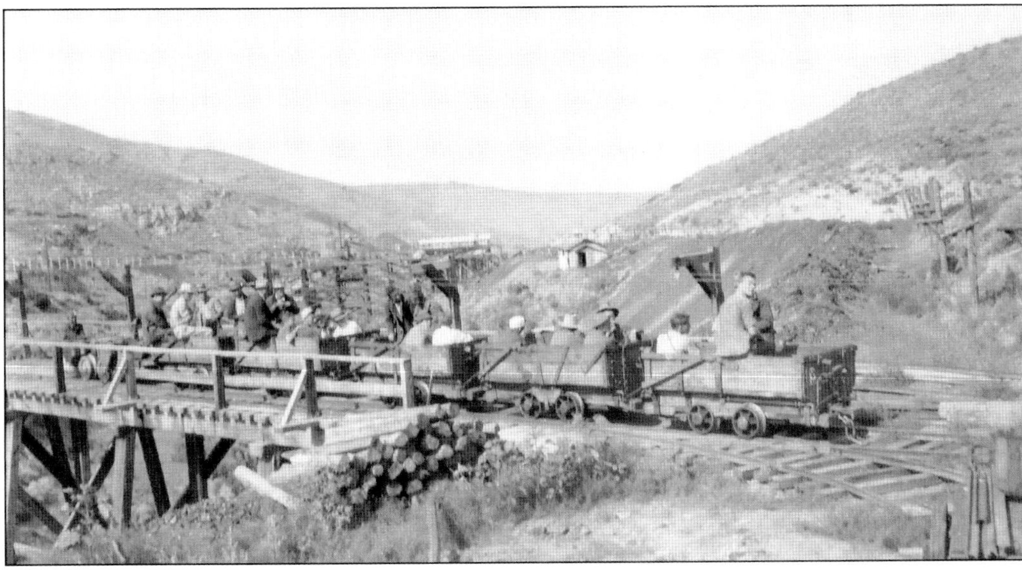

A group of non-miners approaches the entrance to the Smokeless and Sootless Coal Company Mine. They are likely members of one of Bearcreek physician Dr. John Carl Frederick Siegfriedt's many fossil-gathering expeditions into the local mines. In the distance is the mine's boxcar loading facility. (CCHS.)

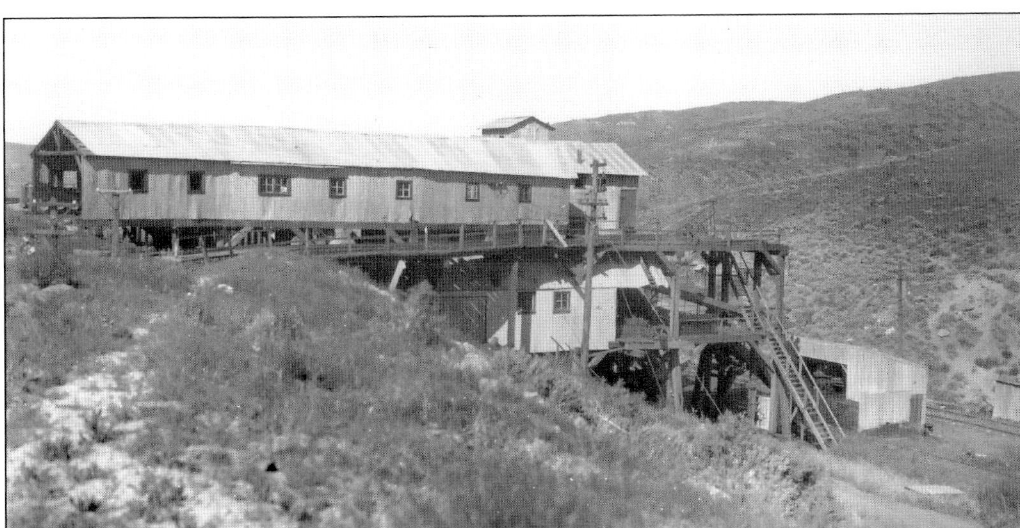

A closer view of the Smokeless and Sootless Coal Company's boxcar loading facility shows railway tracks running beneath the three-story building. A narrow-gauge railway employed smaller cars to transport coal from the mine to this facility. Here workers used gravity to transfer coal from the mining carts to full-scale boxcars. (Planichek.)

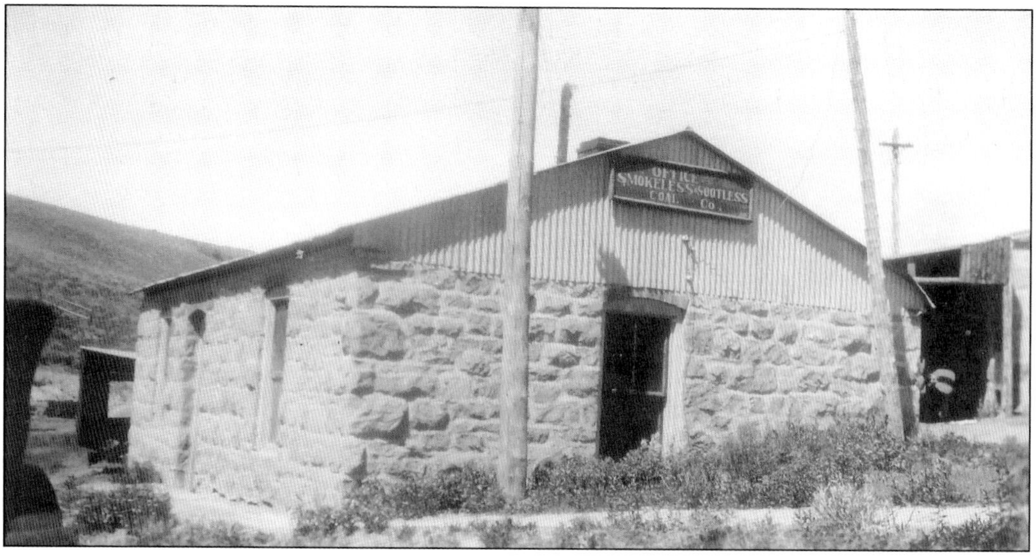

Locally quarried sandstone provided building materials for many of Bear Creek Valley's structures, including the Smokeless and Sootless Coal Company's office building (above) and boardinghouse (below). In the early 1900s, coal-mine development and its need for miners quickly outpaced the ability of neighboring Bearcreek to provide adequate housing. Forced to provide housing for their employees, most corporate mines like the Smokeless and Sootless Coal Company built boardinghouses. The Washoe Coal Company went so far as to build a company town, complete with individual homes to house miners and their families. (Both, Planichek.)

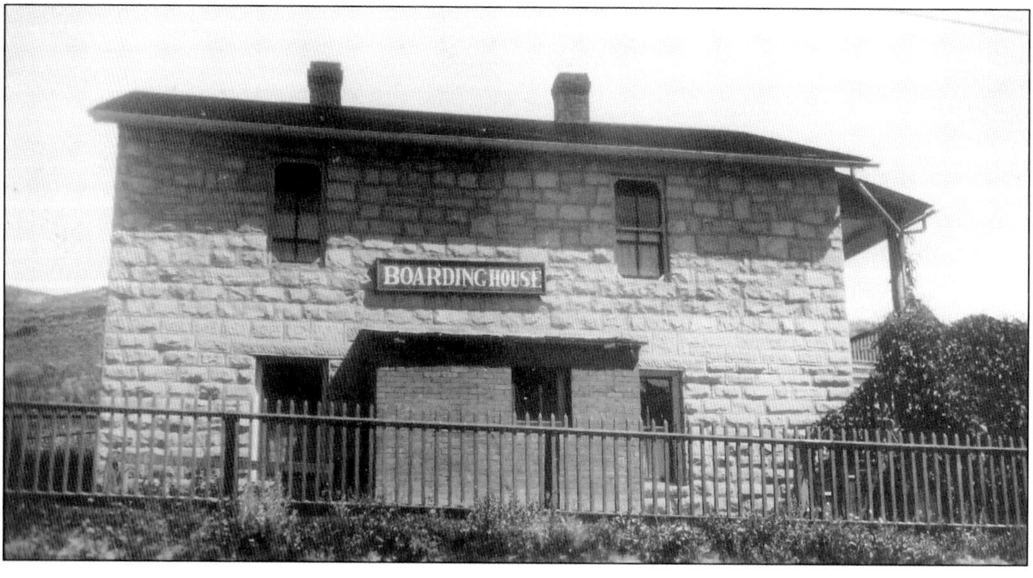

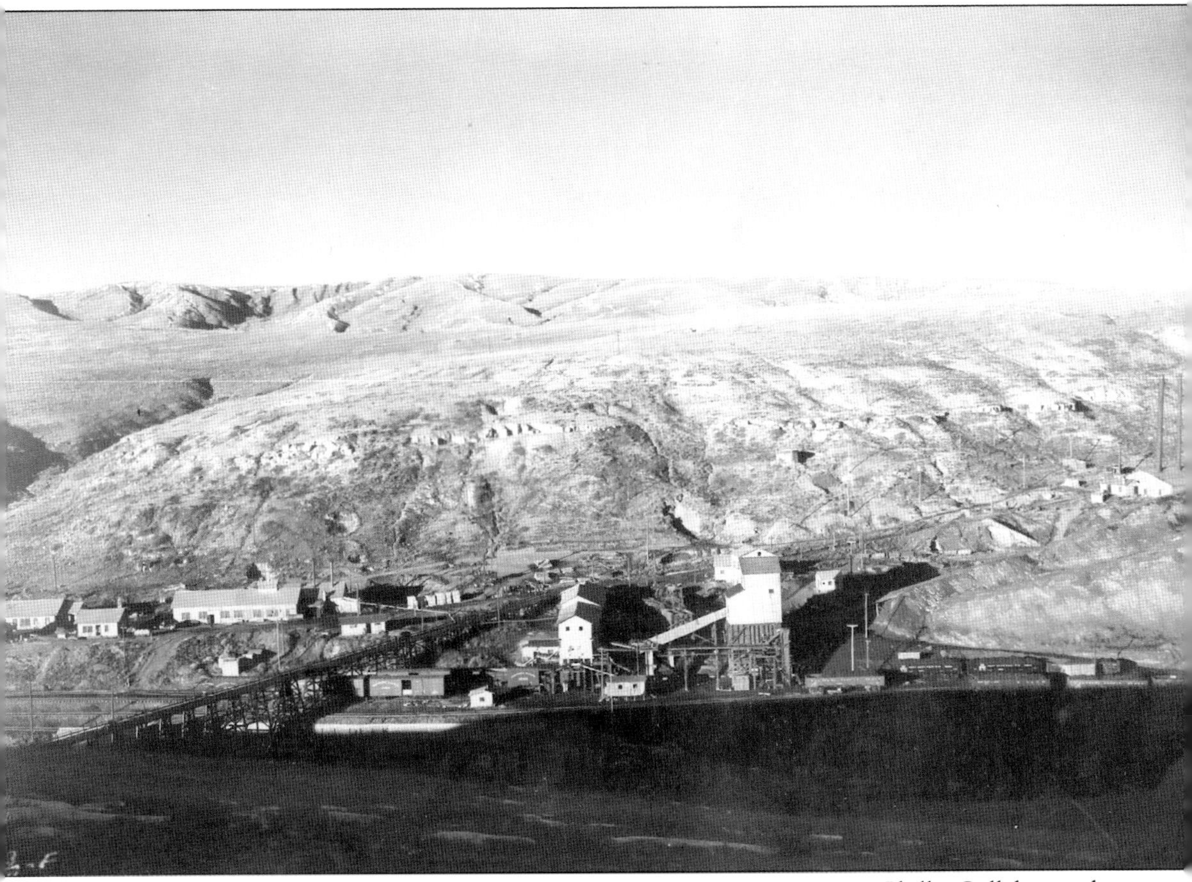

In 1898, the Montana Fuel and Iron Company (founded by George T. Lamport, Phillip Gallaher, and millionaire Elijah Smith) began development of its Smith Mine property at the eastern end of the Keucking Creek Drainage. Soon after its founding, the Montana Fuel and Iron Company became the Montana Coal and Iron Company. By 1907, two entrances were active north of its processing plant and one across Keucking Creek to the south. A trestle across Keucking Creek provided access to the southern entrance—the sole active entrance at the time of the 1943 Smith Mine disaster. After the disaster, the Montana Coal and Iron Company closed this entrance and opened a new one in Scotch Coulee, which operated until 1946. The company continued mining coal in the valley through its Foster Gulch Mine east of Bearcreek until 1953. This photograph captures the Smith Mine in its heyday during the late 1910s to early 1920s. (Flash's Photography.)

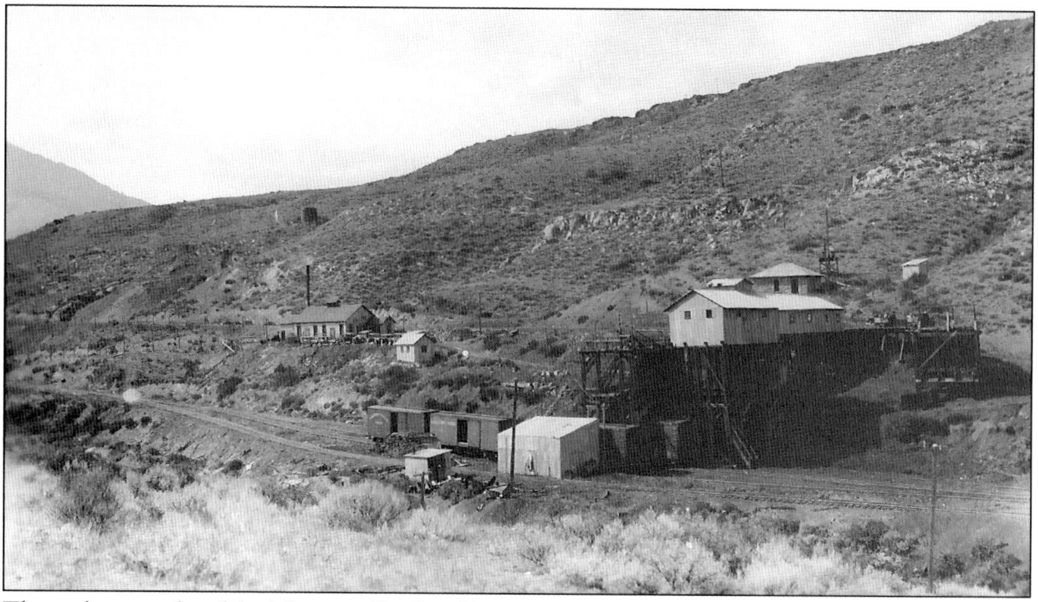

These photographs of the Montana Coal and Iron Company's Smith Mine document the expansion of its processing plant. The early plant consisted primarily of a blacksmith shop to the far left and a large tipple and railway boxcar loader to the right (above). The photograph below shows the almost completed trestle across Keucking Creek (far left). A coal screen and washing facility stands between the trestle and the tipple, a loaded boxcar sits on the new train scale, and a home and office building is in use in the foreground. (Above, CCHS; below, Flash's Photography.)

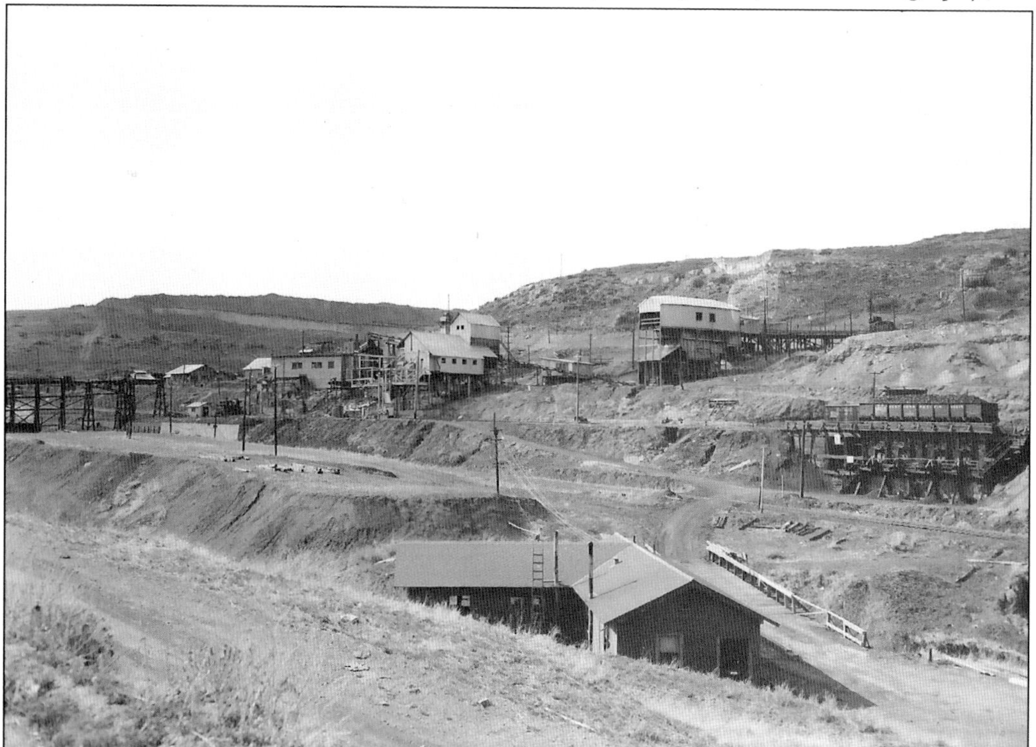

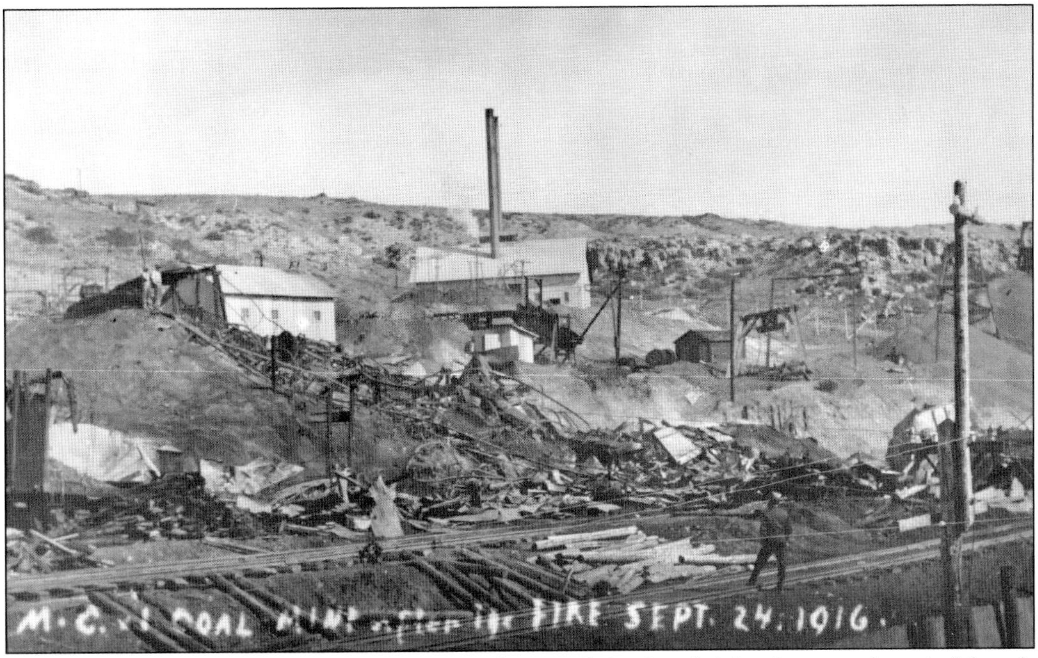

In September 1916, a fire of unknown origin destroyed the Smith Mine's original tipple (above). Within two weeks, its replacement was complete and ready for service (below). This tipple survived just eight years before another mysterious fire destroyed it in September 1924. This second fire occurred just five months after fire destroyed the Washoe General Store and Community Hall and at least two Bearcreek homes. Mine management blamed the second tipple fire on International Workers of the World agitators. Rather than rebuild the tipple again, the Montana Coal and Iron Company purchased the tipple in neighboring Fromberg, Montana, from the Gebo Coal Mine, which had ceased operation in 1921. (Both, CCHS.)

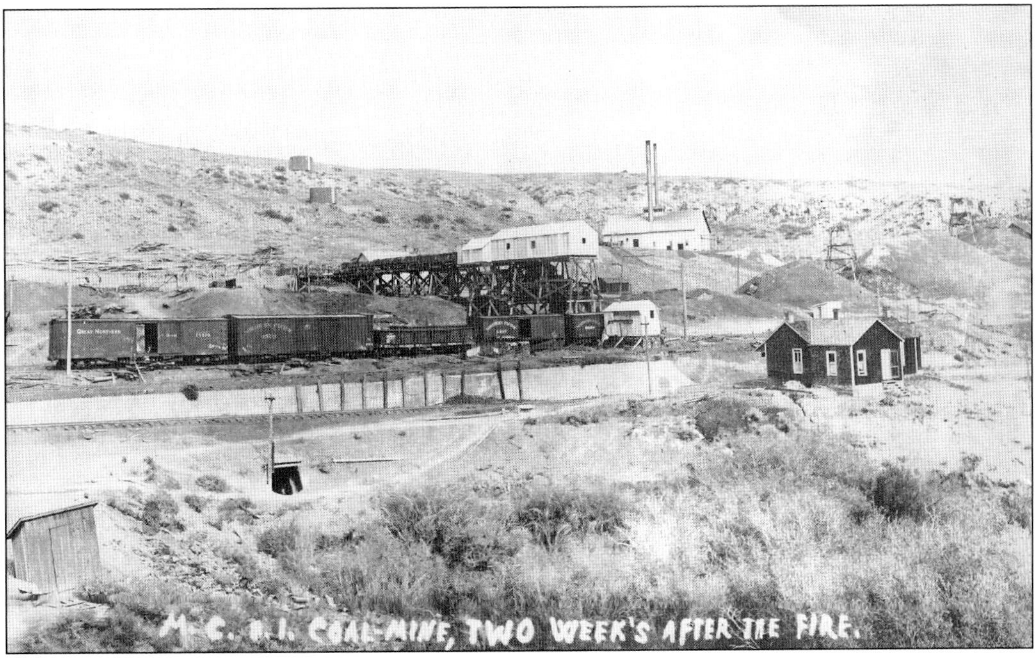

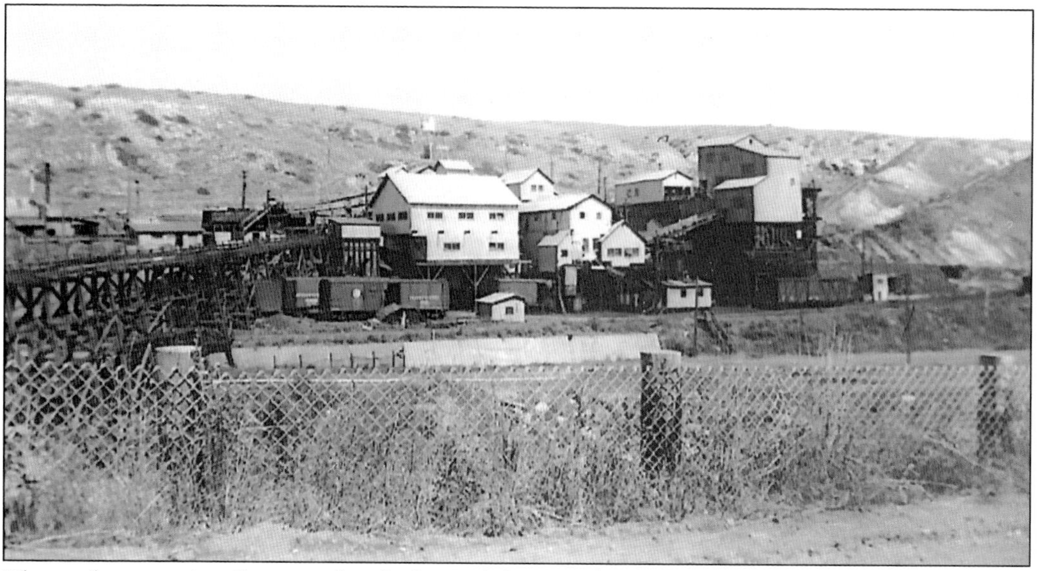

These photographs illustrate the decline of the Smith Mine's processing plant. The *c.* 1937 photograph (above) reveals the fullest complement of buildings used by the Smith Mine. The photograph below shows that most of the front-facing buildings had been lost to a 1945 fire, revealing smaller buildings behind. A concrete retaining wall has also been removed. With the exception of the trestle and the home to its left, most of the buildings shown below around 1950 still stand on the Smith Mine site. (Above, Wakenshaw; below, Mourich.)

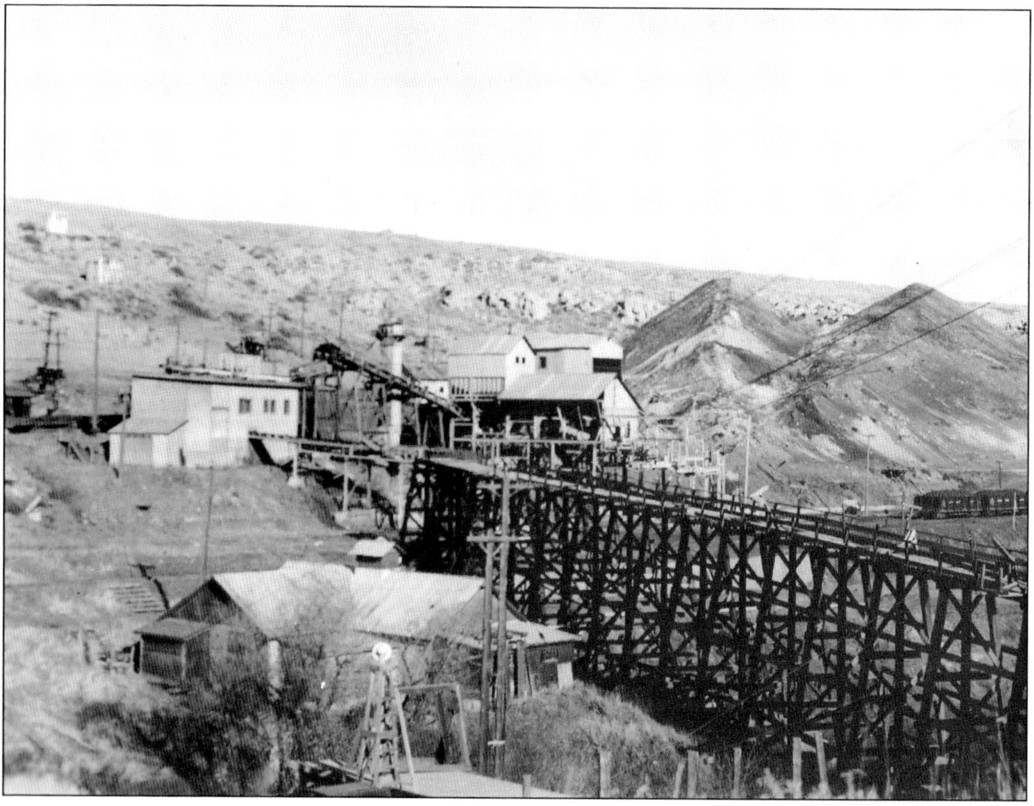

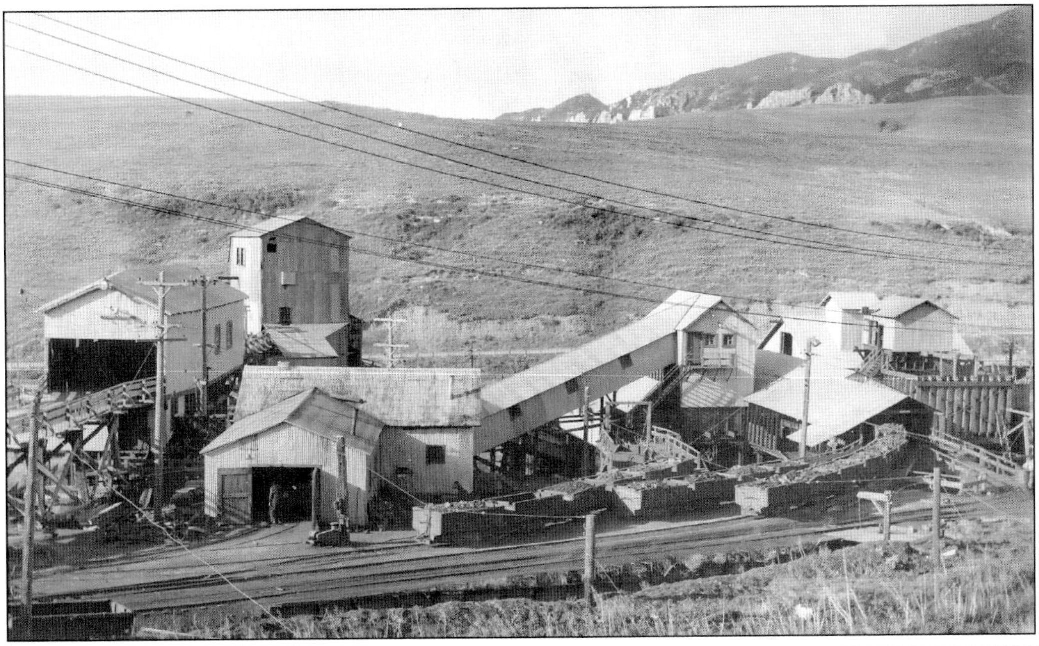

These rare photographs of the Smith Mine processing plant's north side illustrate its operation. All coal extracted from the Smith Mine's three entrances approached the plant from the north. The two northern entrances provided coal cars with direct access to the tipple (above left), while coal cars from the mine's southern entrance crossed the trestle above Keucking Creek and continued along tracks wrapping around the western end of the complex to the tipple (above right). Conveyor belts and bucket lifts moved coal through the plant. An enclosed bucket lift (center right) moved coal vertically while a covered conveyor belt behind it moved coal at lower angles. (Above, Flash's Photography; right, CCHS.)

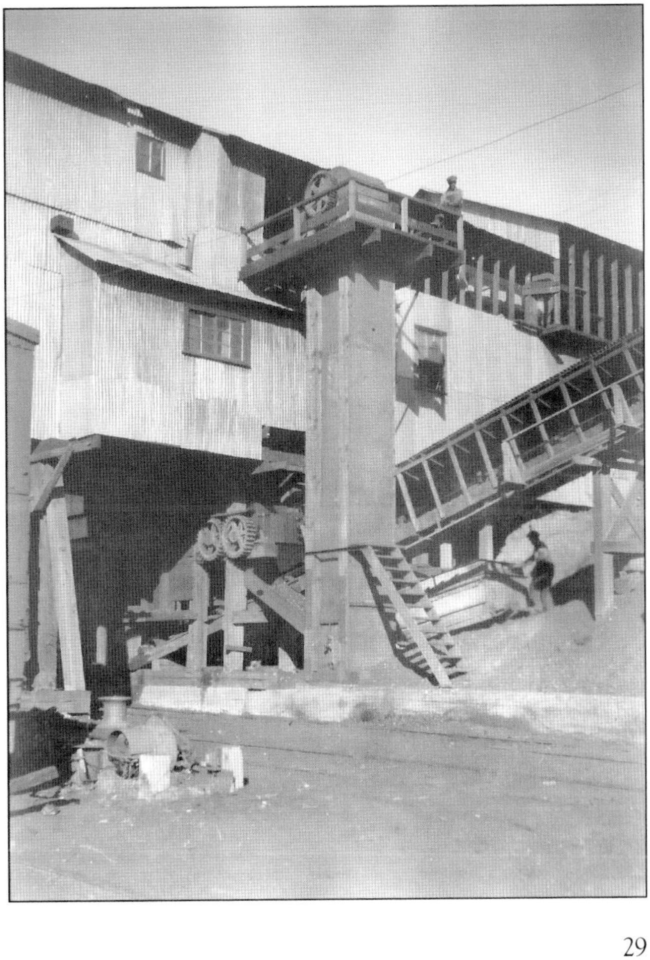

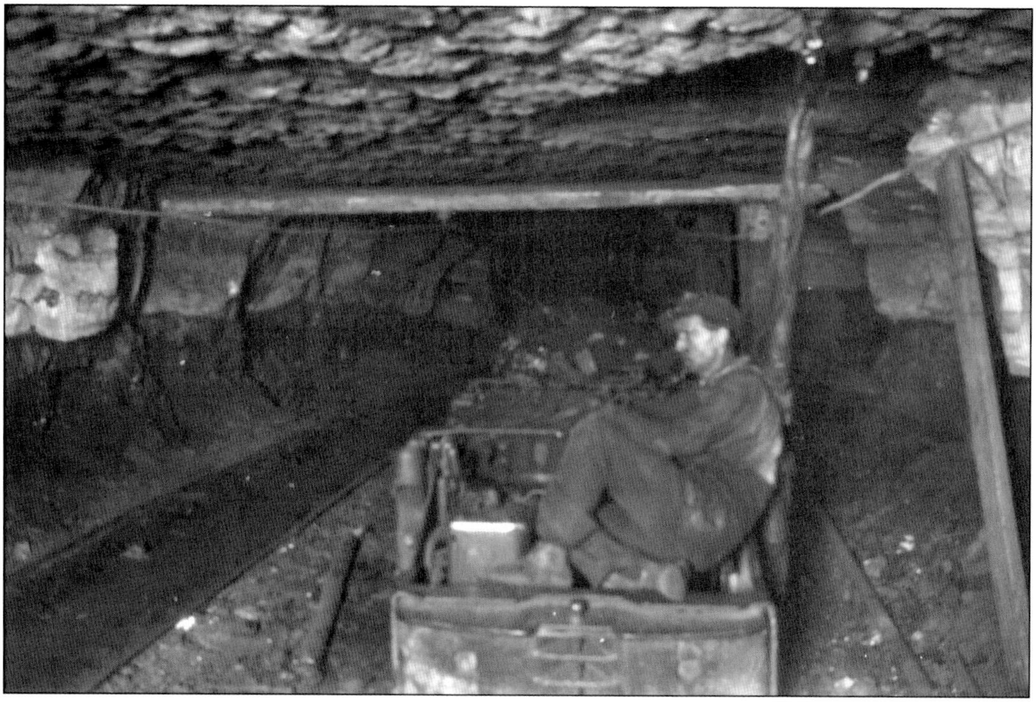

A Smith Mine nipper rides at the front of a train of coal cars leaving the mine. A nipper and motorman worked in pairs, with the nipper acting as the motorman's assistant. The nipper's duties included opening and closing underground doorways as the coal train passed through them. (Flash's Photography.)

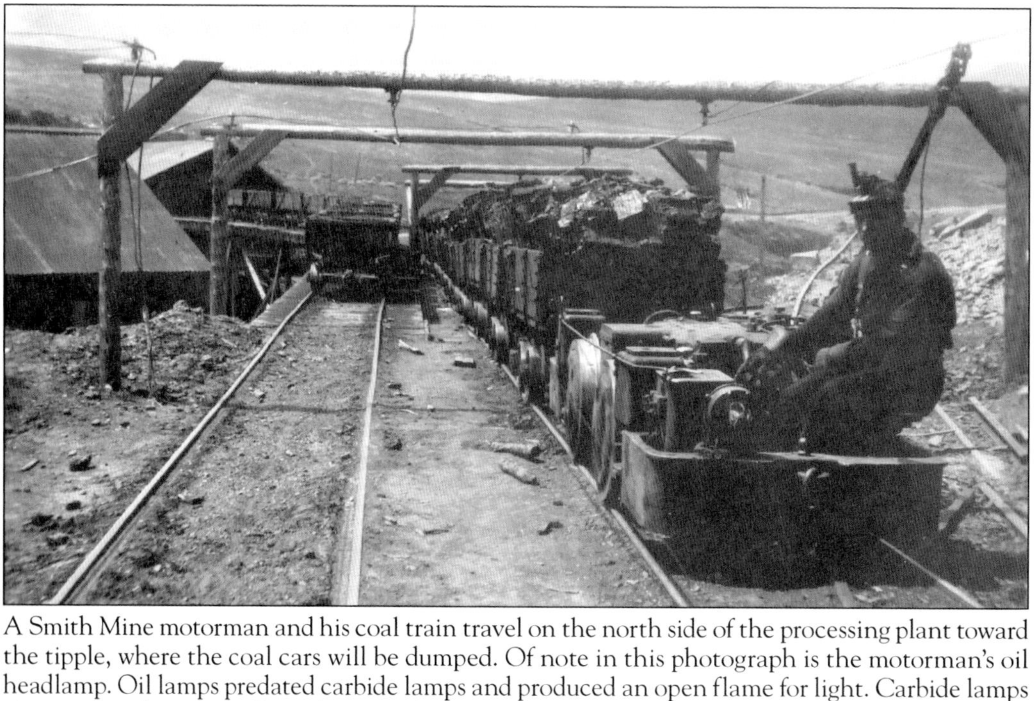

A Smith Mine motorman and his coal train travel on the north side of the processing plant toward the tipple, where the coal cars will be dumped. Of note in this photograph is the motorman's oil headlamp. Oil lamps predated carbide lamps and produced an open flame for light. Carbide lamps also produced an open flame but gave better, brighter light. (Montana Historical Society.)

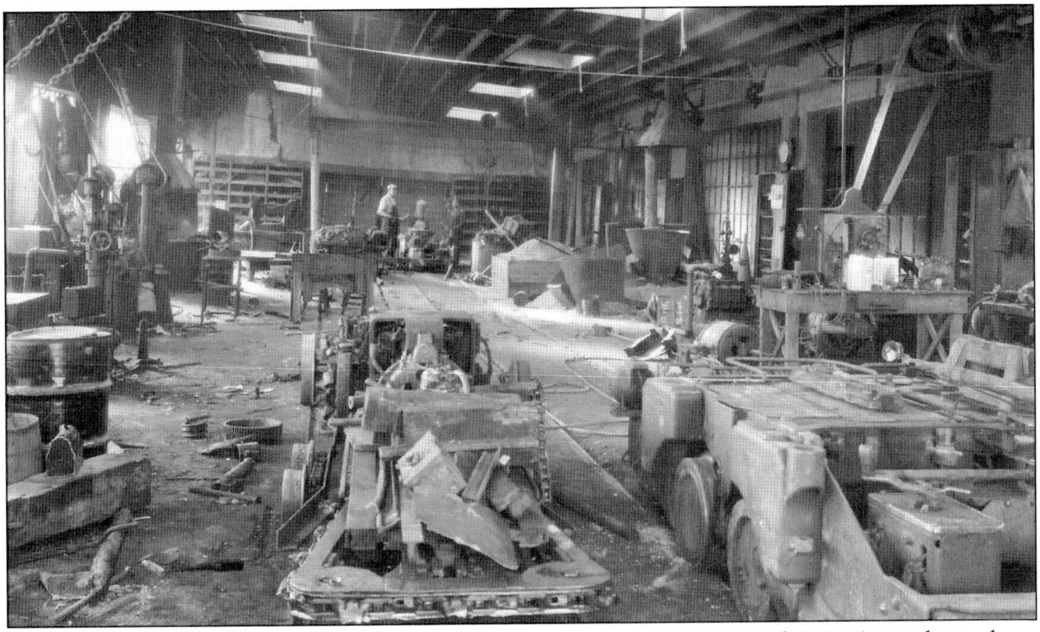

Broken down machinery awaits the attention of repairmen in the Smith Mine's machine shop. These men used a number of power tools and a blacksmith forge in their work. The belt-driven power tools line both sides of the shop with a common rotary power source running along the ceiling. (Flash's Photography.)

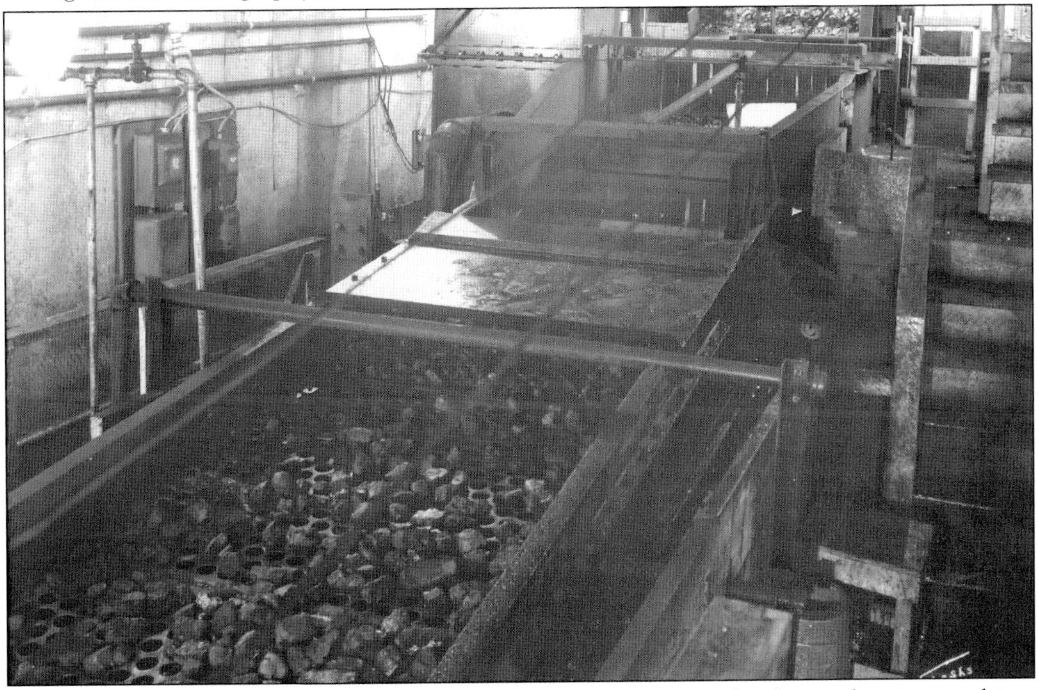

Previously sorted coal travels through the Smith Mine processing plant's wet-cleaning machine. After being dumped from mine cars in the tipple building, the coal traveled through machines that sorted it into like-sized pieces, cleaned it of rock debris, and washed away any dirt that might still cling to it. (Flash's Photography.)

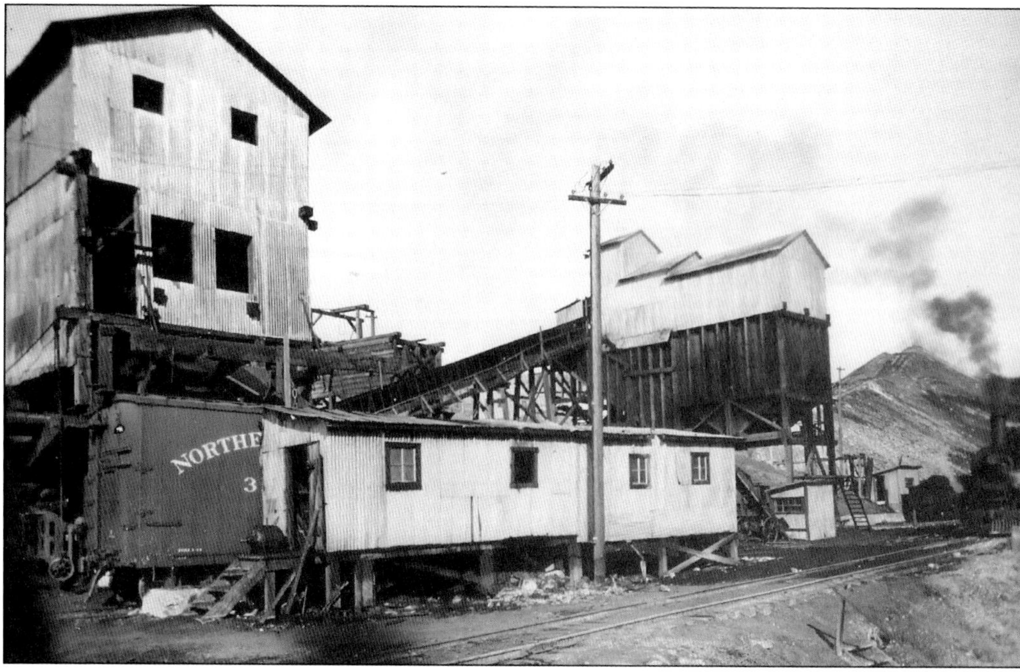

The last step in the coal's long journey through the Smith Mine's processing plant involved loading it onto railway boxcars for delivery to market. In the photograph above, a Montana, Wyoming, and Southern Railroad locomotive steams into the loading facility while a Northern Pacific car waits in the docks to be filled. The photograph below shows a boxcar in the middle of the coal-loading process, a task accomplished by several conveyor belts. The size of the coal being delivered dictated which conveyor system was used. (Above, CCHS; below, Flash's Photography.)

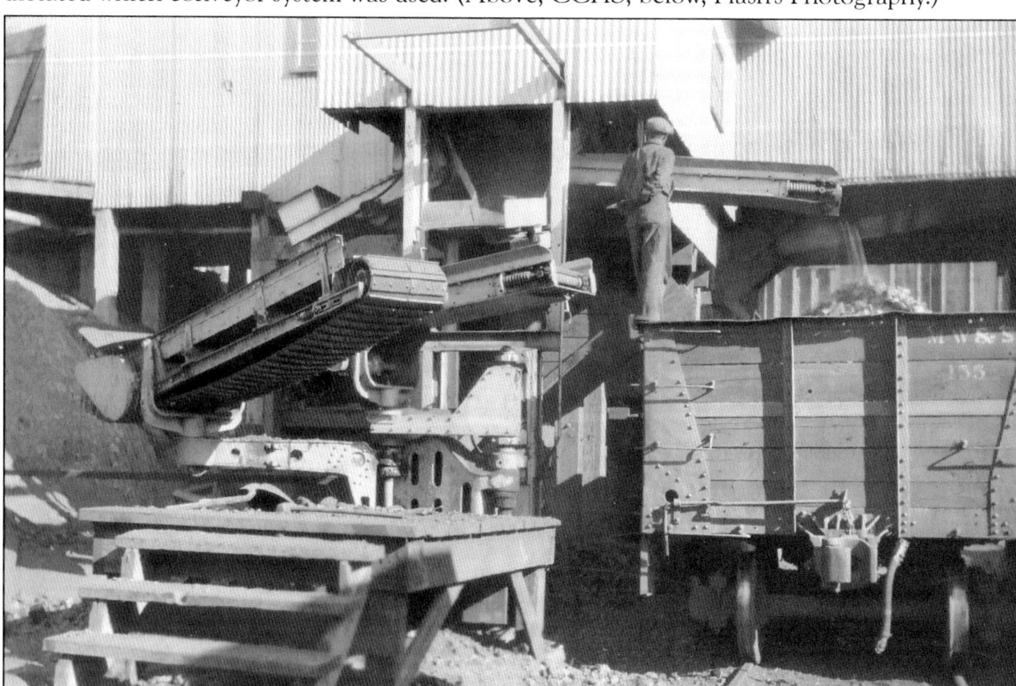

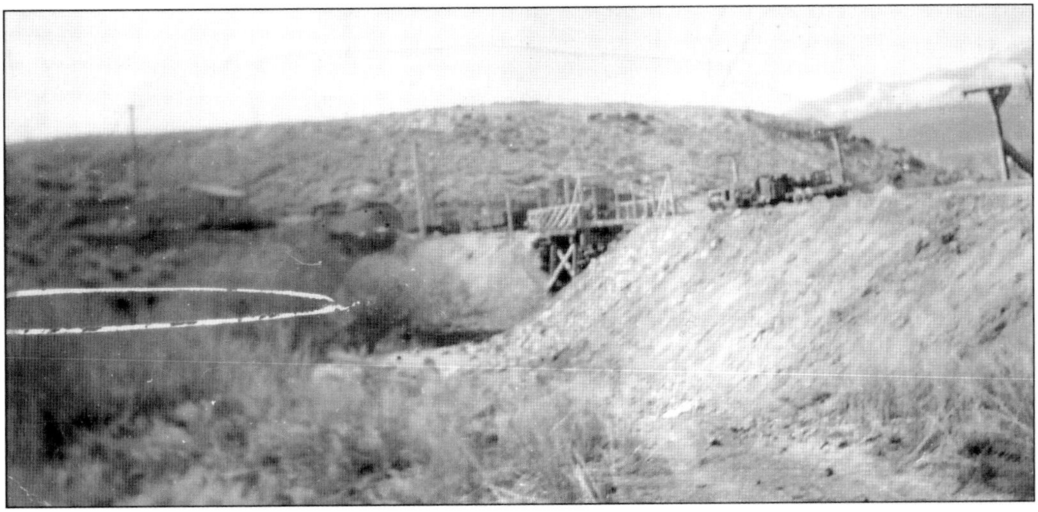

In Bear Creek Valley's early days, George T. Lamport opened his Lamport Mine a short distance up Scotch Coulee, to the southeast of the Smith Mine. The Lamport Mine produced very little coal in relation to other mines in the valley and quickly fell into disuse. After the 1943 Smith Mine disaster, the Montana Coal and Iron Company abandoned its Keucking Creek entrance and resumed operations through this mine—but only until March 1946. At this point, the Montana Coal and Iron Company focused operations solely on its Foster Gulch Mine, southeast of Bearcreek. (Both, Planichek.)

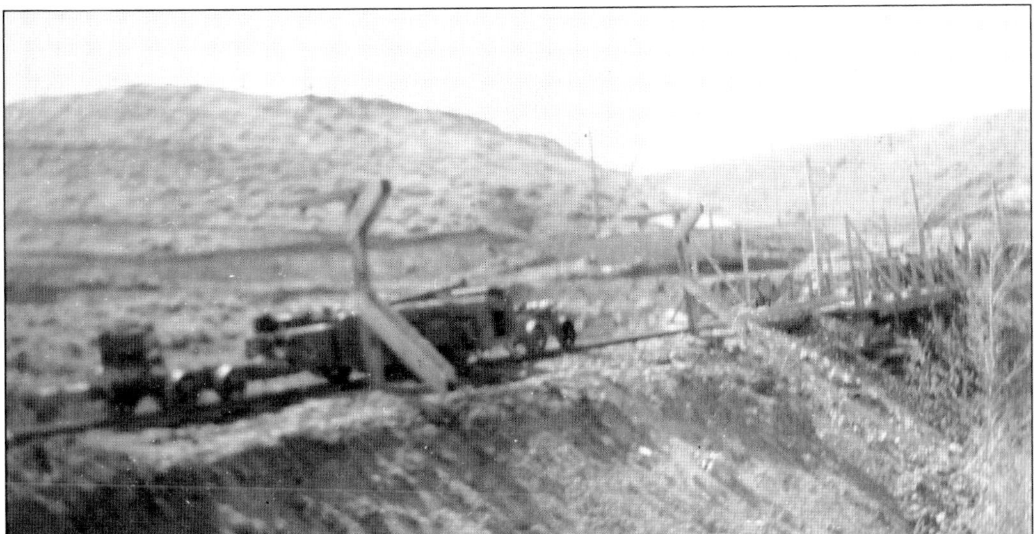

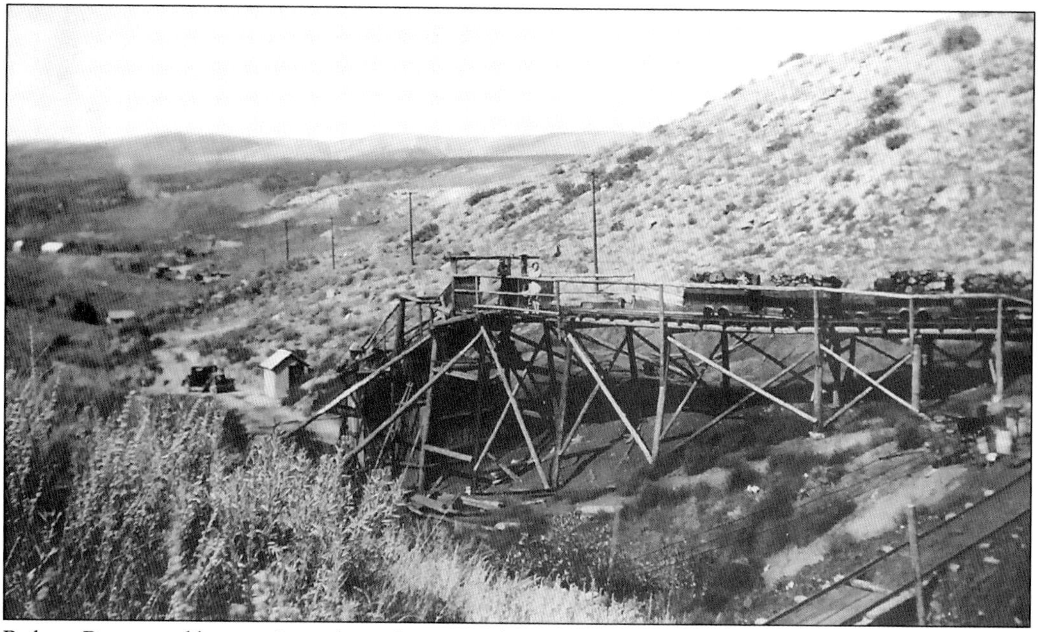

Robert Burns and his son Irvin leased a tract of Scotch Coulee land from the Montana Coal and Iron Company in the late 1920s to begin their own mine. The Burns Mine supplied local markets with heating and cooking coal. Demand from this market fell off sharply during the summers, allowing time to make needed repairs to the mine. The Burns family sold the rights to the mine in the mid-1950s. The Burns Mine trestle and tipple are shown above. The plume of smoke in the distance rises from the constantly smoldering Smith Mine coal waste pile. The entrance to the Burns Mine is shown below. (Both, Burns.)

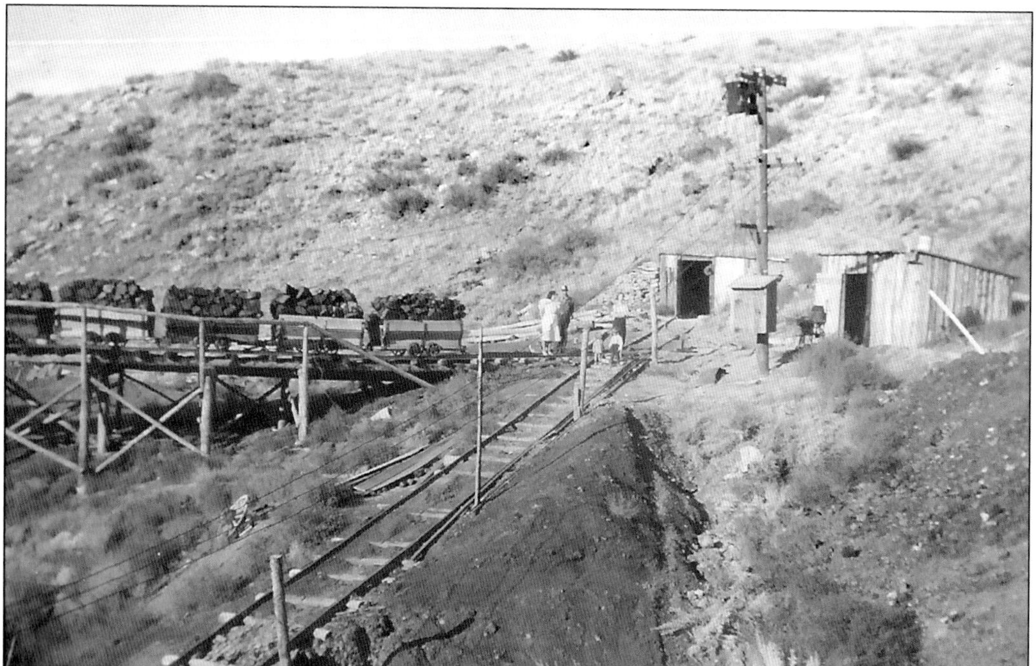

Three generations of Burns men pose for a photograph at the family mine in 1937. From left to right are Robert "Bob" Burns, his grandson Kerry Burns, and his son Irvin "Bud" Burns. The occupation of coal mining usually followed family lines; fathers taught the trade to their sons, who, in turn, taught it to their own. This was true of mine owners as well as mine employees. (Burns.)

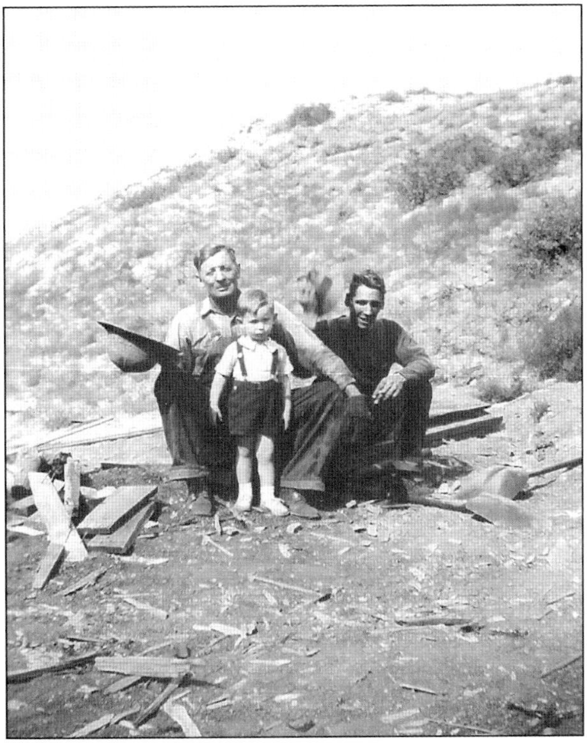

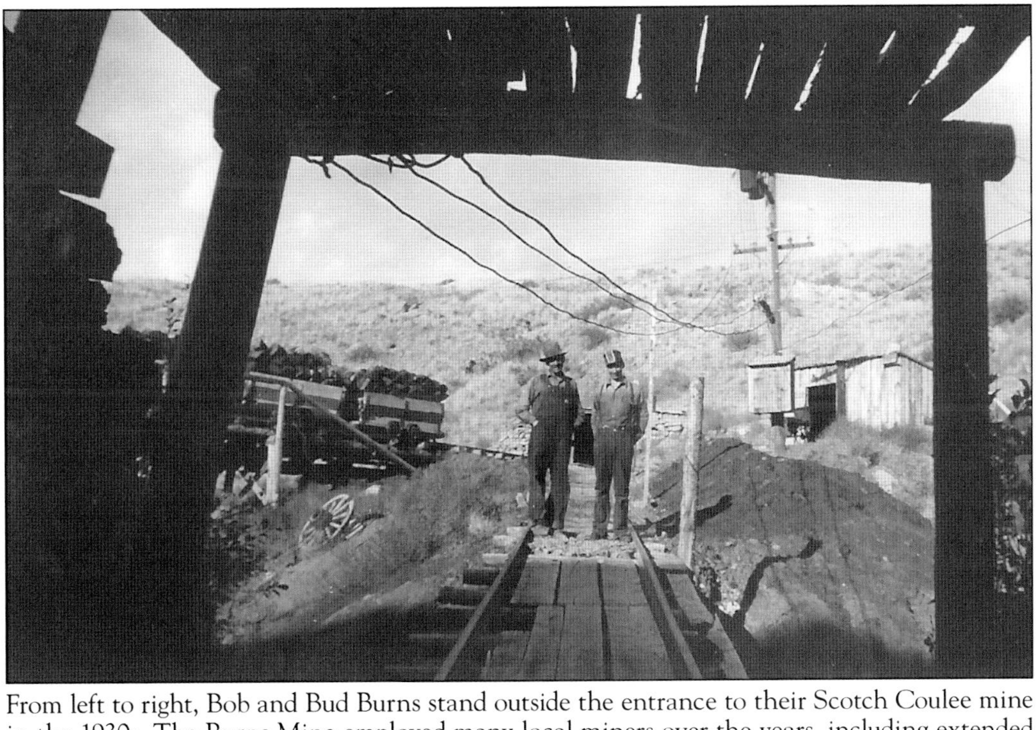

From left to right, Bob and Bud Burns stand outside the entrance to their Scotch Coulee mine in the 1930s. The Burns Mine employed many local miners over the years, including extended family members and longtime friends. Bob acted as the surface boss, while the younger Bud served as underground boss. (Burns.)

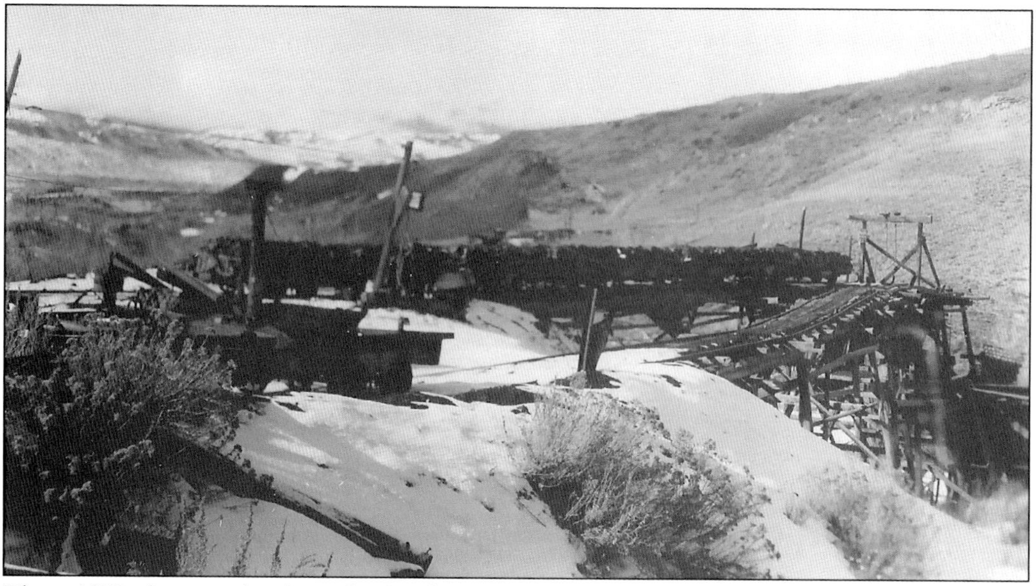

These 1970 photographs show the Janskovitch Mine and its owners. In 1932, the Janskovitch brothers, Leopold "Poly," Frank, Joe, and Tony, acquired land previously deeded to Lodenia Lamport and began operating a privately held mine (above). Their mine was known as the Roadside Mine, or Janskovitch Mine. Tony Janskovitch died when the roof of the mine collapsed on him after he ignited a blasting charge to loosen coal. This was the only serious accident the mine experienced in almost 40 years of operation. Despite this impressive record, the State Bureau of Mines ordered the mine closed in 1970 due to improper machinery and air-conditioning facilities. The photograph below shows the Janskovitch brothers. They are, from left to right, Poly and Frank. (Both, CCHS.)

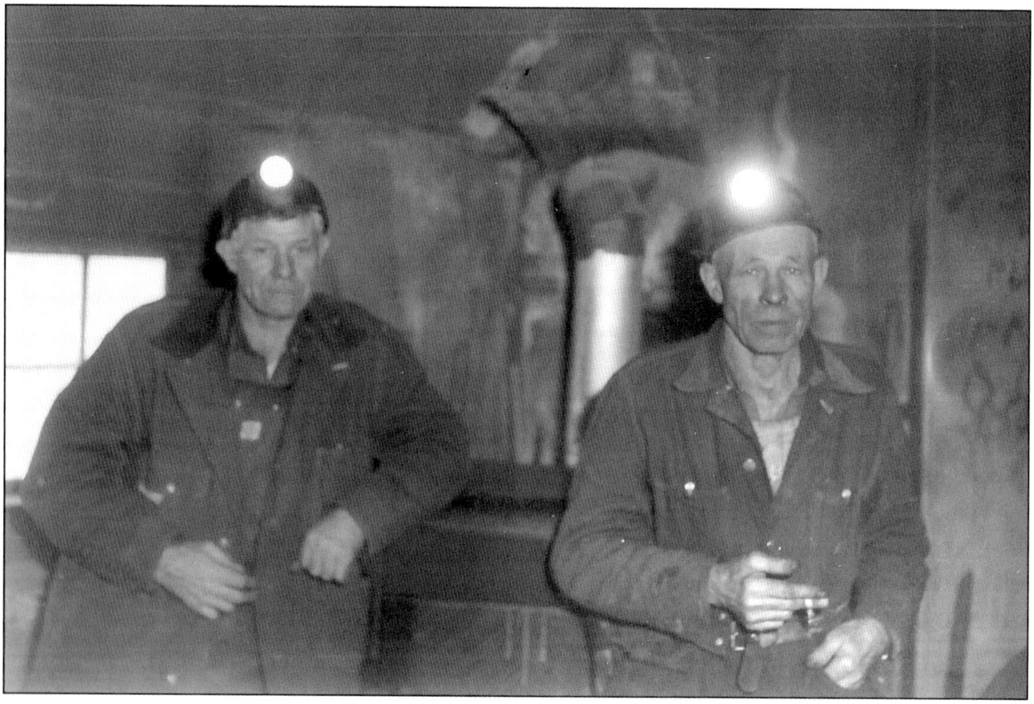

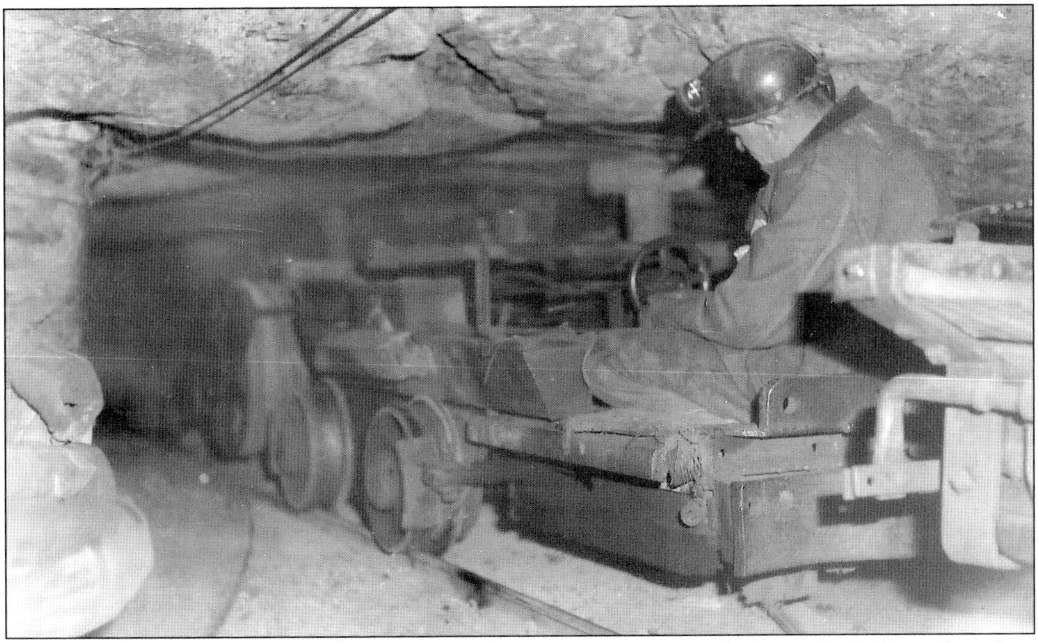

The Janskovitch brothers mined one of the smaller coal seams underlying the hills and coulees of Bear Creek Valley. The seam averaged only 3 feet thick. This small seam required the brothers to work in extremely cramped quarters and to modify standard-issue mining equipment, or build their own, to fit into these confined spaces. A homemade engine hauls homemade coal cars in the photograph above. Timber braces support the rock roof above a mined section of coal in the photograph below. The 3-foot coal seam mined by the Janskovitchs is visible behind these braces. (Both, CCHS.)

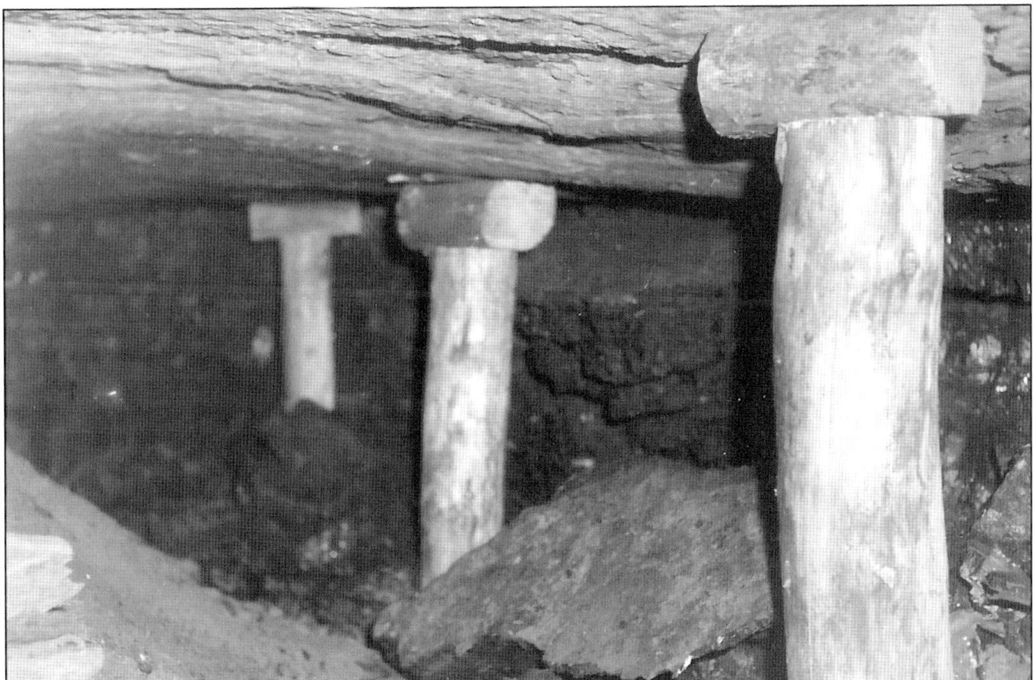

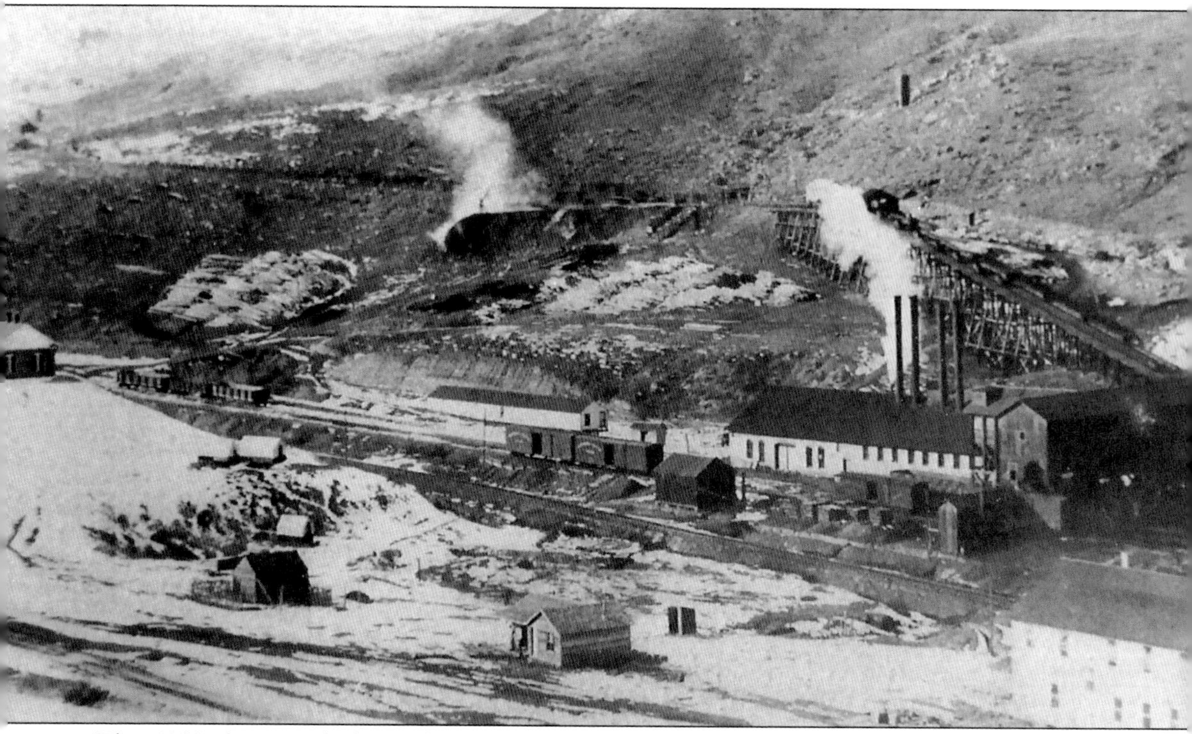

This 1909 photograph shows the Bear Creek Coal Company Mine. Philip Gallaher, Peter and Christian Yegen, and George T. Lamport, all prominent Billings businessmen, formed the Bear Creek Coal Company in the late 1890s and acquired land one-half mile west of the town of Bearcreek. The mine soon generated all of Bearcreek's electricity. By 1906, a report in *The Mining World* praised the company's mine as "the best developed, and in fact the only one ready to mine any amount of commercial coal" in Bear Creek Valley. In just 14 years, however, all the commercially viable coal had been removed from the property, and competing coal interests owned the surrounding land. After a 1920 windstorm destroyed the mine's trestle, the mine closed for the simple lack of ability to expand. (CCHS.)

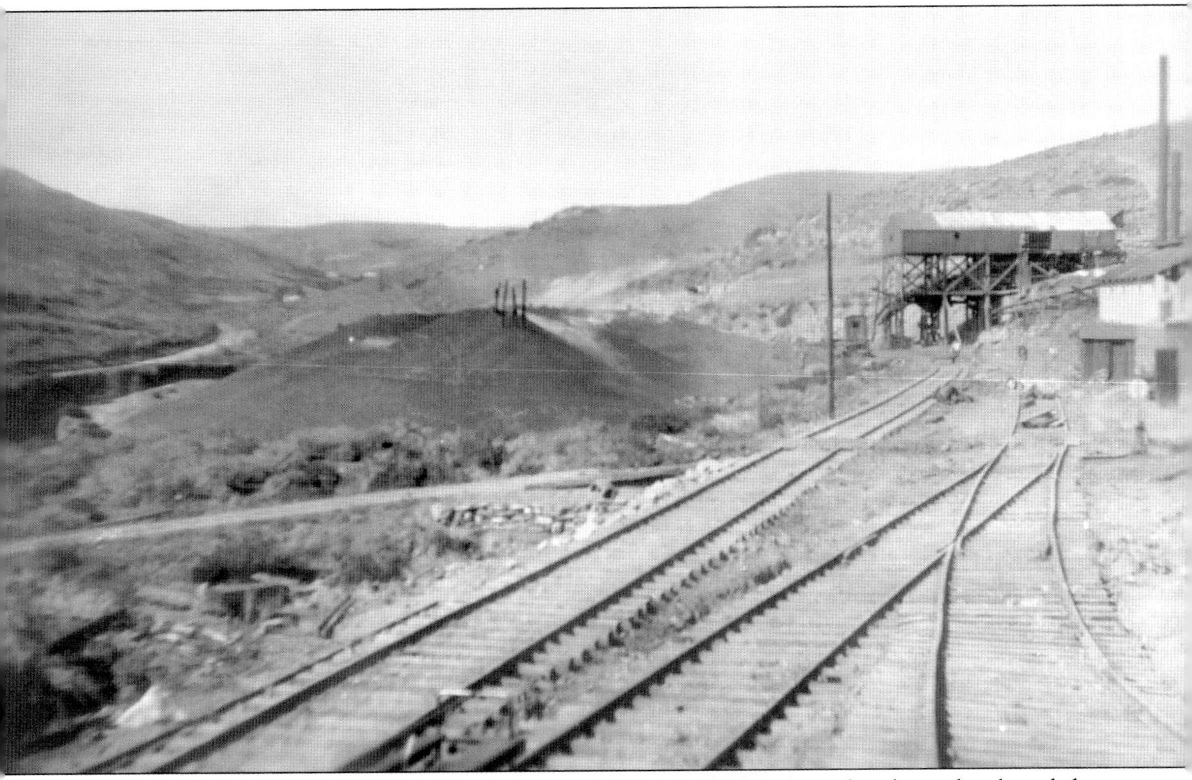

William A. Talmage, a local businessman and a partner with the Yegen brothers, developed the International Coal Company at the eastern end of Virtue Gulch in 1906. Like the Bear Creek Coal Company Mine, it shut down in the early 1920s. This 1928 photograph shows the mine's processing plant seven years after closing. In the far distance, at the head of Virtue Gulch, stands the processing plant of the Smokeless and Sootless Coal Company Mine. The International Coal Company struggled for years to remain viable, securing more than $170,000 in loans from Bearcreek's Clark-Wright Bank to remain afloat. After fire destroyed the majority of its processing plant in the early 1920s, the company was unable to afford to rebuild. It closed and defaulted on its financial obligations, and this resulted in the failure of the Clark-Wright Bank as well. (Kidwell.)

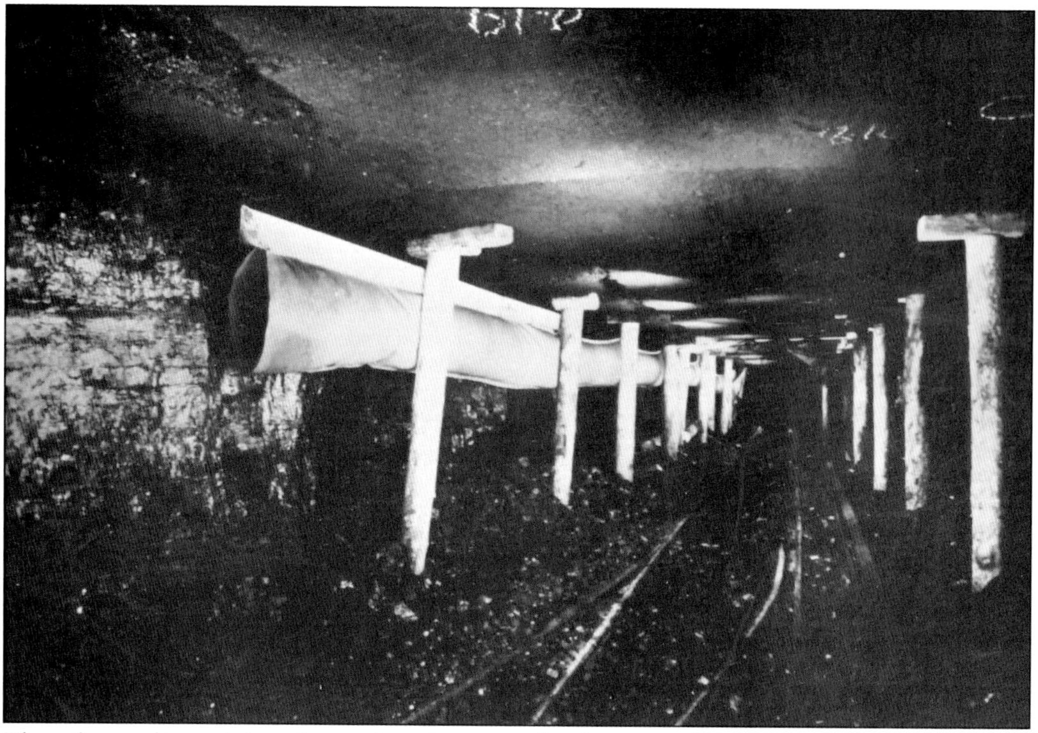

Three factors dictated the safety and productivity of coal mines in Bear Creek Valley: roof supports to prevent cave-ins, water pumps to prevent flooding, and ventilation to flush deadly methane gas to the surface. Without these, no mine could succeed. In this photograph, timbers support the roof, and a cloth conduit guides fresh air from the surface to active areas of the mine. (CCHS.)

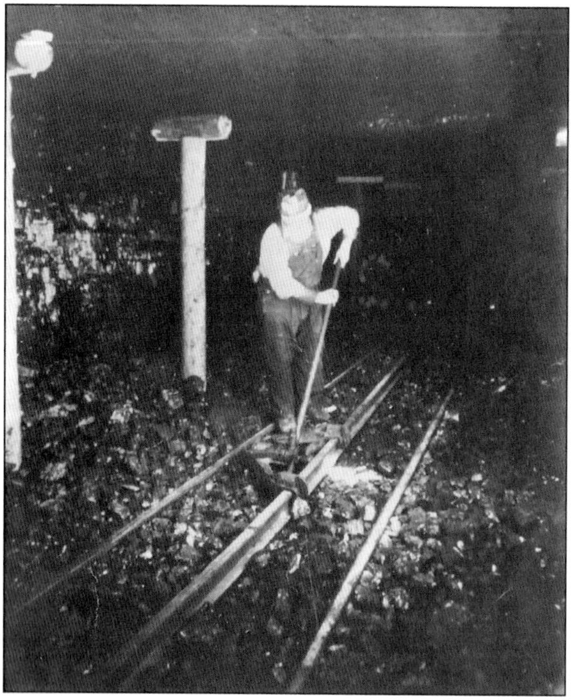

The narrow-gauge rail lines used in coal mines underwent a cycle of construction, maintenance, and removal as material was reused to mine other areas. A trackman uses an alignment tool to straighten a section of track (left). As mining progressed from one area of the mine to another, trackmen removed rails from the previously mined areas for use in the active sections. (CCHS.)

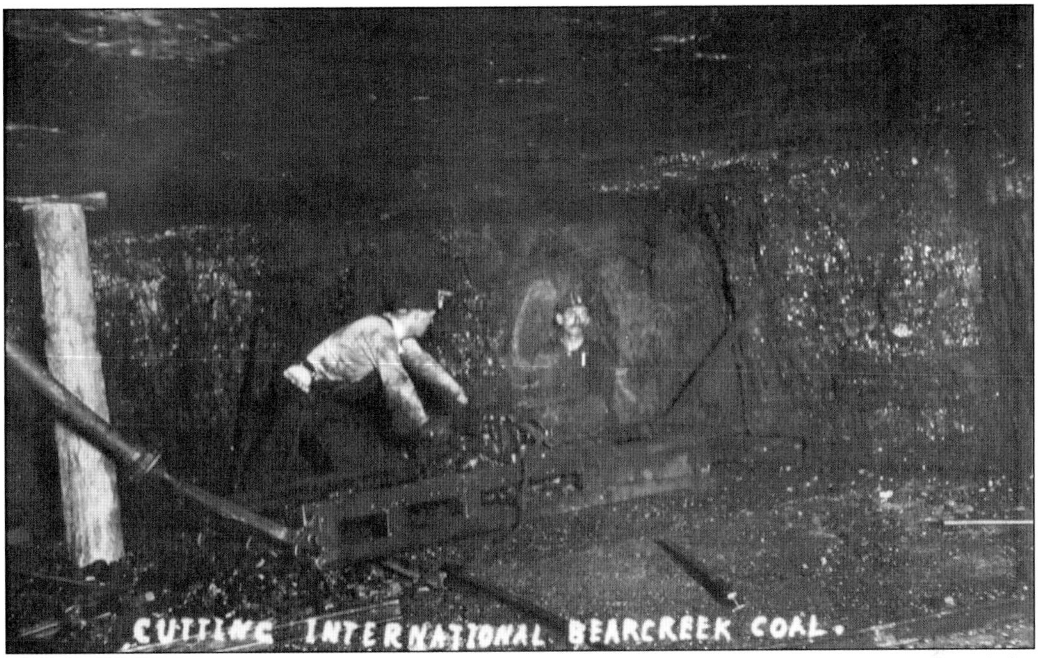

After tracks were laid to the face of the coal seam, mining machines operators (above) used the tracks to guide their machines to the coal face and undercut a section it. Undercutting provided a clean breaking point for the coal when it underwent blasting—the next step in the process. Blasting involved inserting explosives into the coal face and igniting them. (CCHS.)

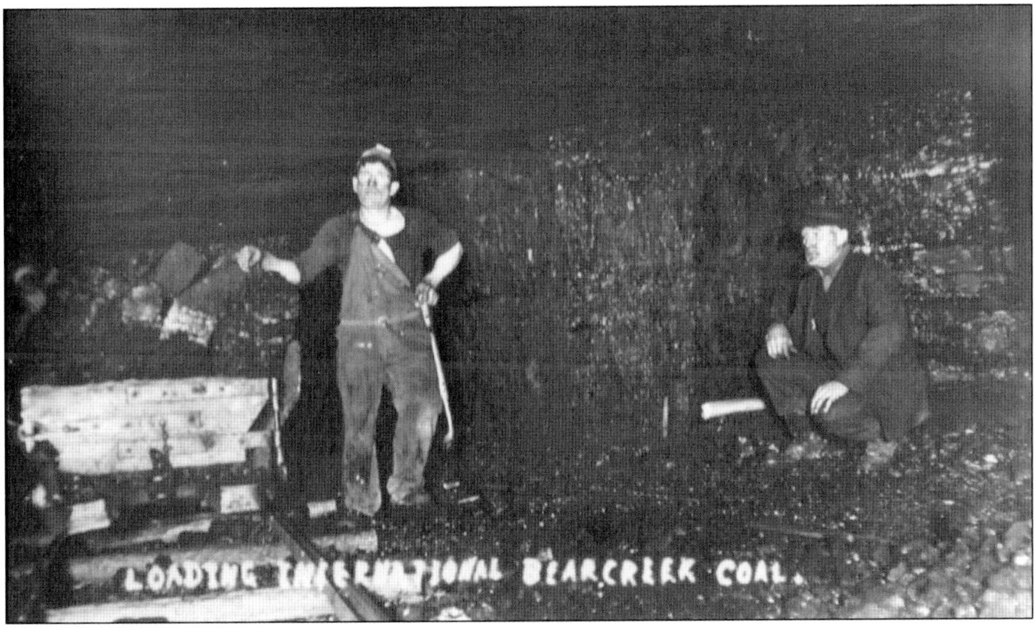

After the coal dust settled from blasting, the backbreaking work of hand loading the coal began. This was a particularly dangerous time because blasting often left the surrounding roof and walls unstable. A faceman entered the recently blasted area first to check for these hidden hazards and correct them. Even so, the work remained treacherous, and by 1920, most mines in Bear Creek Valley used automatic loading machines. (CCHS.)

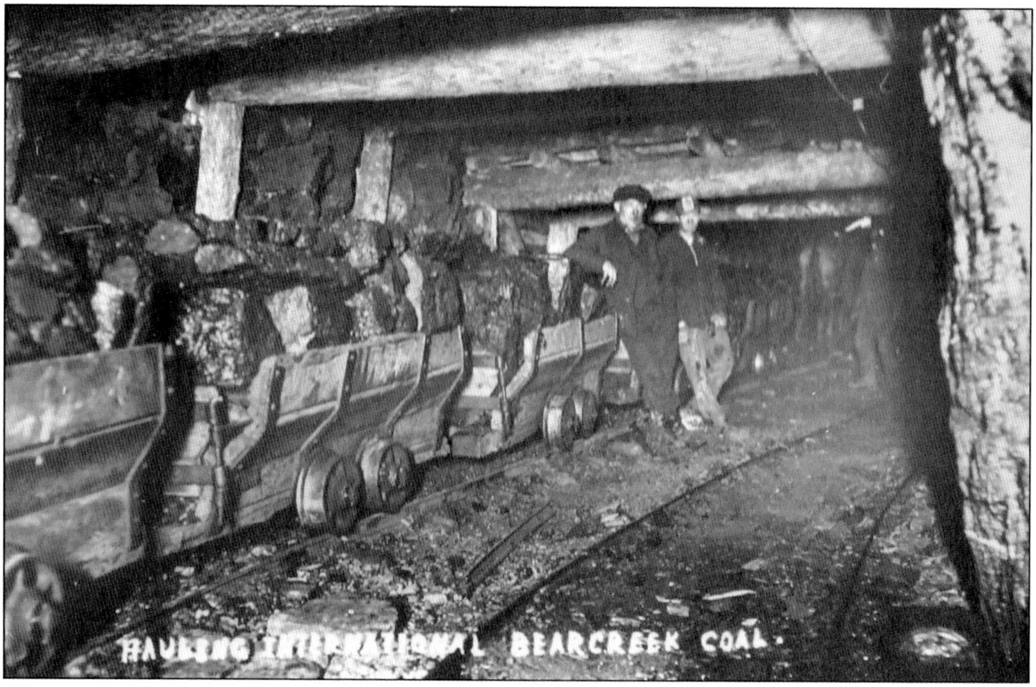

The next step in mining coal required bringing fully loaded coal cars to the surface. At first, horses and mules pulled the loaded coal cars from the mine. Later electric motors replaced them. The mechanization of the coal cutting, loading, and hauling processes greatly increased the mines' productivity—at the cost of lost jobs for the everyday miner. (CCHS.)

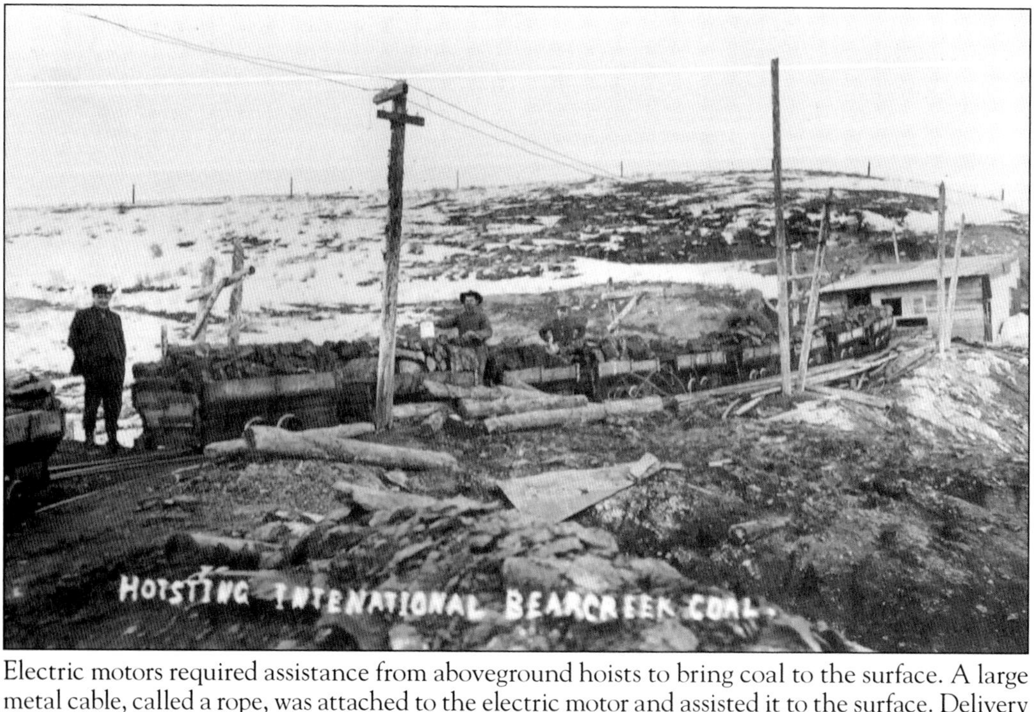

Electric motors required assistance from aboveground hoists to bring coal to the surface. A large metal cable, called a rope, was attached to the electric motor and assisted it to the surface. Delivery of the coal to the tipple marked the end of the mining stage of operations. (CCHS.)

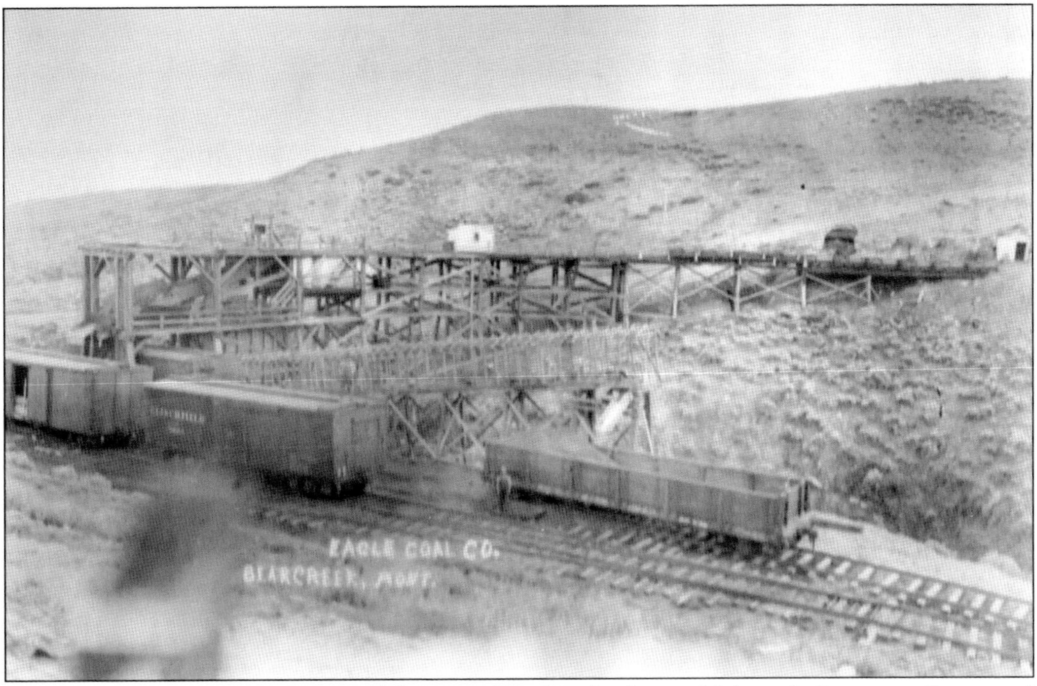

Local businessman John Thomas Flaherty and Red Lodge lawyer Hubert A. Simmons Sr. opened the Eagle Coal Company Mine in Foster Gulch near the beginning of the 20th century. Flaherty arrived in the area in 1890. Before his death in 1926, he served as both an alderman and as the mayor of neighboring Red Lodge. Foster Gulch was not extensively mined until 1917, when the Montana, Wyoming, and Southern Railroad constructed a railway line from Bearcreek into the gulch. Dr. John Carl Frederick Siegfriedt and other paleontologists discovered a huge array of fossilized plants and animals in the Eagle Coal Company Mine. (Above, CCHS; below, Flash's Photography.)

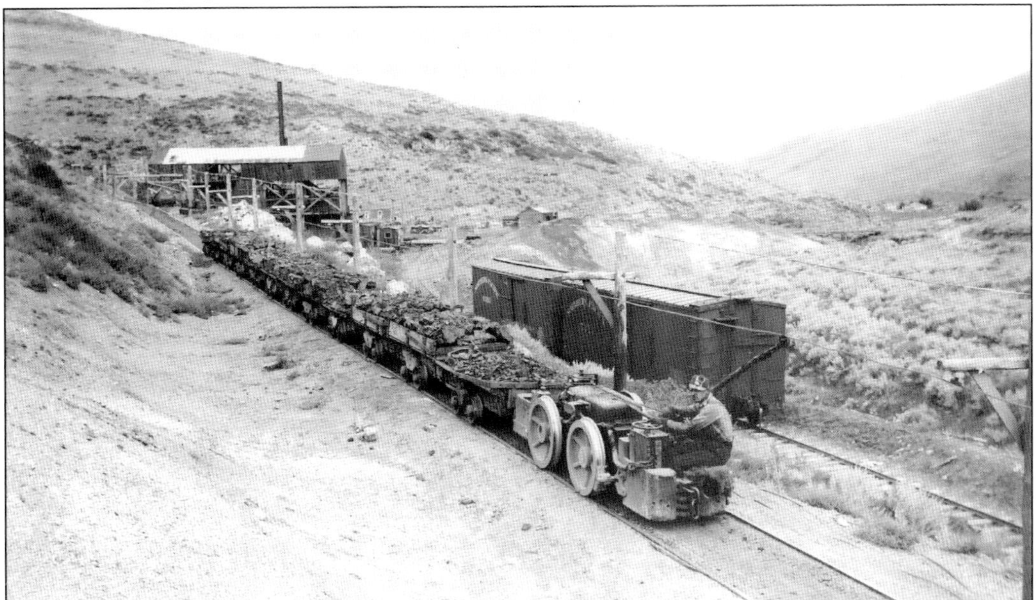

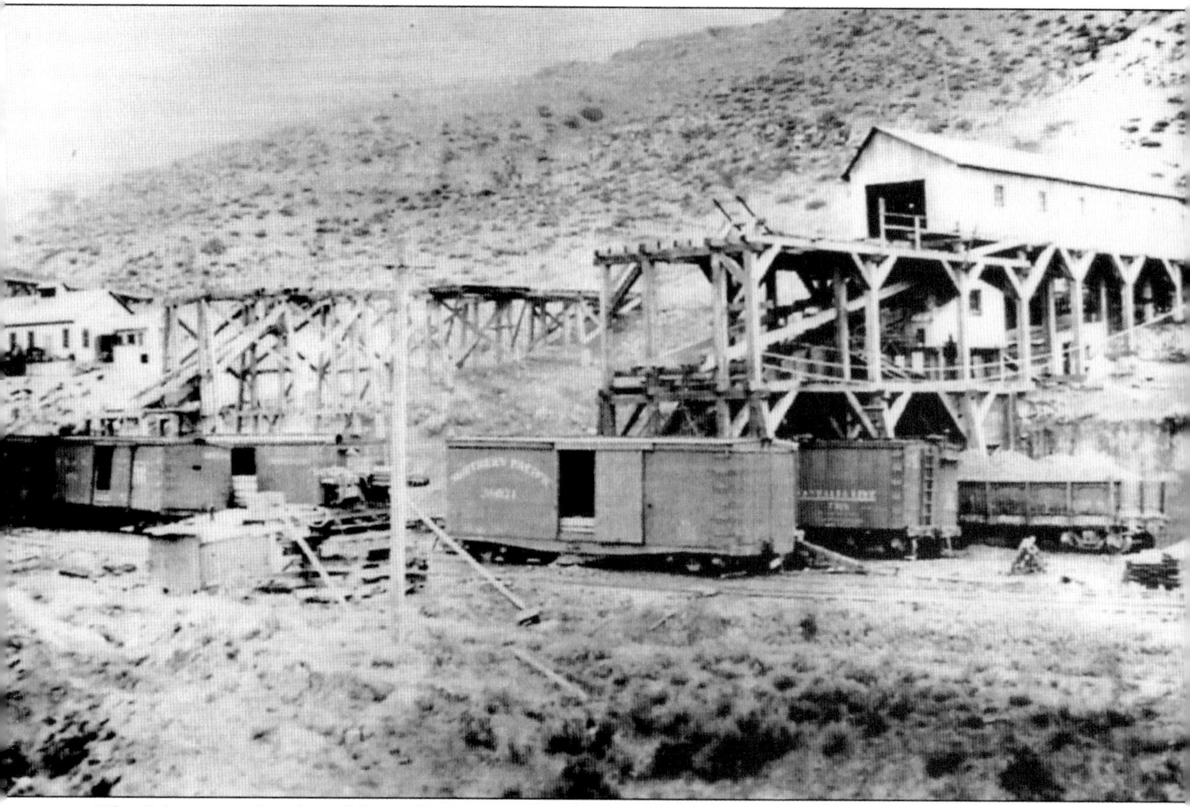

The Montana Coal and Iron Company purchased land at the southern end of Foster Gulch in 1905 and began development of the Foster Gulch Mine by 1907. Extensive development of this mine did not begin until the arrival of the railway in 1917. In the quarter-century from that time until the Smith Mine disaster in 1943, the underground workings of the Montana Coal and Iron Company's Smith and Foster Gulch Mines grew so extensive that their tunnels connected beneath the surface. After the Smith Mine disaster, and the subsequent attempt by the Montana Coal and Iron Company to mine in Scotch Coulee, the Foster Gulch Mine became the company's sole producing mine in the valley. Production in the mine continued until 1953, when the Montana Coal and Iron Company closed it after losing the mine's largest remaining customer, the Great Western Sugar Company in Billings, Montana. (CCHS.)

Three

Towns and Neighborhoods

The introduction of large-scale mining to Bear Creek Valley brought with it a flood of new citizens from across the United States and Europe. Neighborhoods sprang up in the newly created towns of Bearcreek and Washoe, and at all points in between. These neighborhoods, bearing names as eclectic as the people who built them, grew to form a nearly continuous village between Washoe and Bearcreek. The valley's population reached its peak between 1910 and 1920 and has declined steadily since.

The western end of the valley held the town of Washoe and its Company Row neighborhood. East of Company Row and halfway between Washoe and the Smith Mine stood a collection of homes called Caledonia.

Immediately northwest of the Smith Mine sat Cousin Row. The Horseshoe Bend neighborhood occupied the area just east of the confluence of Keucking Creek and Bear Creek. Directly south of Horseshoe Bend, homes lined both sides of Scotch Coulee.

Chickentown was located east of Horseshoe Bend and west of the Virtue Gulch intersection. These homes were built on the north side of the main valley road and to the south of Bear Creek. Stringtown was between the Virtue Gulch intersection and the western city limit of Bearcreek. These homes were built to the south of the main valley road and north of Bear Creek.

East of Stringtown is the town of Bearcreek. The south-central Bearcreek neighborhood known as Hi-Bug housed many of the town's more affluent citizens, as well as Bearcreek High School. The Uptown neighborhood centered around the business district at the intersection of Main Street and First Street, not far from Bearcreek Elementary School.

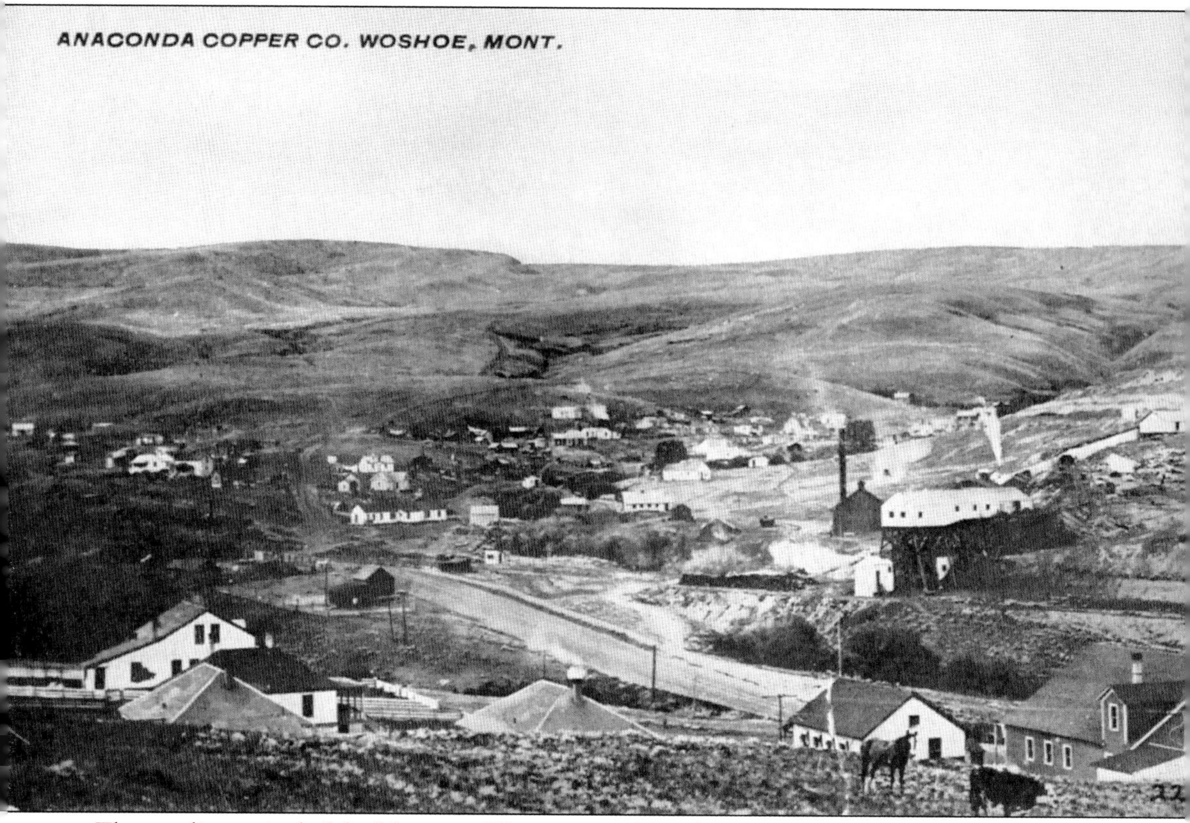

The pending arrival of the Montana, Wyoming, and Southern Railroad spurred the establishment of the town of Washoe and its two coal mines beginning in 1905. A crew of 50 carpenters completed the majority of the town, coal-processing plant, and support buildings by 1907. The crews could haul their construction materials toward the town site by train but only so far as the tracks advanced. Beyond this, they relied upon horse-drawn wagons. The plans for the town/mine complex called for the construction of 51 structures, including tenement homes, offices, superintendent and cashier homes, boardinghouses, a blacksmith shop, stables, tipples, boxcar loaders, and a power plant. This photograph looks west toward Red Lodge from a hill near the elementary school. In the left foreground stand the white-sided superintendent's and cashier's homes. The buildings in the lower right are the mine office and the darker-colored general store. The Washoe Coal Company Mine No. 2 lies in the distance. (Wakenshaw.)

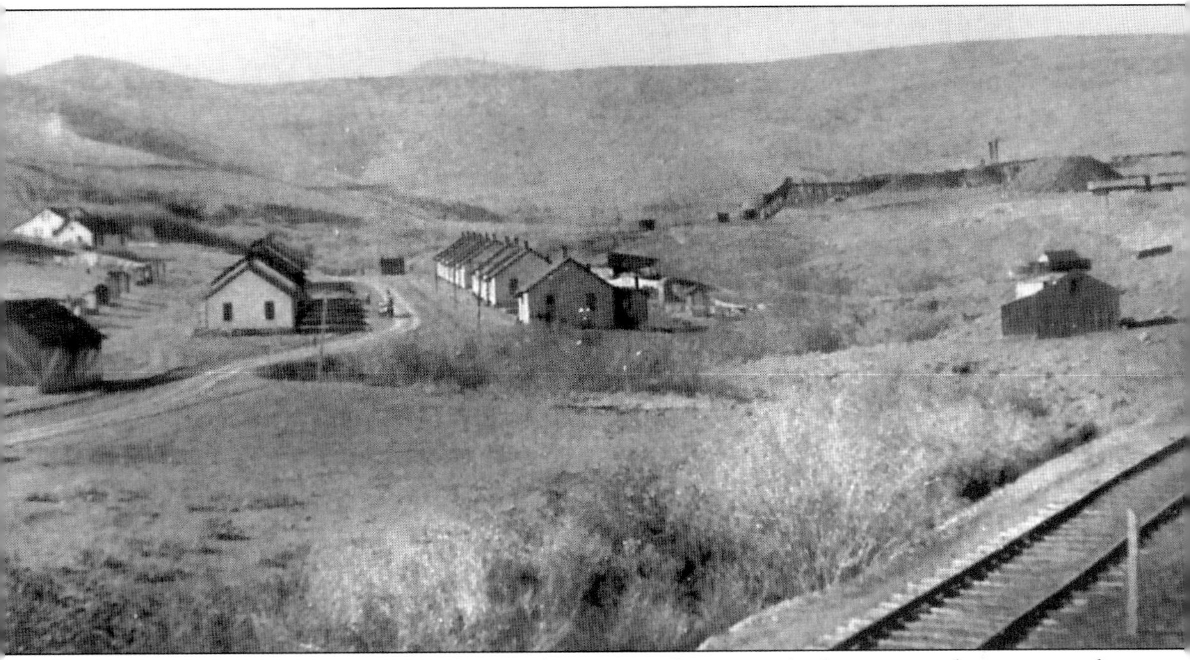

This photograph presents a detailed view of two rows of company-built tenement homes east of Washoe and south of Keucking Creek. This small neighborhood came to be known as Company Row. The background provides a rare glimpse of the Washoe Coal Company Mine No. 1, shown on the right. (CCHS.)

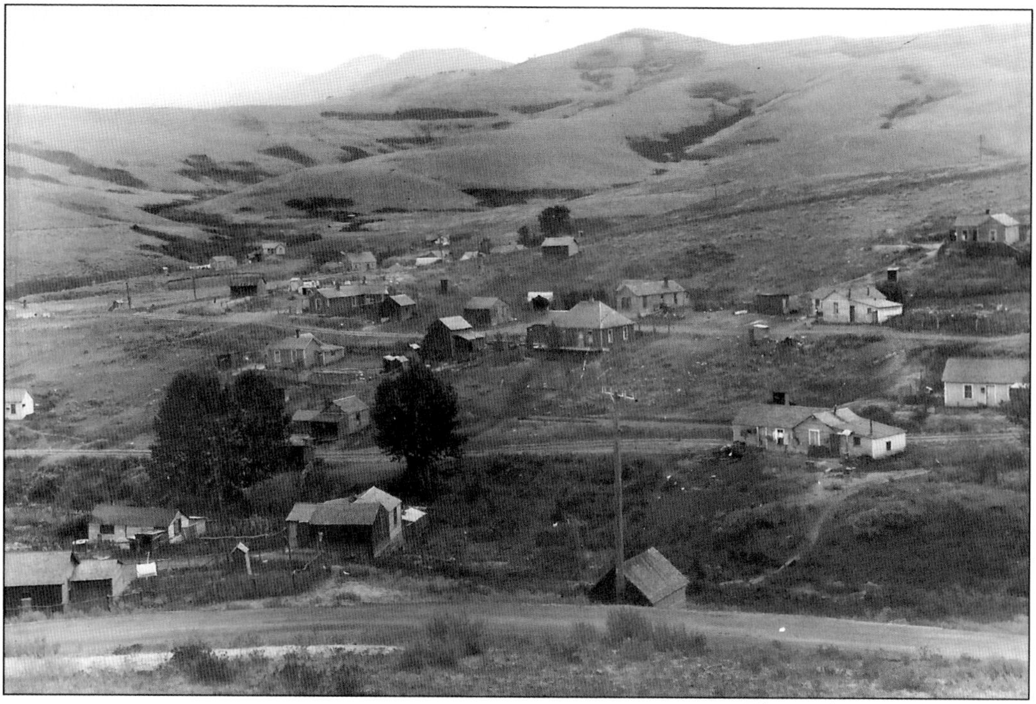

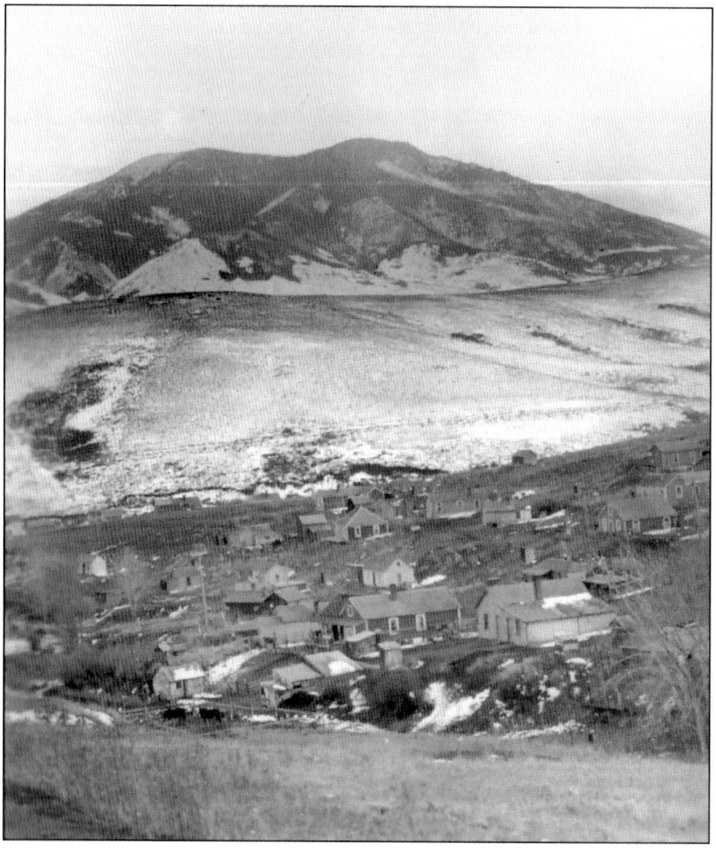

These photographs capture Washoe's residential west end. The town's west side geography consists of two small coulees leading to the top of the high ridge that separates Bear Creek Valley from Red Lodge. Both of these photographs show the northern portion of these two coulees, where the majority of homes stood and the Washoe-to-Red Lodge road passed. The photograph above shows the Washoe-to-Red Lodge road in the foreground. Keucking Creek flows eastward out of the Beartooth Mountains, through the southern coulee, and feeds into Bear Creek, flowing out of Scotch Coulee several miles from Washoe. (Above, Flash's Photography; left, Planichek.)

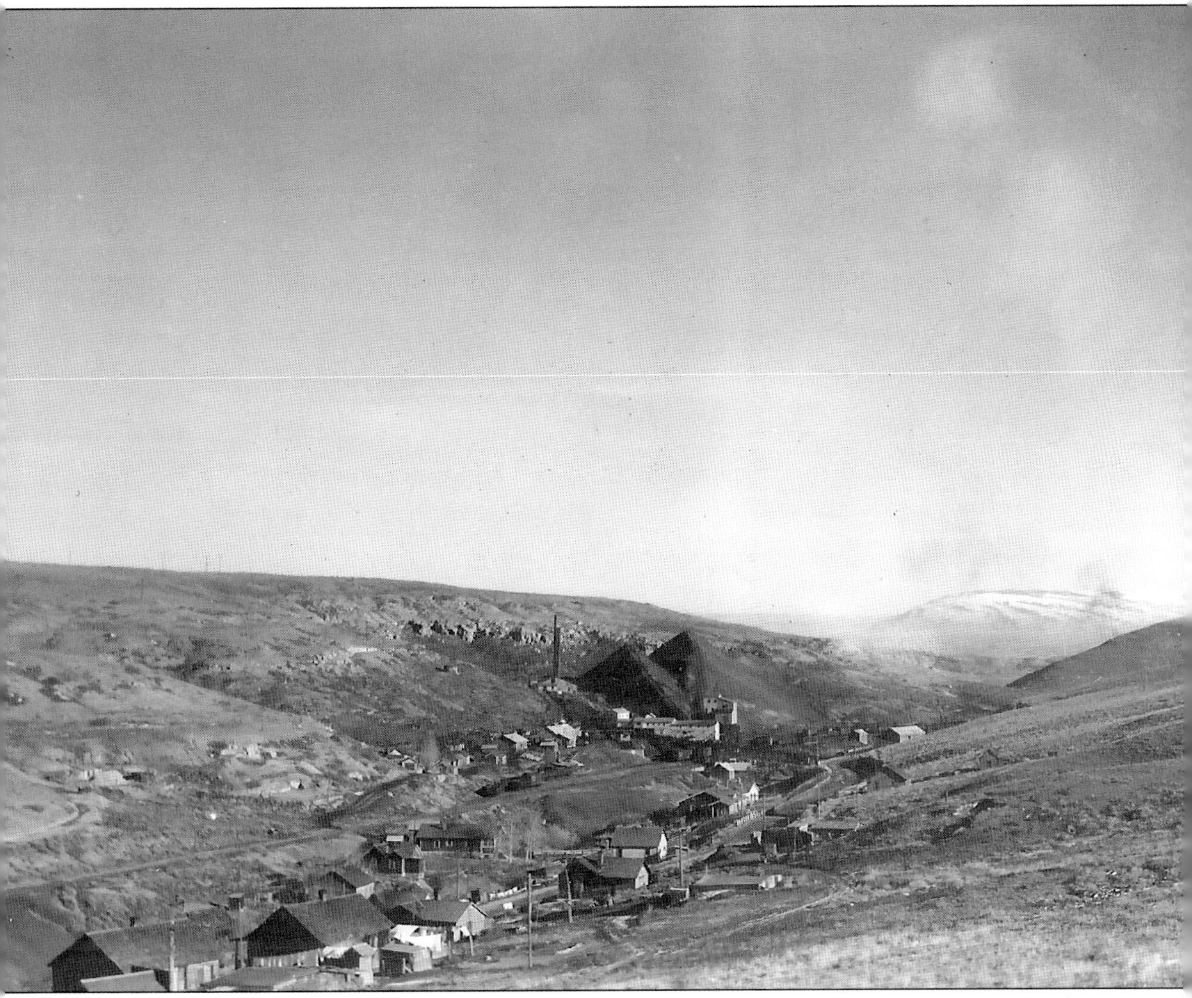

With the Smith Mine as its backdrop, this photograph shows two of the six neighborhoods that existed between Washoe and Bearcreek. The homes in the foreground are the eastern end of the Caledonia neighborhood. Aptly named, many of Caledonia's residents were Scottish immigrants. The group of homes beneath the Smith Mine's power plant smokestack and towering slack piles was known as Cousin Row because many of its residents were blood relations. During the Smith Mine disaster, the residents of Cousin Row opened their homes to provide rescuers with a convenient place to eat, drink coffee, and rest before their next shift. In between Cousin Row and Caledonia lies the track bed of the Montana, Wyoming, and Southern Railroad. Eastern Montana's snow-covered Pryor Mountain range looms in the distance. (Flash's Photography.)

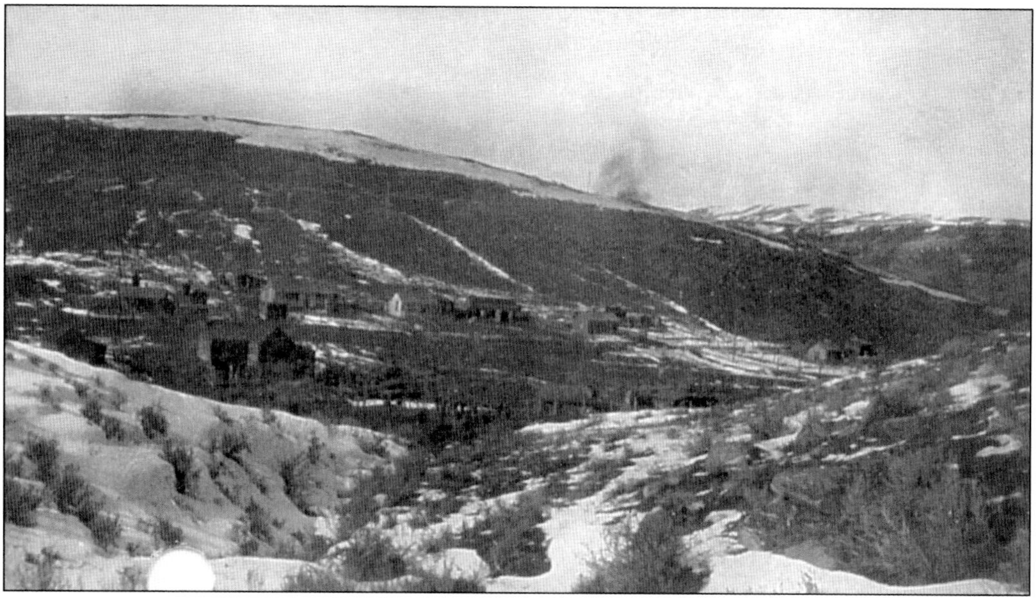

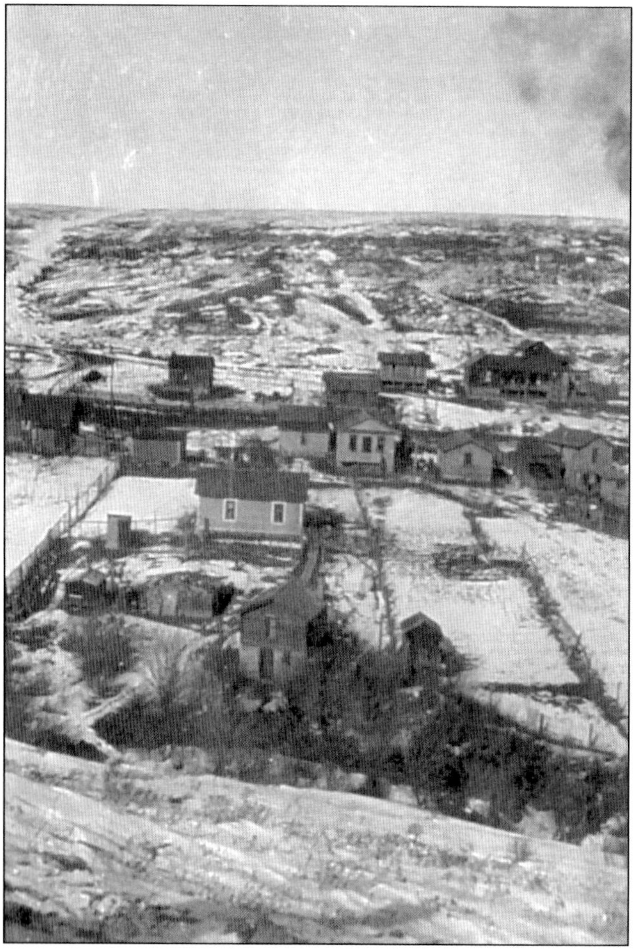

These 1910s panoramas of Scotch Coulee homes give a rare glimpse of this once-thriving community. Both photographs look westward toward the Smith Mine. In these photographs, a plume of smoke from the Smith Mine's coal-fired power plant rises from behind the hillside. Bear Creek flows out of the mountains, through the coulee, to be joined by its tributary, Keucking Creek, just east of the Smith Mine. Homes lined Scotch Coulee for more than 1 mile south from this point. Although the name of this coulee suggests that its residents were of Scottish descent, Scotch Coulee was predominantly home to immigrants from Serbia, Croatia, Montenegro, Austria, Czechoslovakia, and Slovenia. (Both, Planichek.)

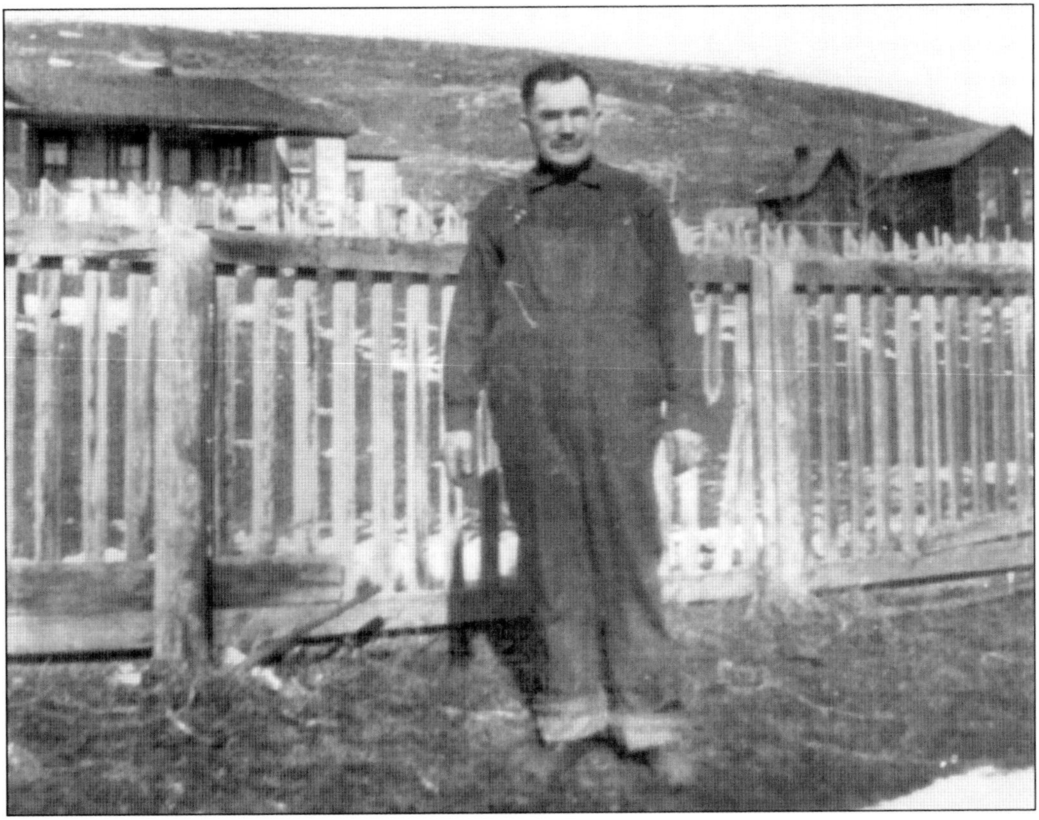

These photographs provide a more detailed look at the homes of Scotch Coulee. Picket fences surrounded most homes, and porches were an integral architectural feature. The majority of homes shown on this and the preceding page were hand-built by the homeowners and their neighbors. Jacob Mourich, shown above, undoubtedly had a hand in building many of the Scotch Coulee homes, including that of his grandson, Tony "Tonch" Planichek, on the eastern side of the coulee (right). This photograph was taken from near the spot where the Scotch Coulee Hall stood. (Both, Planichek.)

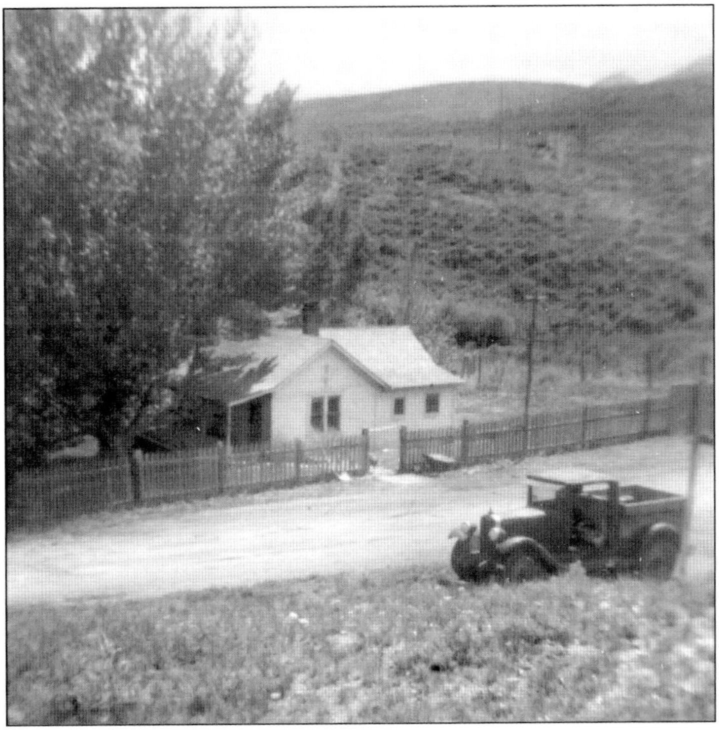

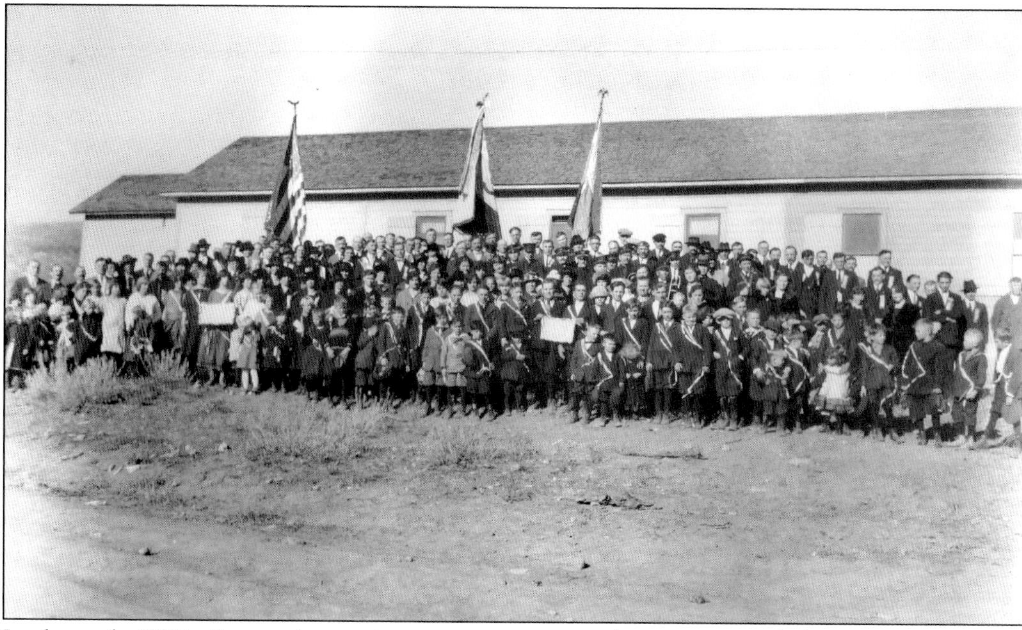

In the early 1920s, fraternal organizations representing the countries of Slovenia, Croatia, and Serbia erected a community hall in Scotch Coulee. Members of these organizations, including many Scotch Coulee residents, built the hall on the western side of the coulee near the backcountry road connecting the coulee with Washoe. These photographs capture the community-wide celebration that followed completion of the project. The photograph above shows more than 200 people and gives a sense of the large population living in the coulee at the time. Scotch Coulee Hall was sold in the early 1950s and was moved to a farm near the neighboring town of Fox, Montana, where it still serves as an outbuilding. (Above, Mourich; below, Planichek.)

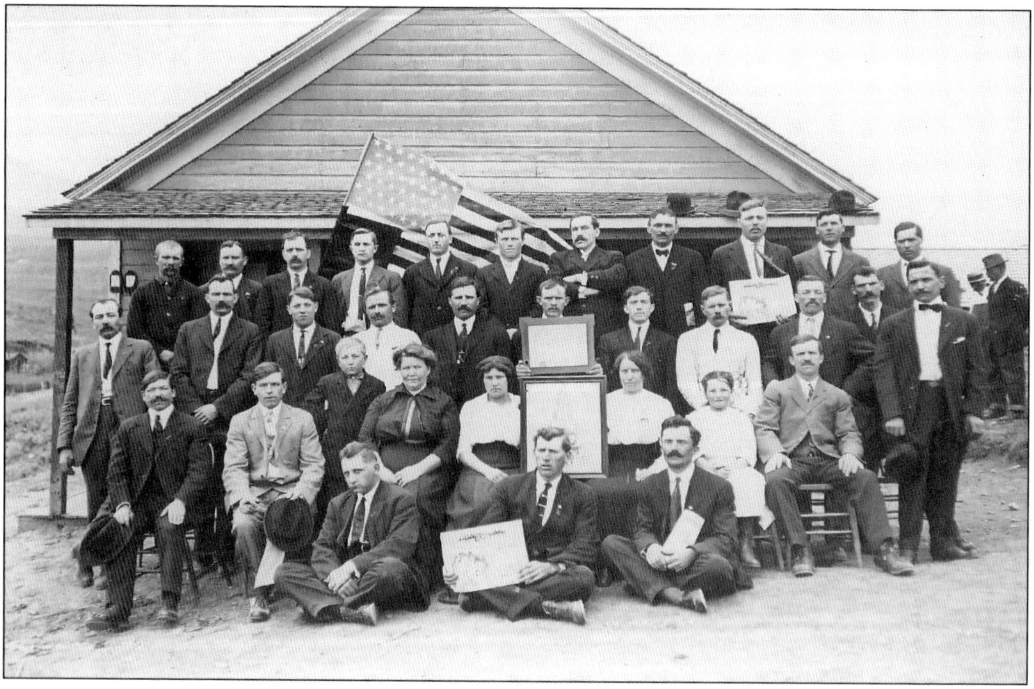

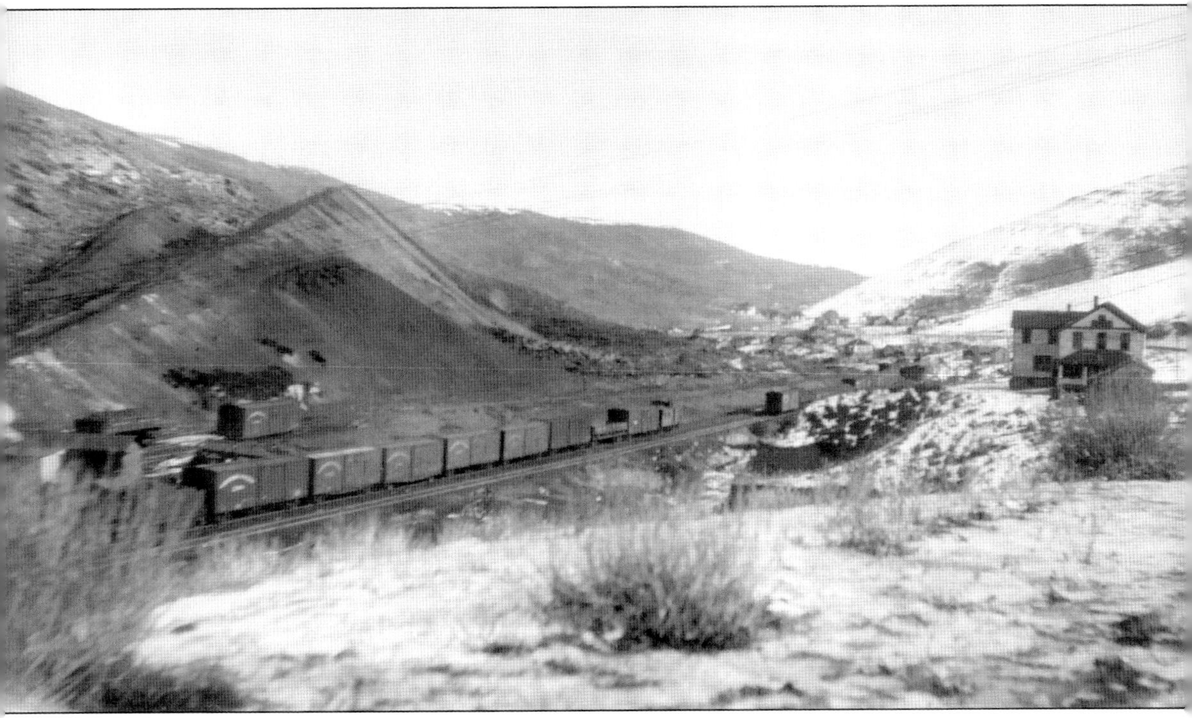

The Horseshoe Bend neighborhood occupied the area just east of the Keucking Creek and Bear Creek confluence and north of the Bear Creek Coal Company Mine. The name Horseshoe Bend came from the original shape of the main valley road at this point. The Bear Creek Coal Company boardinghouse (right) defined the northern border of this locality. Note the horseshoe shape the road takes in skirting the Bear Creek Coal Company boardinghouse. The remainder of the neighborhood extended out of frame south of the boardinghouse. The western end of Bearcreek lies in the distance; the distinctive, white, grade-school building marks the town's western city limit. (Kidwell.)

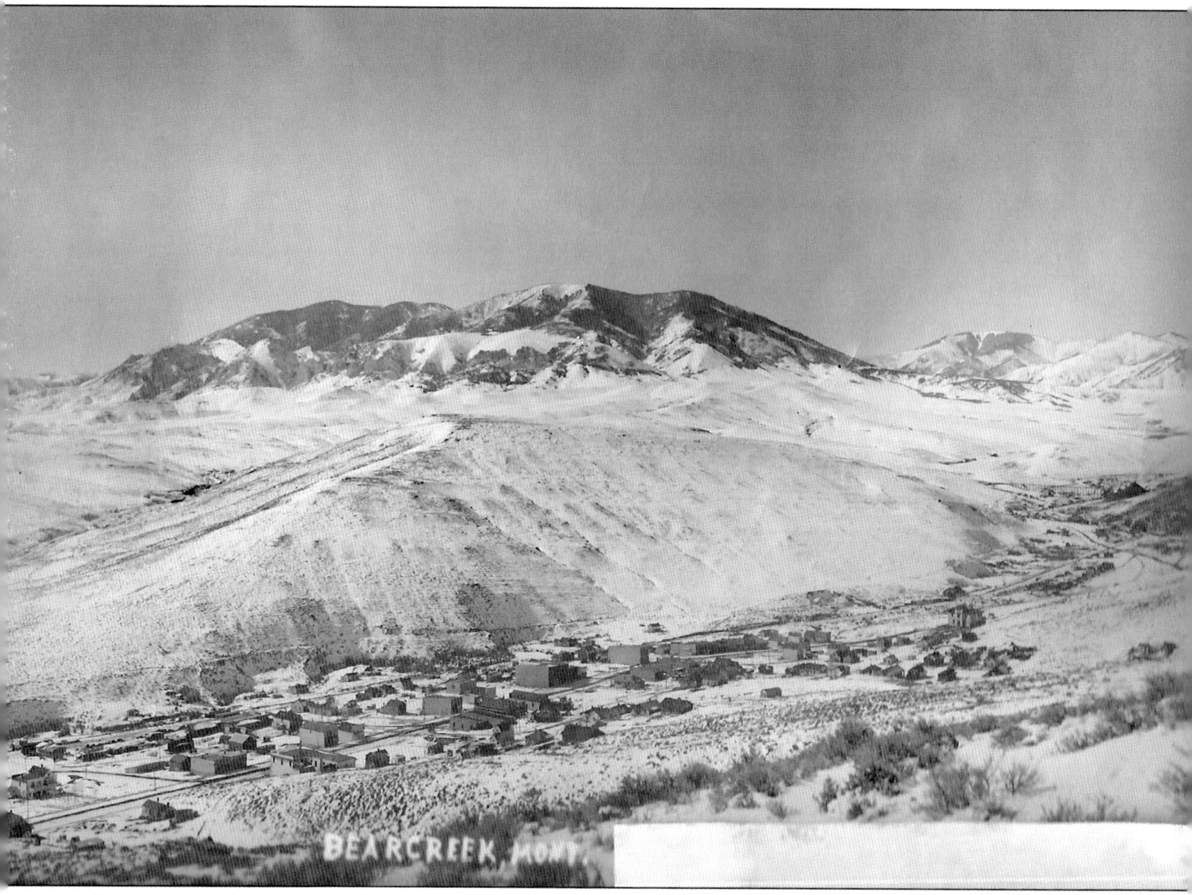

Two neighborhoods existed between Horseshoe Bend and Bearcreek's western city limit. Chickentown occupied the area east of Horseshoe Bend and west of the Virtue Gulch intersection. It began near the Bear Creek Coal Company Mine and ended where Bear Creek crossed under the road. These homes were built on the north side of the road and to the south of Bear Creek. Chickentown (center right) is the cluster of homes at the foot of the hill just below the black slack piles of the Bear Creek Coal Company Mine. The other neighborhood, Stringtown, stood between Chickentown and Bearcreek's western city limit. These homes formed a line to the south of the road between Bearcreek and Washoe and north of Bear Creek itself. They can be seen in this photograph between Chickentown and the two-story Bearcreek Elementary School. (Mourich.)

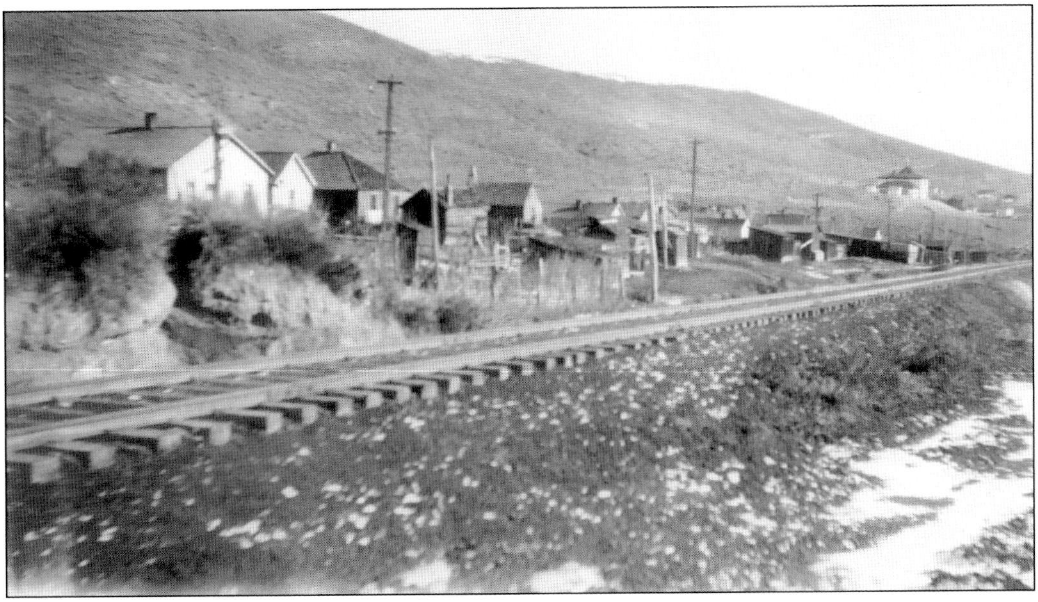

These photographs illustrate the eastern (pictured above) and western (shown below) ends of the Chickentown neighborhood. The homes on Chickentown's eastern end came perilously close to the railway tracks for its children but were within easy walking distance to the Bearcreek Elementary School. The western end of Chickentown had its own access road as well as a Montana, Wyoming, and Southern Railroad water tower and turntable. The water tower is visible along the railway tracks at center left of the photograph below. The Montana, Wyoming, and Southern Railroad bed served as a popular promenade for evening strolls during fair weather. (Both, Kidwell.)

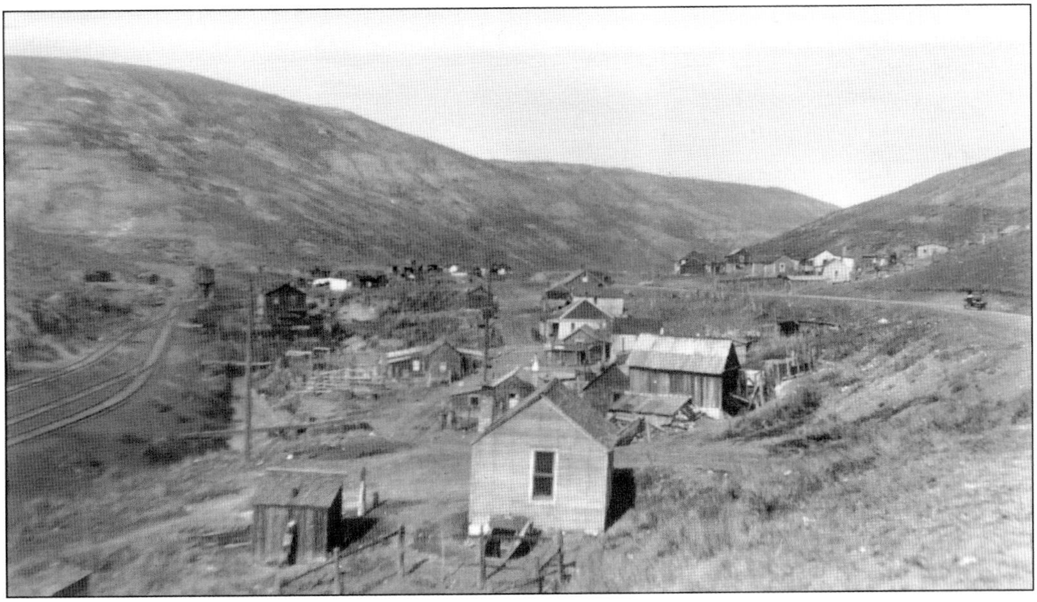

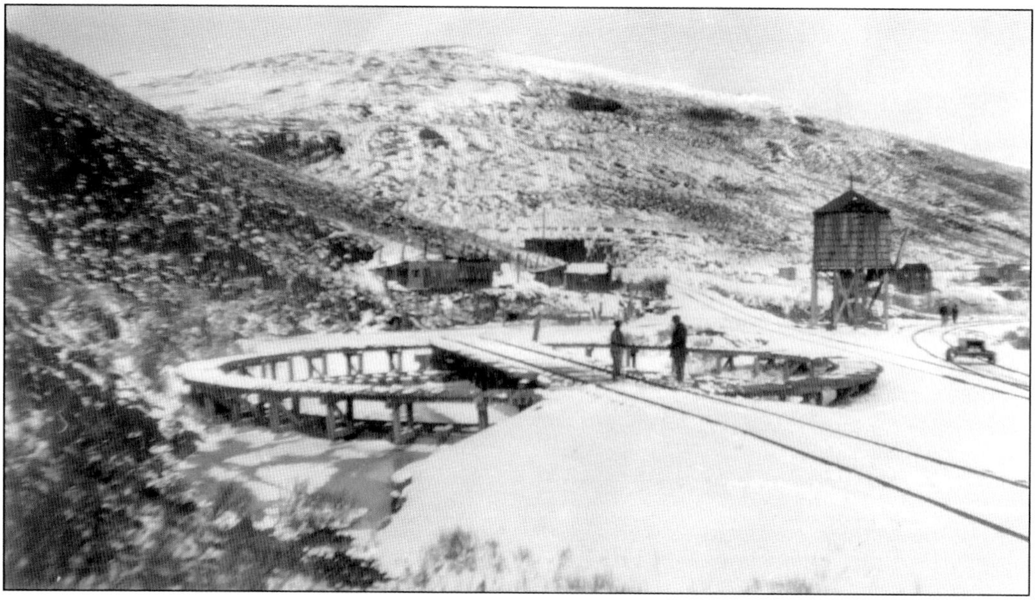

These photographs show the Montana, Wyoming, and Southern Railroad's water tower and turntable in Chickentown. Locomotive turntables provided the railway with the ability to reverse the direction of its locomotives for the return trip out of the valley's gulches and back to Belfry. The turntable in these photographs serviced locomotives traveling into Virtue Gulch and to Washoe. Another turntable at the eastern end of Bearcreek serviced locomotives traveling into Foster Gulch. In the photograph above, a handcar can be seen on the tracks to the right of the picture. In the photograph below, a railroad worker stands ready to throw a switch as a locomotive approaches. (Both, Kidwell.)

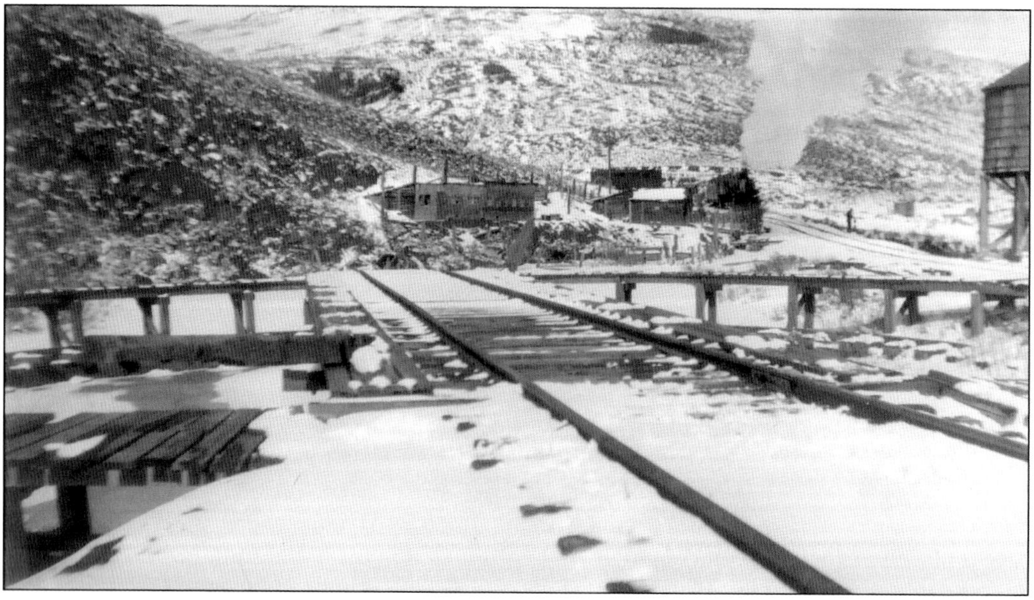

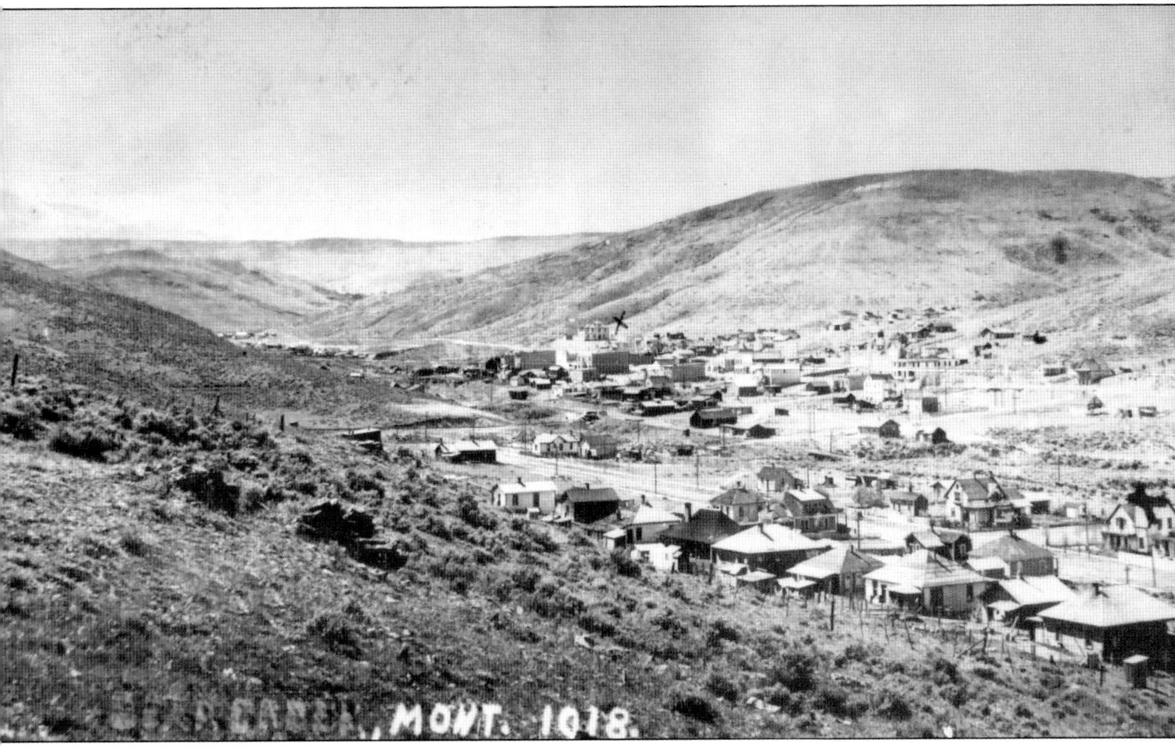

This 1918 photograph, taken from the hillside above Bearcreek High School, shows the western end of Bearcreek. The "X" in the center of the photograph marks the location of Bearcreek Elementary School. In the far distance, to the left of the dirt road, stand the homes of Stringtown. Residents of Bearcreek referred to the area surrounding the high school as Hi-Bug. George T. Lamport and Robert Leavens, who first platted Bearcreek in 1905, made their homes in Hi-Bug. In December 1906, Bearcreek incorporated as a town. It soon sported such big-town amenities as electric street lamps, telephone and water systems, and concrete sidewalks. During the next decade, the population of the valley continued to grow steadily. World War I, however, triggered a genuine population boom. Seven commercial mines, employing in excess of 1,000 miners, operated six days a week to produce coal for the war effort. (CCHS.)

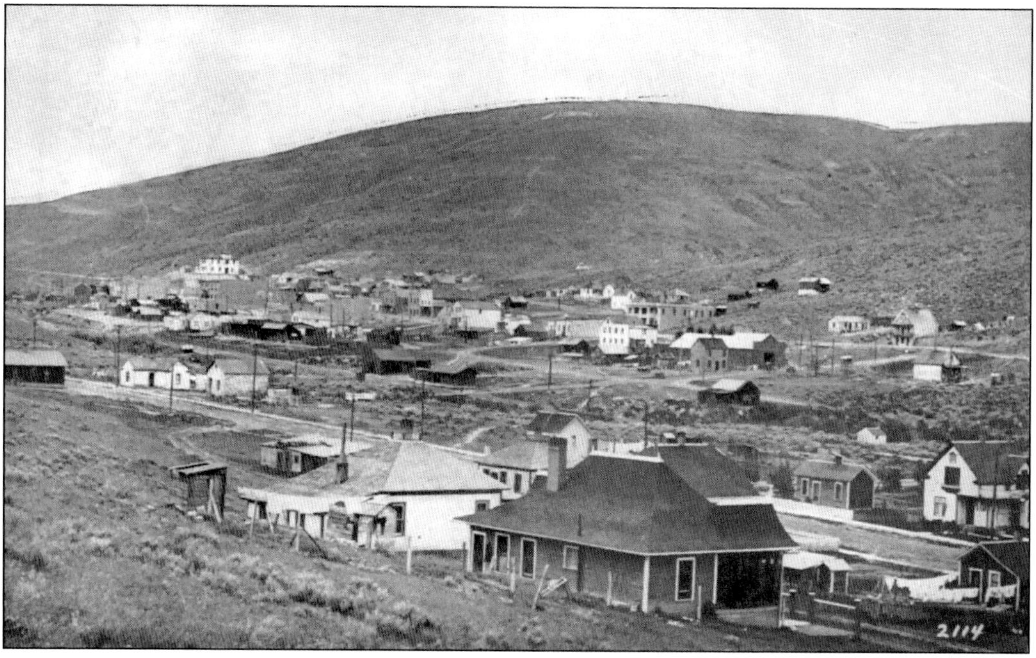

Opposing views of Bearcreek are shown on this page. The late-1910s photograph above documents the western end of Bearcreek from Hi-Bug looking toward Bearcreek Elementary School. The Lamport Hotel, with its distinctive columns and balcony, occupies the center of the photograph. The photograph below captures the eastern end of Bearcreek. It was taken from the hillside above the Lamport Hotel looking toward Bearcreek High School, the dark, two-story building in the distance. This image, showing significantly more structures, was taken in the mid-1920s. (Above, Wakenshaw; below, CCHS.)

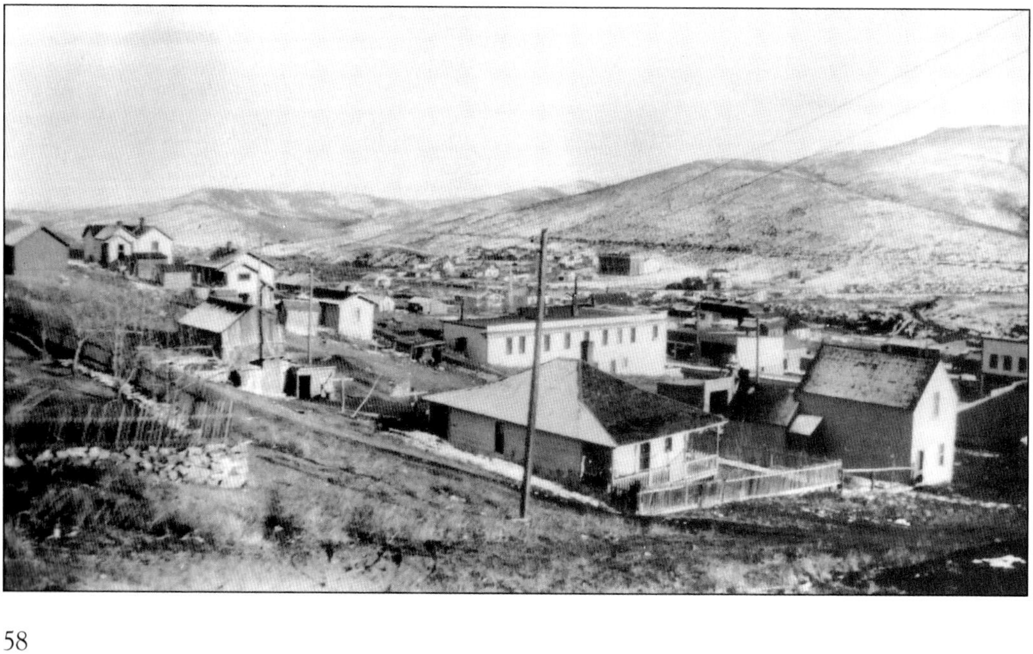

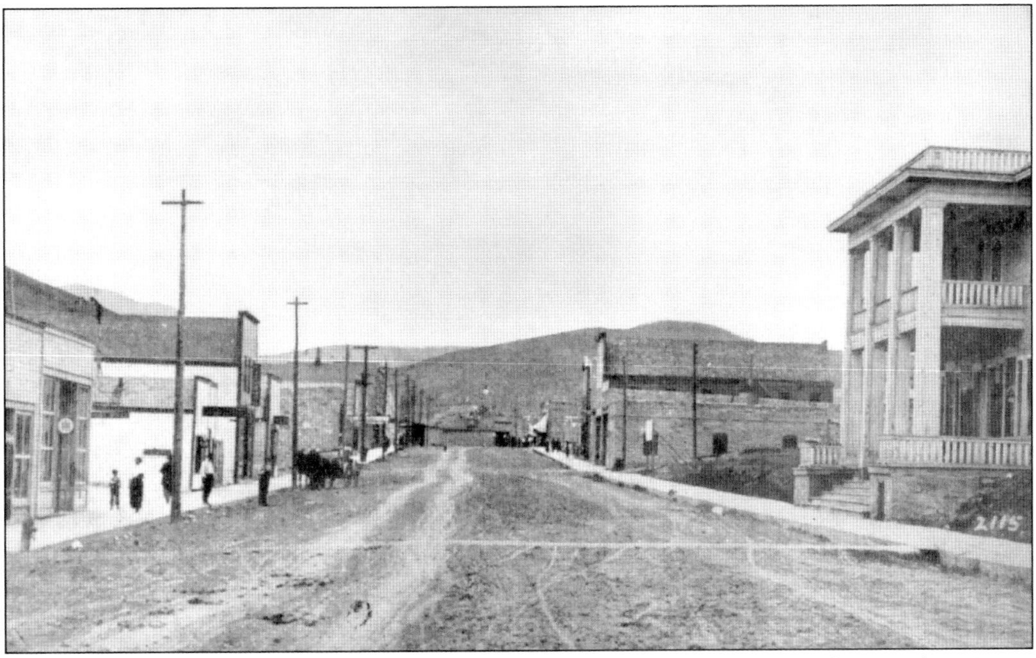

This c. 1920 photograph captures the western end of Bearcreek's business district along Main Street. On the right are the Lamport Hotel and the F. and S. Garage. Businesses across the street from the Lamport Hotel included a mercantile, the town post office, a bakery, and a barbershop. (CCHS.)

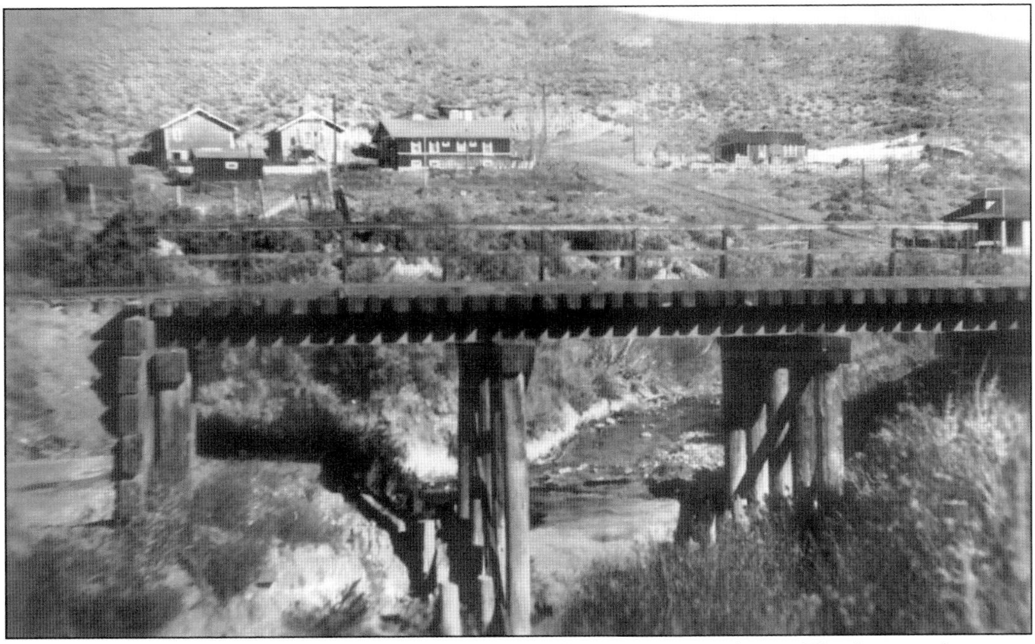

A railway bridge crosses Bear Creek near Bearcreek's eastern city limit. The homes shown in this c. 1915 photograph were owned by, from left to right, Pete and Marian Pryde, Alex Young, the Nish family in front of the Walters' family home (later purchased by the DeVille family), Bud Wakenshaw (who purchased his home from the Fleming family), and the Johnsons. (Kidwell.)

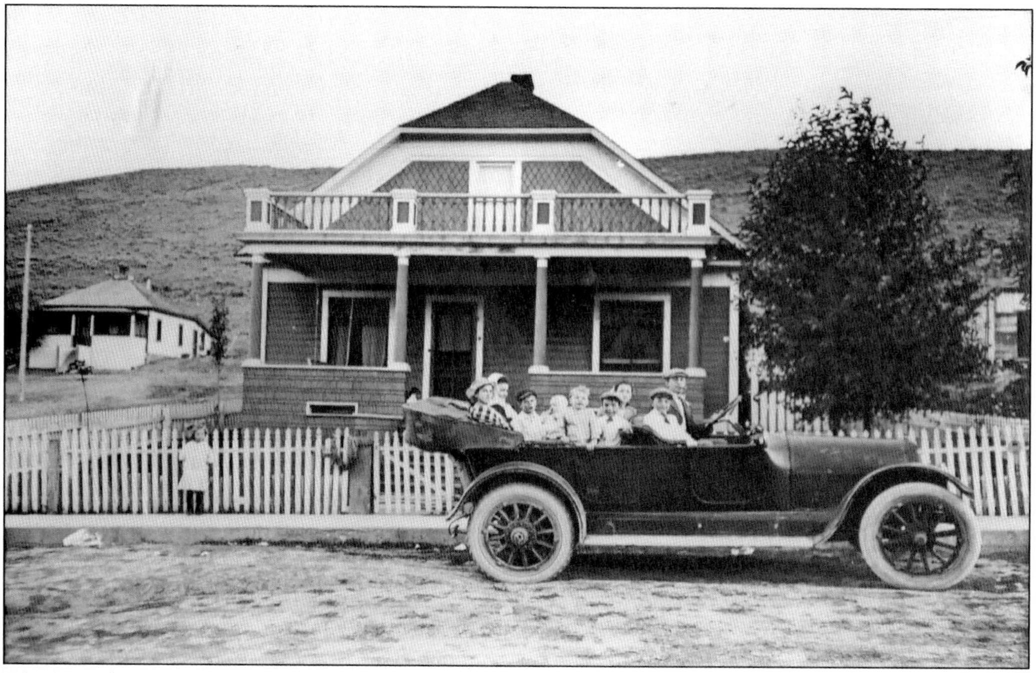

The Joseph Henry Wright family prepares for a summer drive in 1915. The Wright family home stands in the background at Block Five, lots one and two, in Bearcreek's second addition. Like many homes in the area, this house was sold and moved to another town when the coal industry left the valley. It now resides in Red Lodge at 723 South McGillen Avenue. (CCHS.)

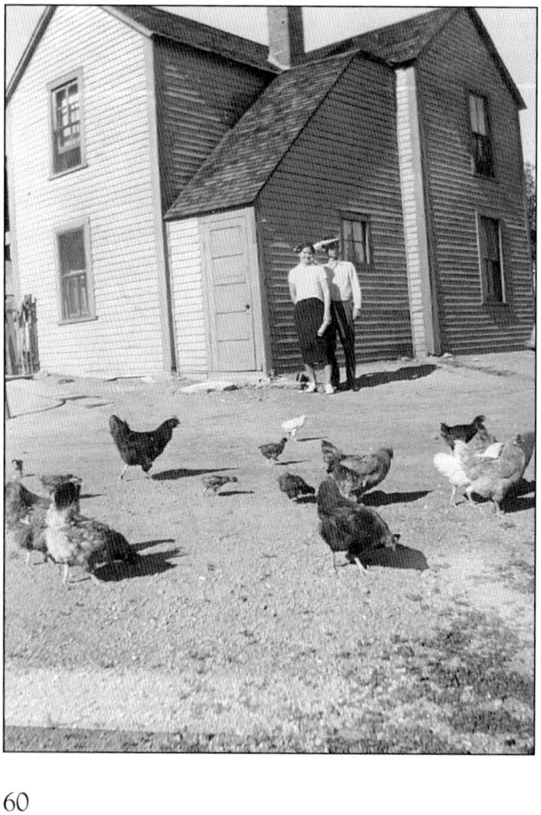

Siblings John and Mildred Chesarek stand by their home on the western end of Bearcreek's Main Street. The chickens pictured in the foreground of this photograph were a common sight in Bear Creek Valley. Families raised them as an inexpensive way to supplement their diets with meat and eggs. (Vorachek.)

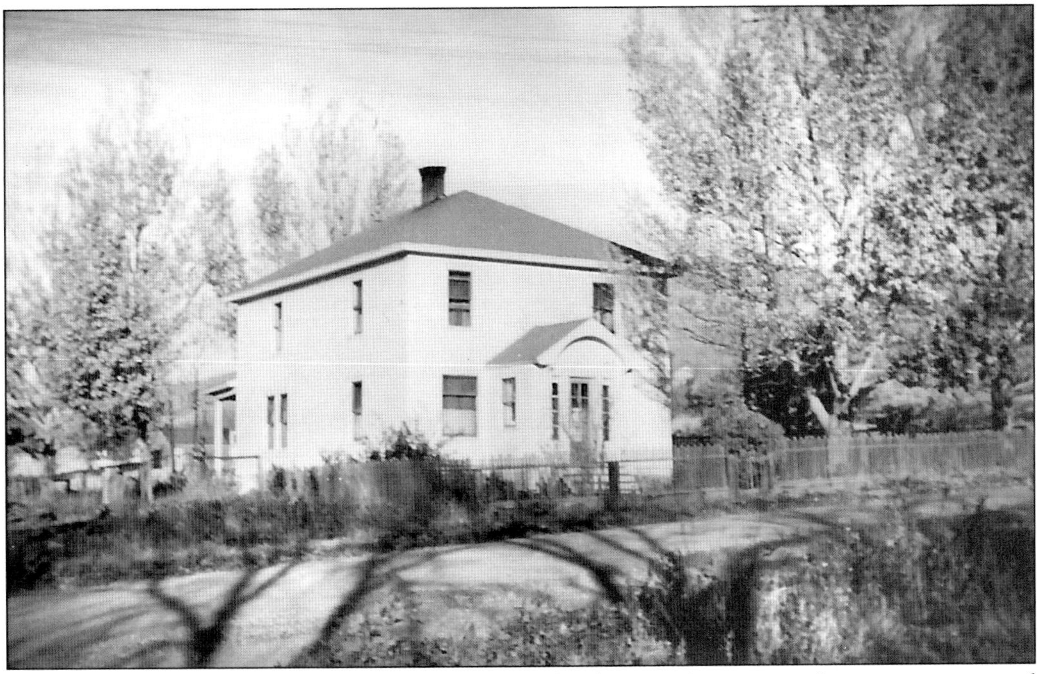

The Irvine home in Bearcreek also served as a boardinghouse. Many private homeowners opened their homes to boarders as a means of supplementing their incomes. The trees surrounding this home were planted at the time of its construction. Prior to the development of Bear Creek Valley, deciduous trees existed only along streams, creeks, and springs. (Mourich.)

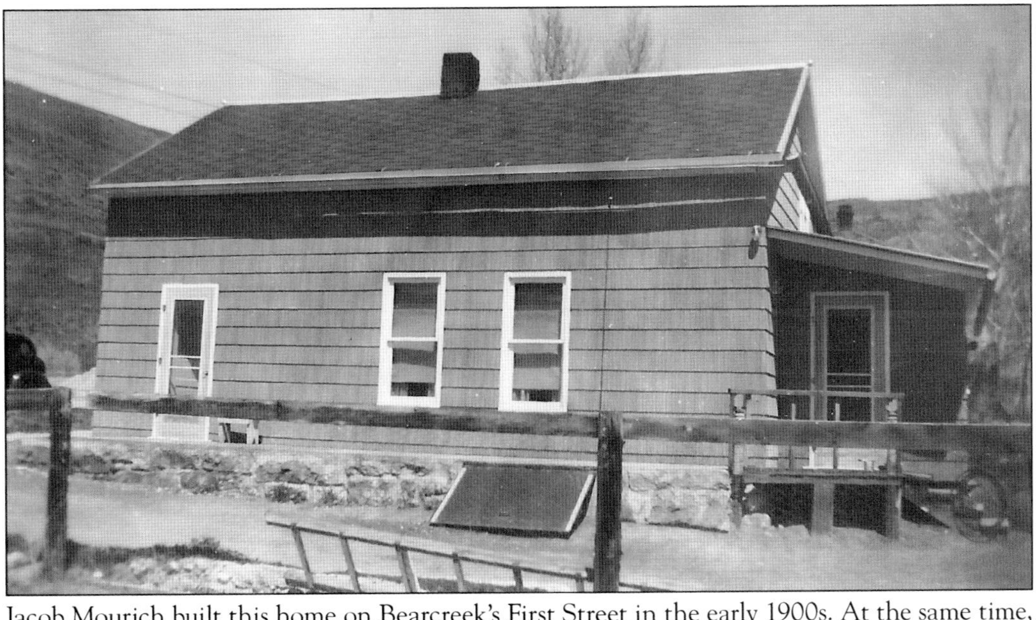

Jacob Mourich built this home on Bearcreek's First Street in the early 1900s. At the same time, Jacob purchased two adjoining lots on First Street and built a second home on one of them, leaving an empty lot between them. Jacob gave this home to his son Jack as a wedding present in 1929 and the second home to his son Frank in 1924, again as a wedding present. (Mourich.)

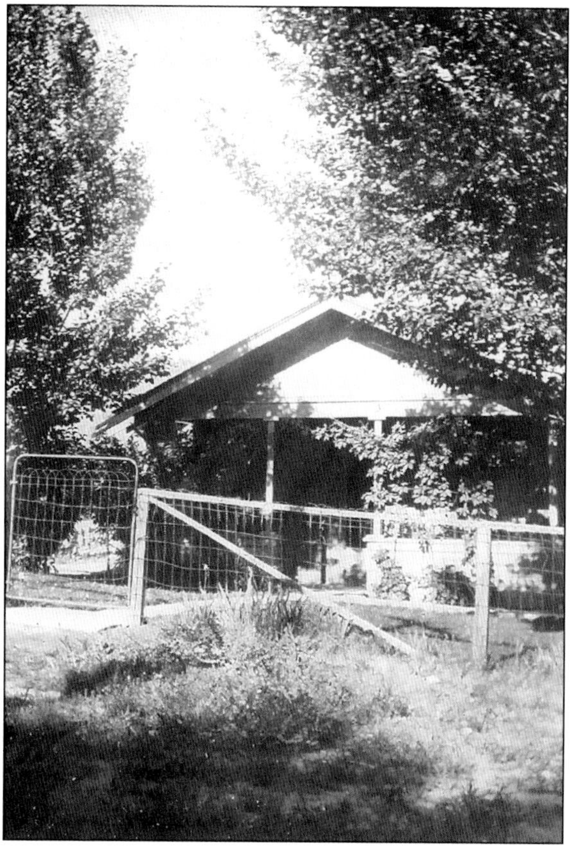

These c. 1940 photographs show the Bud and Mary Wakenshaw home on Bearcreek's Fifth Street. Again note the abundance of trees surrounding this home. Rooted far from natural water sources, many of the trees planted by Bear Creek Valley's early residents died as homeowners left the area. The photograph below shows Adam and Mag Wakenshaw's chicken coop behind a garden overflowing with vegetables. These vegetables would be canned and used throughout the long Montana winters. Bud and Mary Wakenshaw's home can be seen in the distance. In 1950, Mary Wakenshaw sold her home. The new owners moved it to neighboring Bridger. (Both, Wakenshaw.)

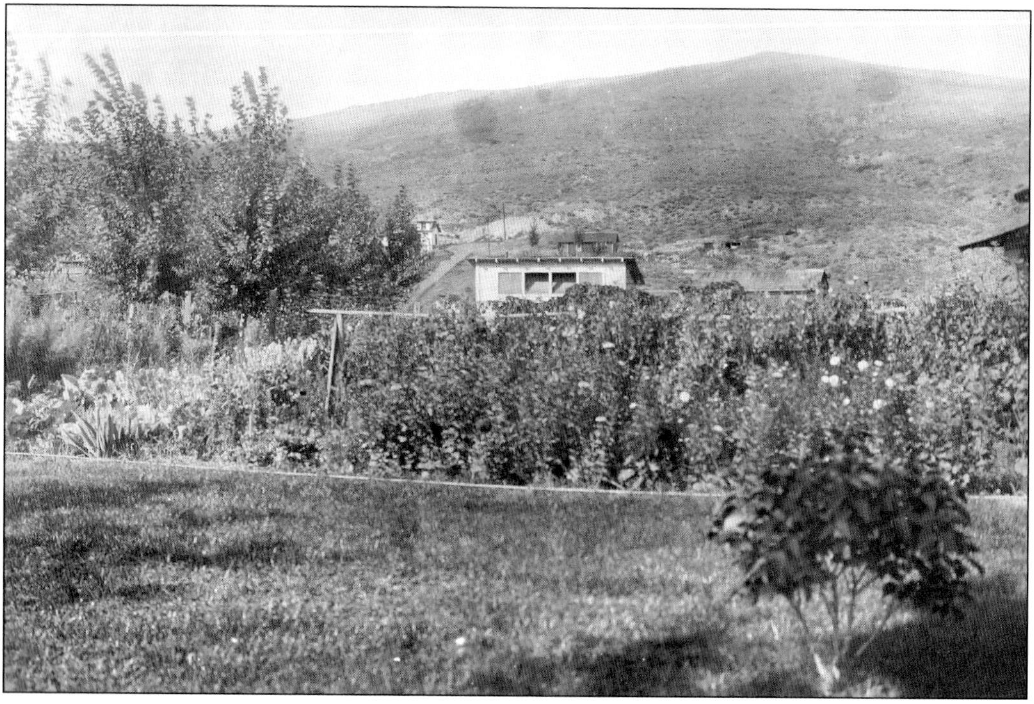

Four

Businesses

In the first decades of the 20th century, an array of businesses helped transform Bear Creek Valley into a self-sustaining community. The bulk of the valley's commerce occurred in Bearcreek's business district along Main Street. Washoe also had a smaller number of businesses grouped along the main valley road near the mine office and company store.

Bakeries, dry good stores, a cooperative store, produce markets, butcher shops, and an icehouse provided the staples of life. The shopkeepers and proprietors of these stores were the valley's unsung heroes, extending credit to miners during times of unemployment, allowing them to feed their families.

A real estate and home building company, numerous private boardinghouses, and hotels provided ample housing options. The valley's mining companies also built their own boardinghouses and allowed employees to build homes on company land. Hardware stores, garages, a lumberyard, and a furniture store supplied the essentials of daily living.

Several physicians, two hospitals, a dentist, and a drugstore tended to the valley's sick and injured. For those beyond saving, the mortuary in Bearcreek offered its services. Barbershops kept the valley's residents groomed, and shoe shops and mercantile stores clothed them. A single bank met the business needs of both the mining companies and individual citizens.

A variety of establishments offered various entertainments. A movie theater initially showed silent films. The youth of the valley could often be found at the confectionery or roller-skating on the second floor of the union hall. A number of bars, pool halls, and dance venues served the adult population, as did a house of ill repute above one Bearcreek bar.

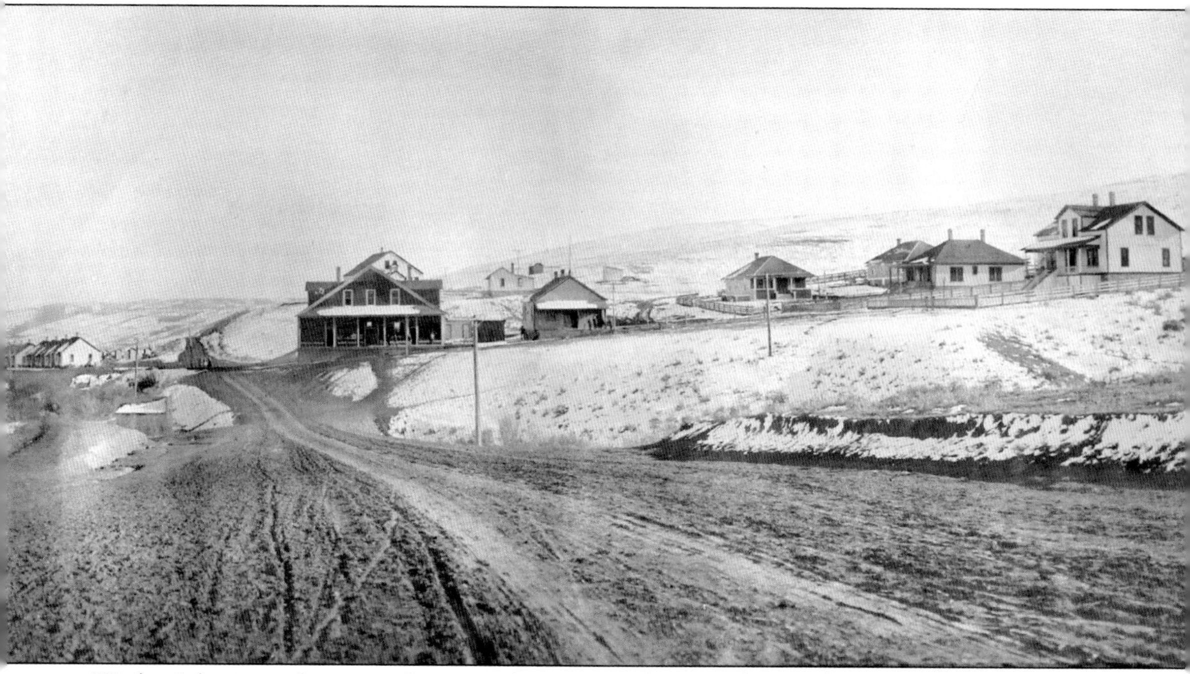

Washoe's business district is shown in this *c.* 1910 photograph. On the left-hand side of the dirt road are two rows of miner homes and out of frame are the Washoe Coal Company Mines and their processing plants, a pool hall, and a barbershop. To the right of the dirt road, the building with a covered porch is the Washoe Coal Company's general store and community hall. To its right is the Washoe Coal Company's mine office. This building served dual purposes, housing a post office that served the western end of Bear Creek Valley. Continuing right are the store manager's home, the company cashier's home in front of the postmaster's house, and the two-story mine superintendent's home. The white building behind the company store is Washoe Elementary School and to its right is the home and office of the company's physician, Dr. Charles E. Beltzer. The school's head teacher lived in a small home behind the school. (Flash's Photography.)

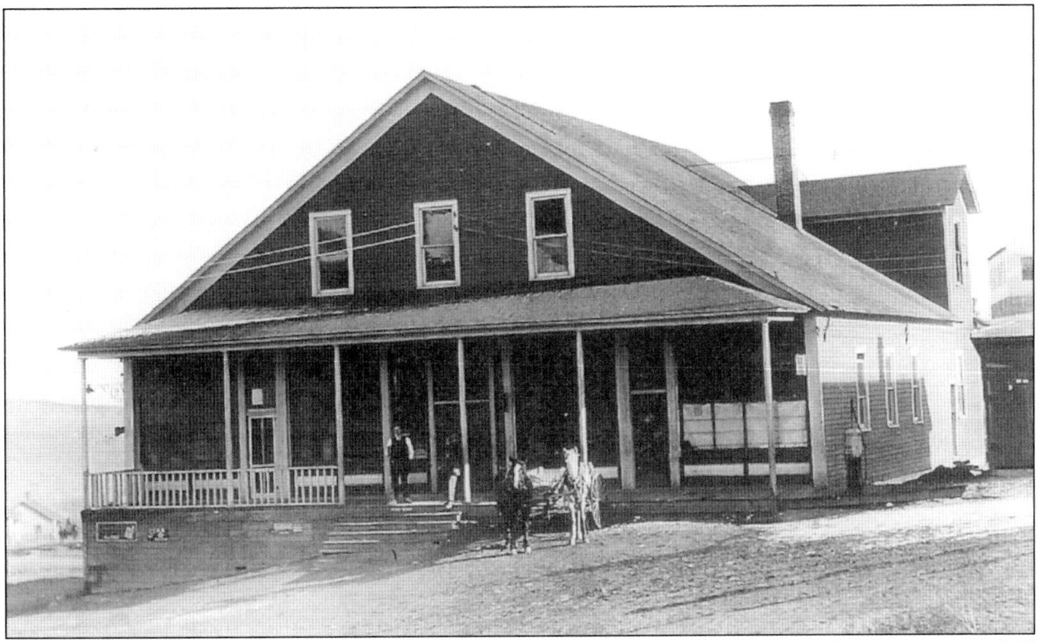

In 1909, two years after its completion, the Washoe Trading Company and Community Hall opened for business. The original proprietors were Kelley and Eggleston. Fire destroyed the two-story structure in May 1924. When rebuilt, it consisted of just one story with separate entrances for the store and community hall. (Flash's Photography.)

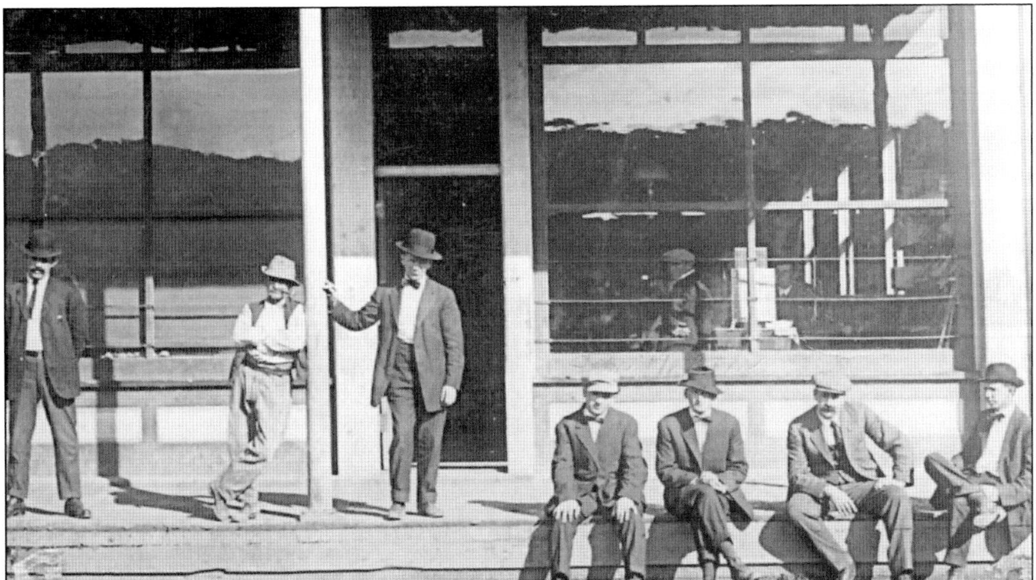

The Washoe Pool Hall and Bar was owned and operated by William Phil Noble and Clement Lodge Sr. This photograph shows a group of Washoe men, including both owners of this establishment. They are, from left to right, unidentified, Ottewell Lodge, William Phil Noble, Edward J. Laird, Clement Lodge Sr., John Curry, and Dr. Charles E. Beltzer. (Lodge.)

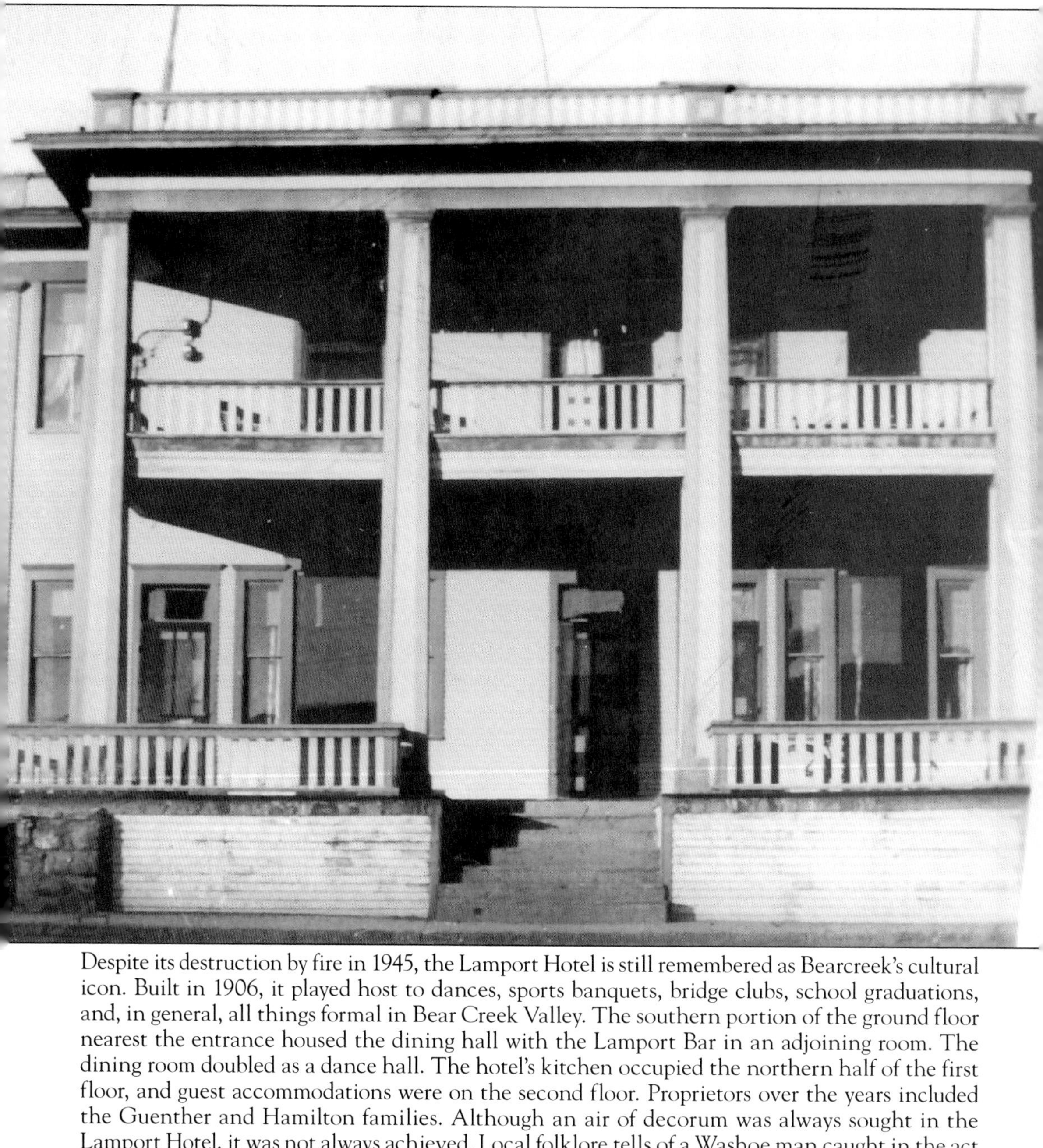

Despite its destruction by fire in 1945, the Lamport Hotel is still remembered as Bearcreek's cultural icon. Built in 1906, it played host to dances, sports banquets, bridge clubs, school graduations, and, in general, all things formal in Bear Creek Valley. The southern portion of the ground floor nearest the entrance housed the dining hall with the Lamport Bar in an adjoining room. The dining room doubled as a dance hall. The hotel's kitchen occupied the northern half of the first floor, and guest accommodations were on the second floor. Proprietors over the years included the Guenther and Hamilton families. Although an air of decorum was always sought in the Lamport Hotel, it was not always achieved. Local folklore tells of a Washoe man caught in the act of chopping down the dance floor's support timbers after an altercation at a dance. (CCHS.)

The Labor Temple building (right) housed a hardware store and bar on the first floor and the Labor Temple on the second floor. It stood on the south side of Main Street between First and Second Streets. The second floor also served as both a dance hall for the valley's adults and as a roller-skating rink for its children. (Author's collection.)

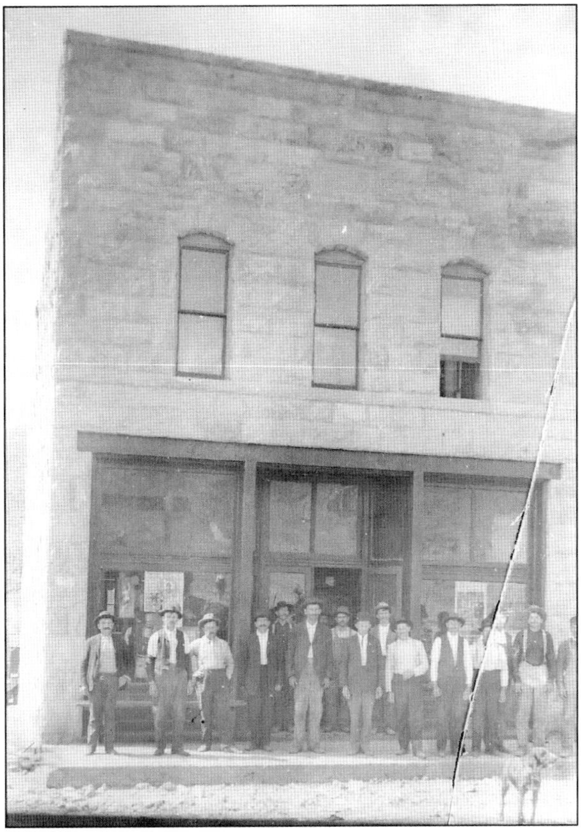

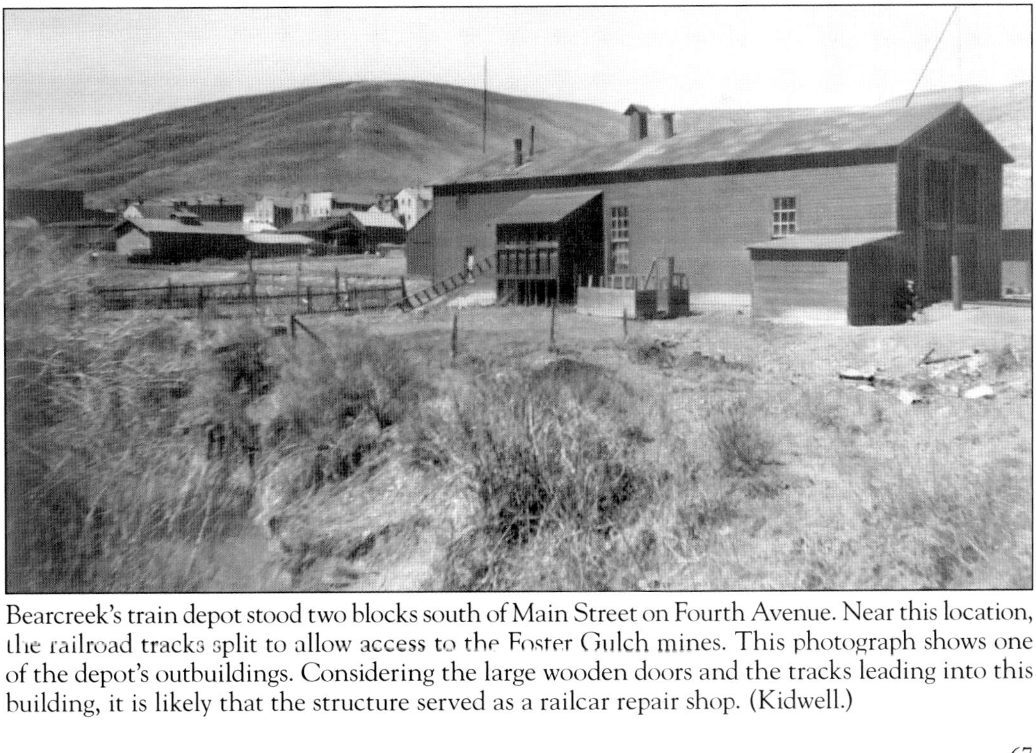

Bearcreek's train depot stood two blocks south of Main Street on Fourth Avenue. Near this location, the railroad tracks split to allow access to the Foster Gulch mines. This photograph shows one of the depot's outbuildings. Considering the large wooden doors and the tracks leading into this building, it is likely that the structure served as a railcar repair shop. (Kidwell.)

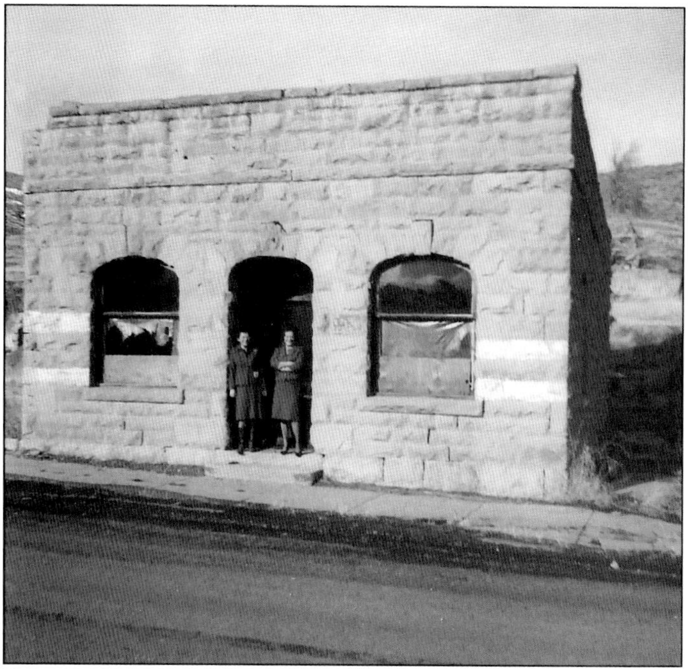

Originally occupied by the Clark-Wright Bank, this sandstone building currently serves as Bearcreek's city hall. The Clark-Wright Bank overextended itself in financing the International Coal Company, and when the coal company failed in 1921, the bank was forced to close as well. Efforts are currently underway to restore this building to its original condition. (Wakenshaw.)

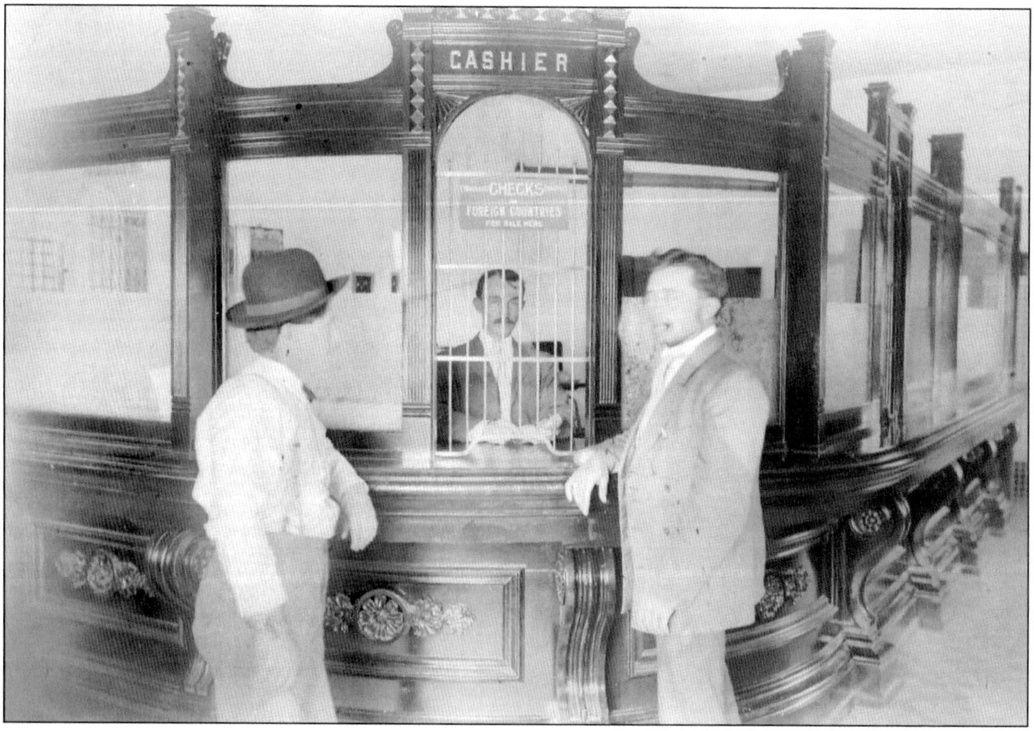

This early-1900s photograph shows the beauty of the Clark-Wright Bank's interior. From frosted glass and tiled floors, to an ornately carved cashier's cage, the bank was elegant in every aspect. In this photograph, Joseph Henry Wright, the bank's co-owner, stands in the cashier's cage. The man on the left is unidentified. Dr. Jesse George Forney, a Bearcreek dentist, is on the right. (CCHS.)

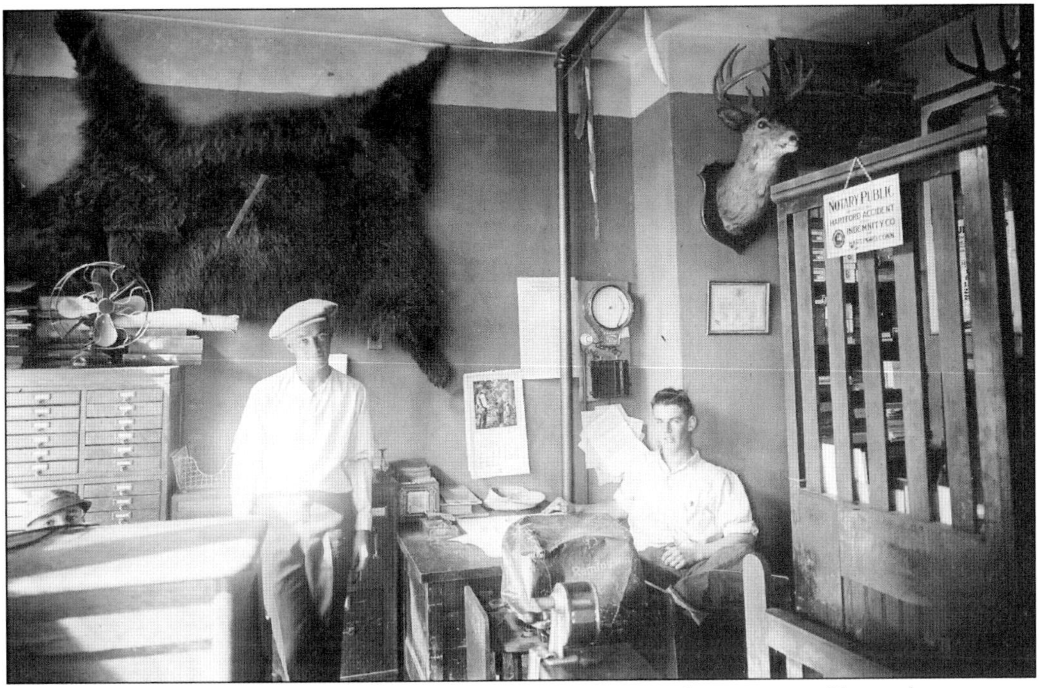

After the collapse of the Clark-Wright Bank, Joseph Henry Wright maintained his realty company office in the building that housed Bearcreek's hardware store and later the F. and S. Garage. This late-1920s photograph shows Wright's office and two of his sons, from left to right, Penrose George Wright and Charles Edward Wright. (CCHS.)

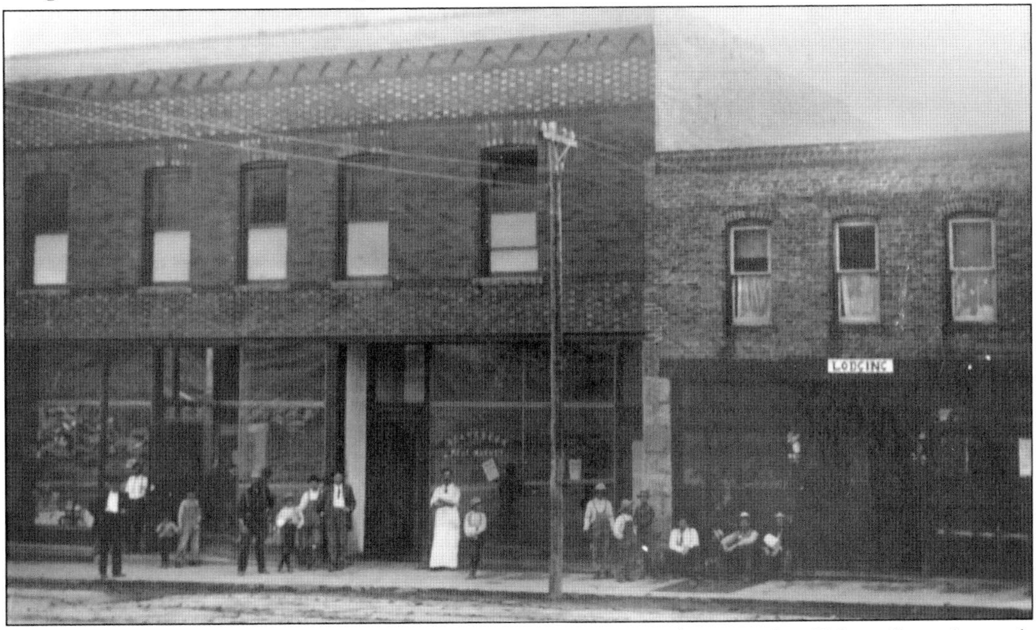

Several early Bearcreek businesses are shown in this c. 1920 photograph of Main Street's north side, between First and Second Streets. They are, from left to right, a sporting-goods store, the Bearcreek Meat Market, and the Bearcreek Hotel. The concrete sidewalks in this photograph were a rarity for coal camps of this time. (Flash's Photography.)

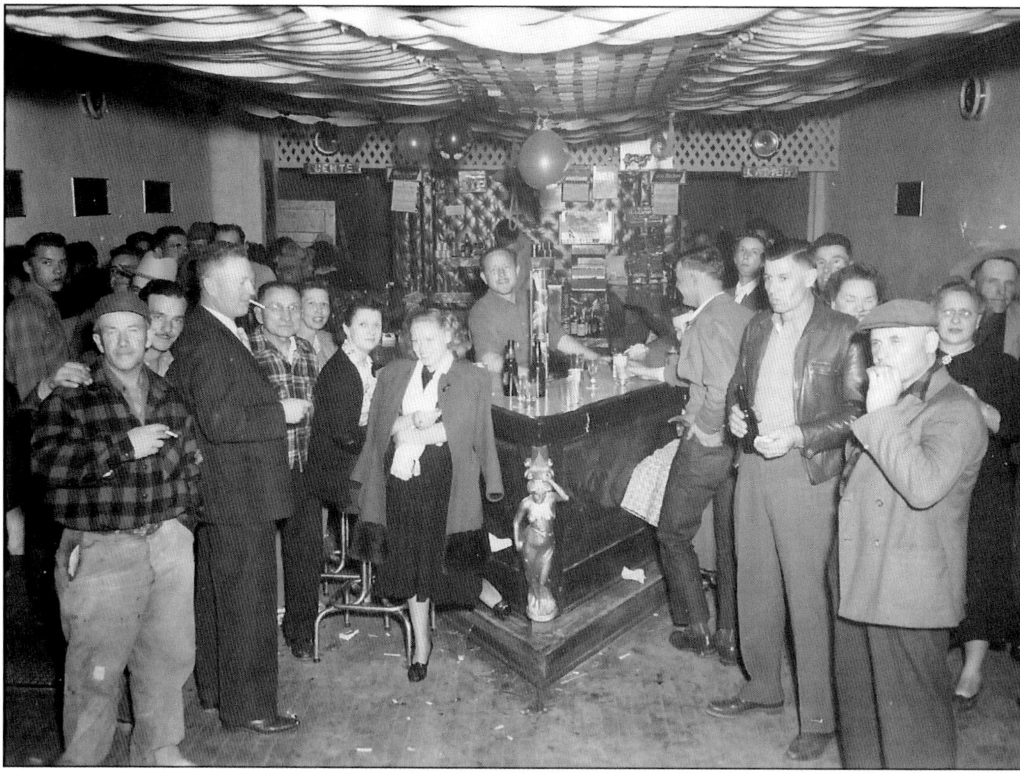

A New Year's Eve celebration takes place in Tony's Club in this *c.* 1950 photograph. Proprietor Tony Ocepek stands behind the unique V-shaped bar. Poly Janskovitch is the man in the leather jacket to the right. His wife, Agnes, sits at the front left of the bar. Previous occupants of this 1913 building, which no longer exists, included the Bearcreek Meat Market, a bakery, and Cole's Barber Shop. (Mourich.)

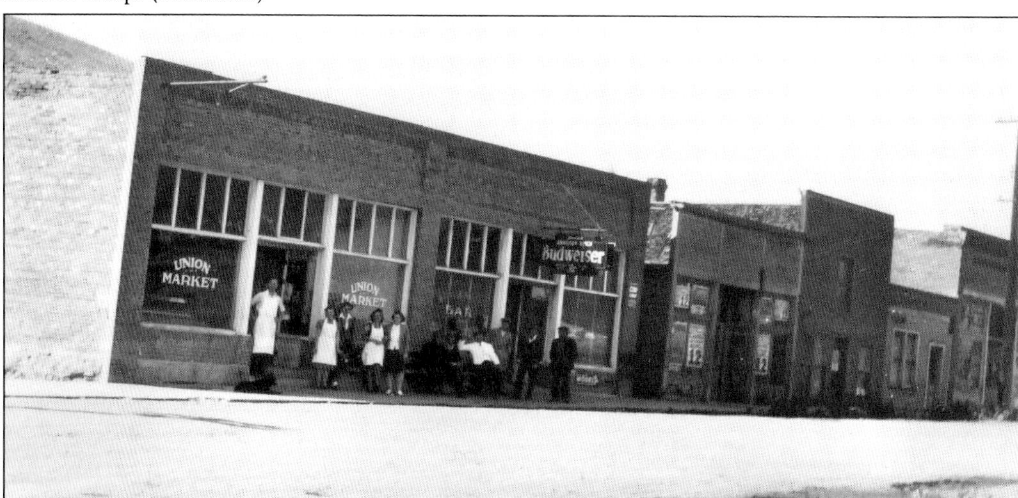

The southwest portion of Bearcreek's Main Street housed a large number of businesses, mostly saloons. In this photograph, Guido Marchello, owner of the Union Market, stands in the doorway of his business. West of the Union Market is the Bearcreek Saloon and the First and Last Chance Saloon (far right). (Mourich.)

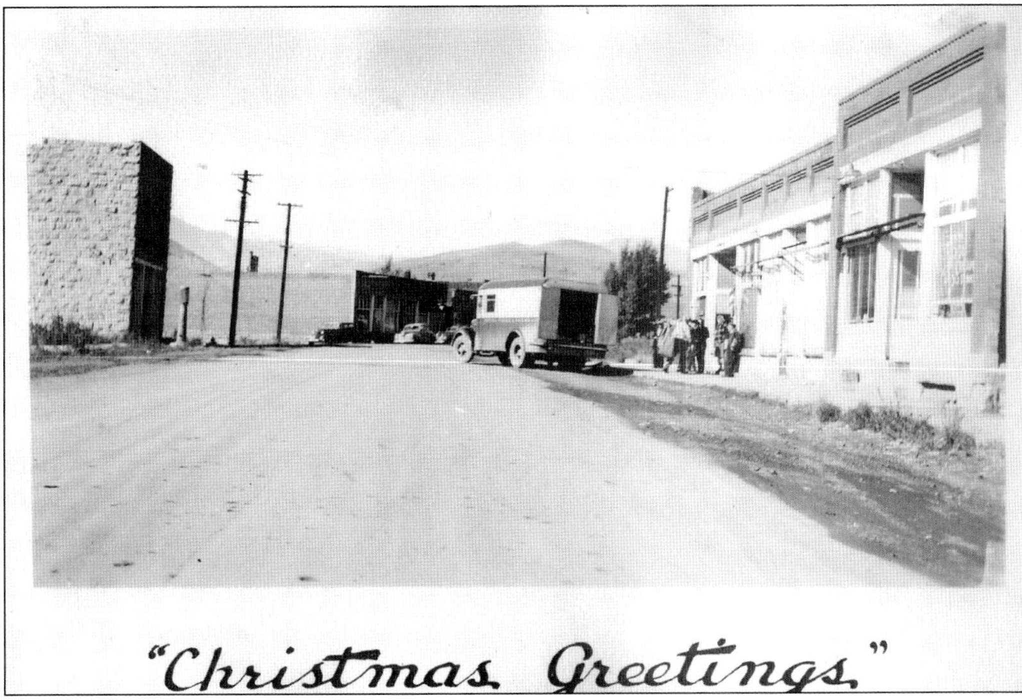

Two post offices served Bear Creek Valley. One, in Washoe, provided service west of Horseshoe Bend; the other, in Bearcreek, served Bearcreek itself, as well as Scotch Coulee. The Washoe Post Office operated from 1907 to 1959. The Bearcreek Post Office, established in 1905, remains in service. The Bearcreek Post Office occupied many locations over the years, including the old bakery building (above) during the 1950s. In the photograph to the right, three Red Lodge ladies pose in front of one of the past locations of the Bear Creek Post Office. They are, from left to right, Margaret Bailey Indreland, Lucy Bailey Pentilla, and Eva Petelin Beitel. (Above, Wakenshaw; right, Indreland.)

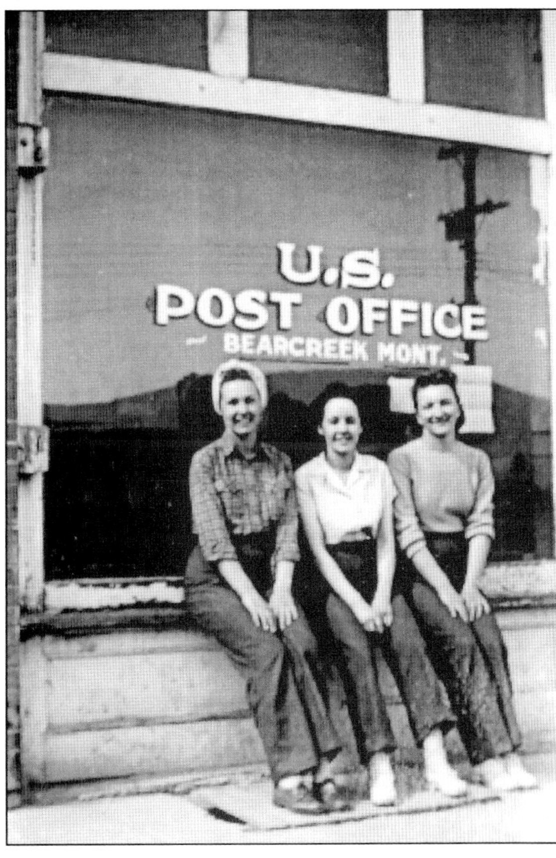

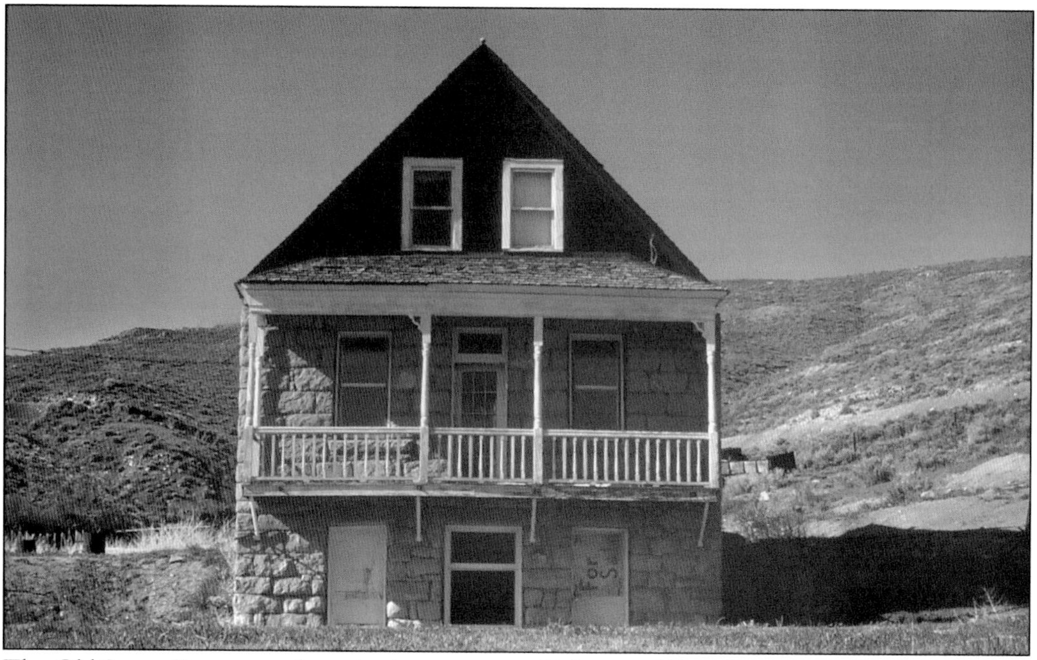

The Old Stone House stands at the intersection of Main and Fourth Streets. In 1906, Fred and Cecelia Jurcak built the home out of locally quarried sandstone. The Jurcaks lived on the first floor and housed boarders on the second floor. In November 1906, a disagreement between two Slovenian boarders, Stephen Novota and Gabriel Sedlack, resulted in Sedlack's murder, a rare event in Bear Creek's 100-year history. Novota shot Sedlack in the neck with a shotgun as the victim drank from the home's well. The murder came as the culmination of two weeks of heavy drinking on Novota's part and the incessant bullying of Novota by Sedlack. Stephen Novota was sentenced to life in prison for his crime. (Above, CCHS; below, Wakenshaw.)

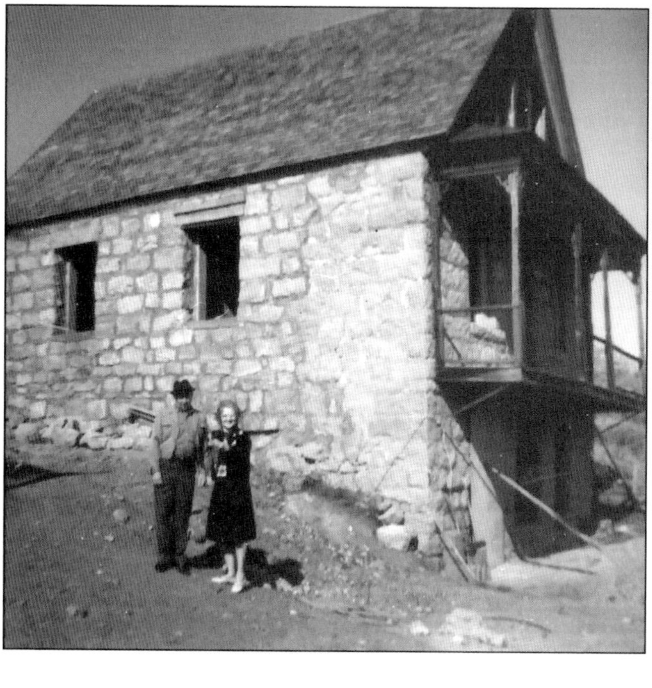

Five

Schools

The residents of Bear Creek Valley were primarily immigrants seeking a better life for their families in America. To achieve this goal, immigrant families devoted themselves to providing for their children's education. Their dedication to learning is best illustrated by Rev. Daniel Spencer McCorkle in an early-1920s report to the Montana Educator's Association:

> By the excellent quality of its coal and its schools, Bearcreek has won for itself merited distinction—just how a village of less than five hundred in a community of about fifteen hundred holds a rank so high is worthy of note. Foremost stands, of course, the will to provide a good school. The Bearcreek school district has always had many children and little taxable property. It is one of the poorest communities in Montana. From an accessed valuation of less than two hundred and forty thousand dollars are supported eleven or twelve teachers; a high school of eighty and an elementary school of two hundred fifty. Every year by means of a special levy, one of the highest in the state, the people provide for their schools.

Reverend McCorkle, a Presbyterian minister from nearby Clark, Wyoming, worked the Bear Creek Valley's mines, ministering to its people, teaching its children, and advocating for the rights of mine workers across the county from the 1910s through the 1930s.

More than any other community endeavor, the residents of Bear Creek Valley supported their schools. They understood the importance of education in improving the lives of their children.

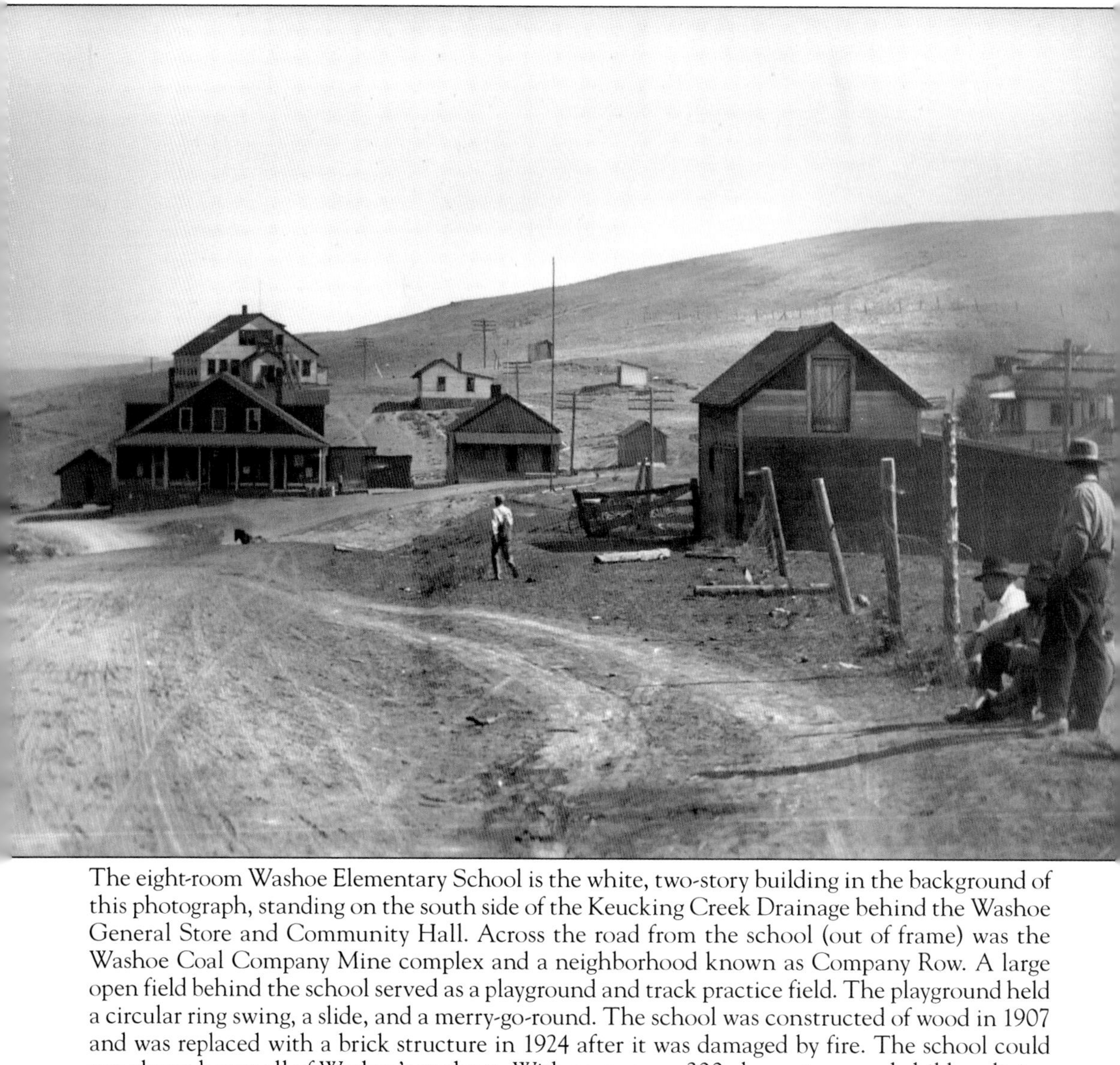

The eight-room Washoe Elementary School is the white, two-story building in the background of this photograph, standing on the south side of the Keucking Creek Drainage behind the Washoe General Store and Community Hall. Across the road from the school (out of frame) was the Washoe Coal Company Mine complex and a neighborhood known as Company Row. A large open field behind the school served as a playground and track practice field. The playground held a circular ring swing, a slide, and a merry-go-round. The school was constructed of wood in 1907 and was replaced with a brick structure in 1924 after it was damaged by fire. The school could not always house all of Washoe's students. With as many as 300 elementary-aged children living in the Washoe end of the valley in the late 1910s and early 1920s, a store and several homes were converted into makeshift schoolrooms to accommodate students. The school pictured here was closed after the 1954–1955 school year and later demolished. (Flash's Photography.)

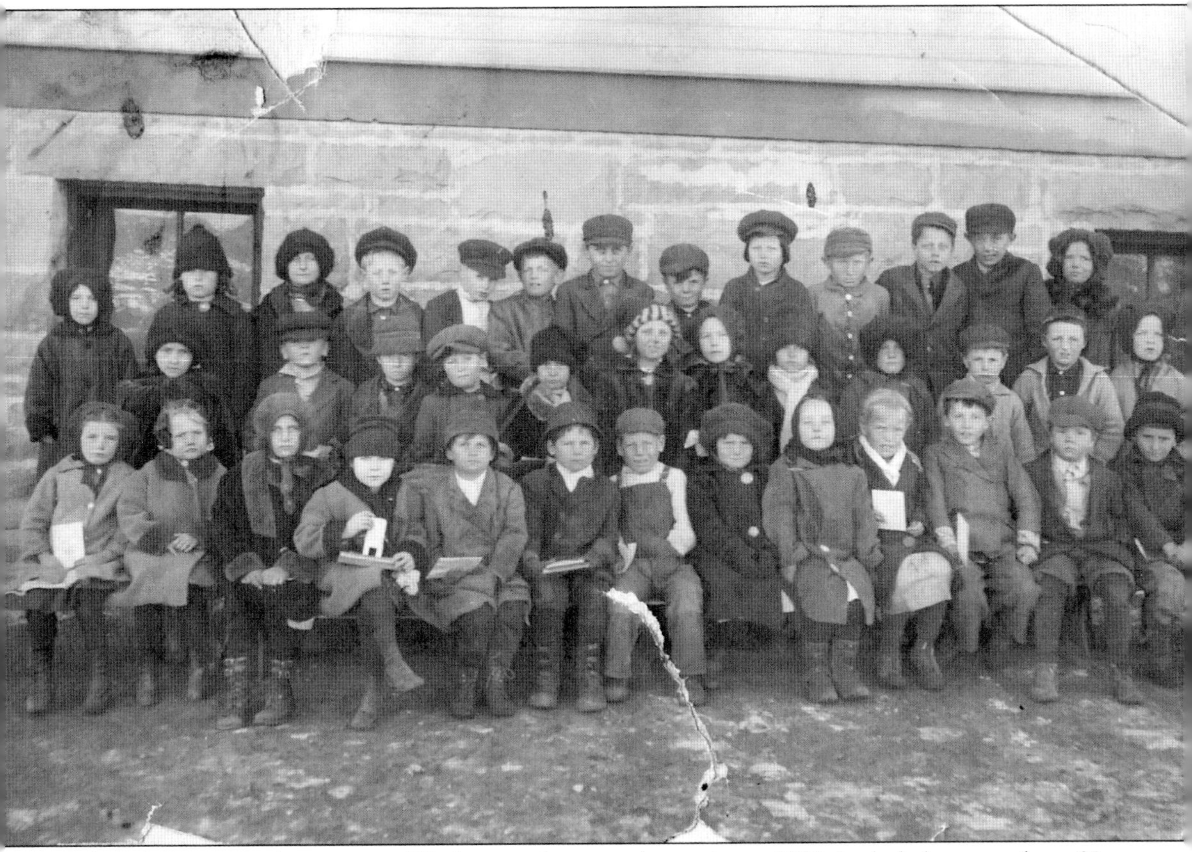

This photograph, showing one Washoe grade, was taken prior to 1915. Included among these 38 children are Jessie Freeman, Ludwig Meyer, James Brophy, Jacob Cameron Jr., Jack Sewell, Jack Bolinger, Susan Cecile McDonald, Catherine McMullen, Mardel McMullen, William Phil Noble, David Leach, Hilda Patana, David Sommerville Jr., Agnes McNeil, and Howard Freemen. Students from Scotch Coulee, the Smith Mine, Washoe, and the west end of Virtue Gulch all attended school here. Scotch Coulee children walked to school through the foothills of the valley along a backcountry road south of the school. The children from the Smith Mine area followed the main valley road connecting Bearcreek and Washoe. The few children living in Virtue Gulch crossed a ridge separating the gulch from the Keucking Creek Drainage and down past the Washoe Coal Company Mines. (Mourich.)

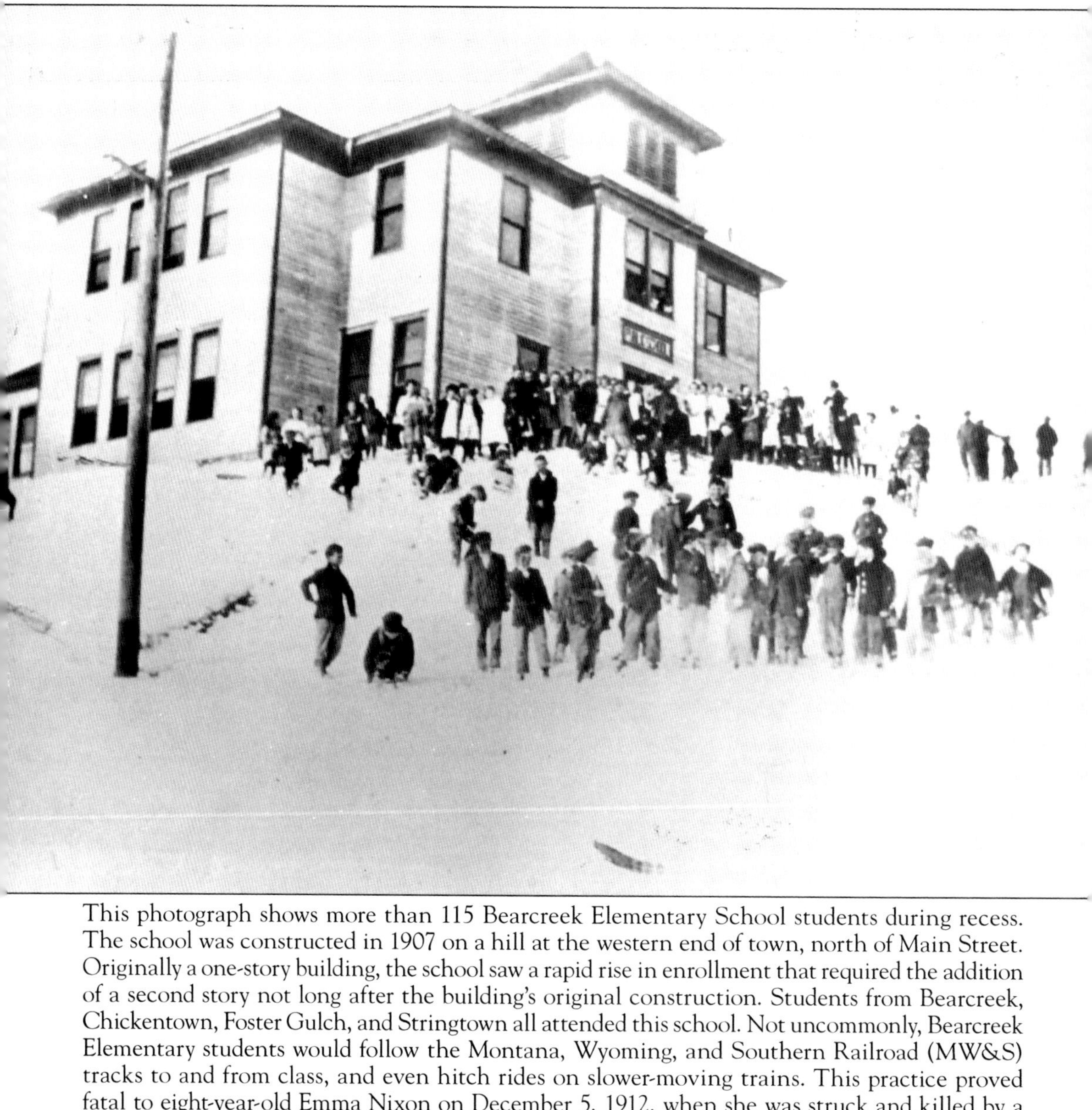

This photograph shows more than 115 Bearcreek Elementary School students during recess. The school was constructed in 1907 on a hill at the western end of town, north of Main Street. Originally a one-story building, the school saw a rapid rise in enrollment that required the addition of a second story not long after the building's original construction. Students from Bearcreek, Chickentown, Foster Gulch, and Stringtown all attended this school. Not uncommonly, Bearcreek Elementary students would follow the Montana, Wyoming, and Southern Railroad (MW&S) tracks to and from class, and even hitch rides on slower-moving trains. This practice proved fatal to eight-year-old Emma Nixon on December 5, 1912, when she was struck and killed by a train. The accident prompted a lawsuit by Emma's father, O. R. Nixon, against the MW&S that reached the Montana Supreme Court, where the MW&S was found innocent of negligence in the case. The building in this photograph closed after the 1941–1942 school year and was eventually demolished. Its students were moved to the high school building. (Mourich.)

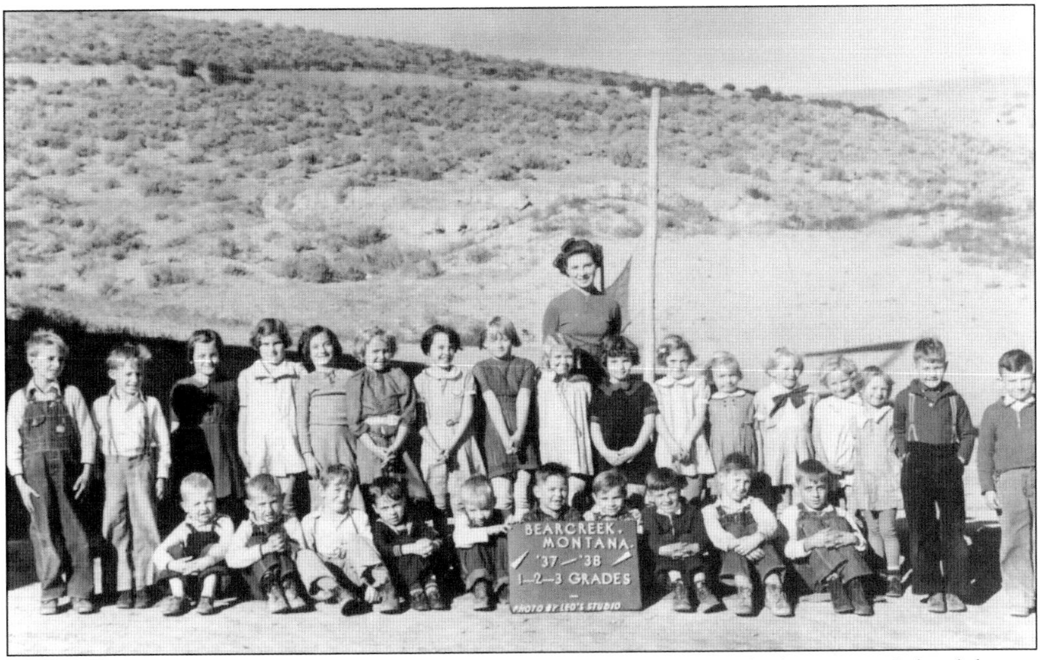

These photographs capture most of the 89 children attending Bearcreek Elementary School during the 1937–1938 school year. They represent the first through third grade classes (above) and the fourth through sixth grade classes (below). Another 24 students were enrolled in the seventh- and eighth-grade classes that year. These photographs were taken northwest of the school on its dirt playground, which included a circular ring swing, a slide, and a merry-go-round. The school's baseball field was south of the school, across Main Street, by the railroad tracks and Bear Creek. The flood control ditch created by the Works Progress Administration runs in the background of both of these photographs. (Both, Mourich.)

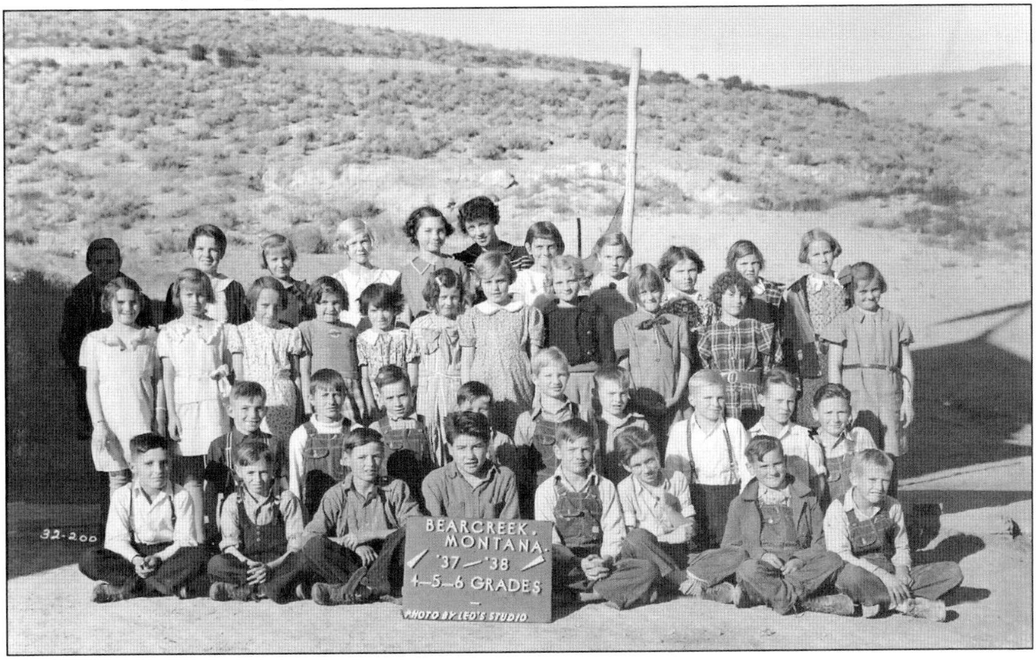

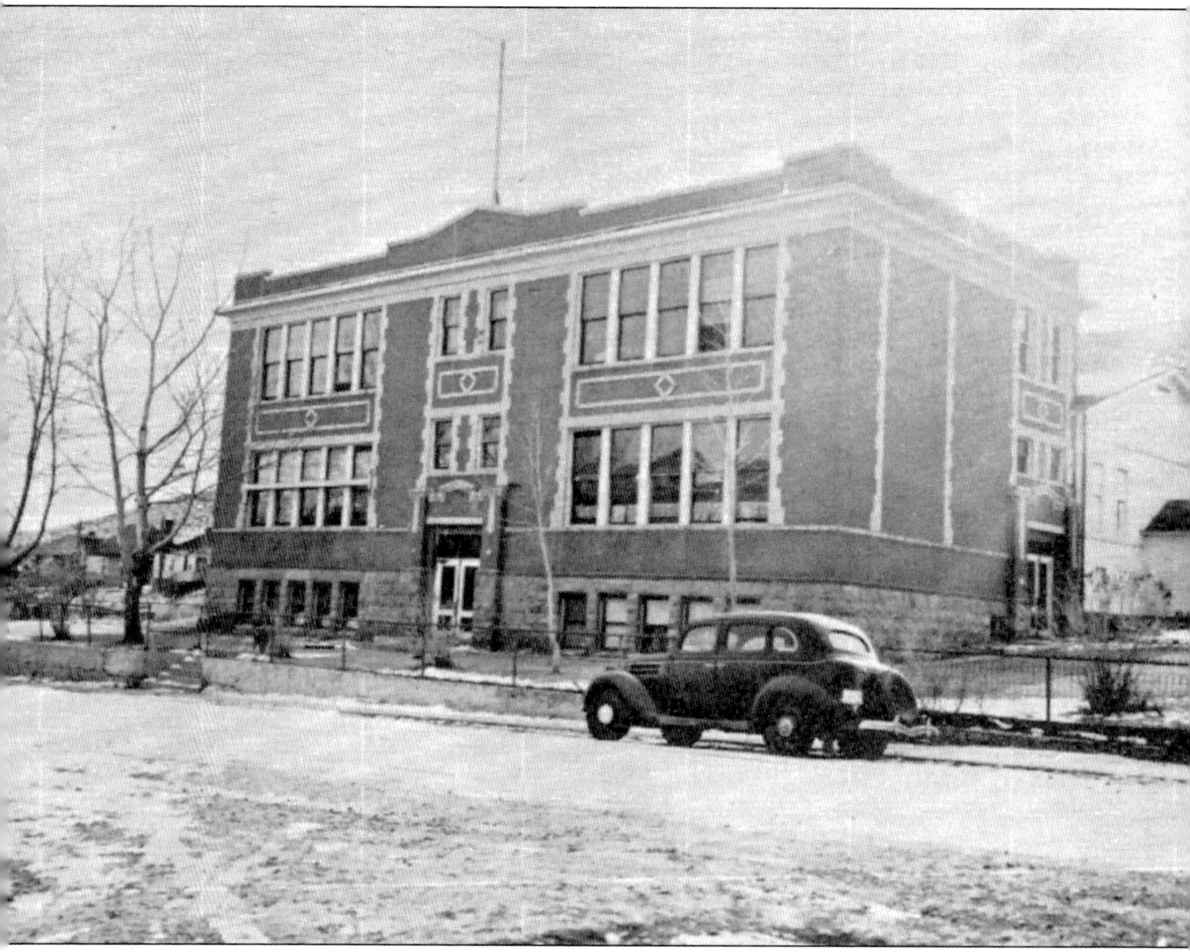

Bearcreek High School classes began in 1916 in the town's elementary school. Construction of a high school started that same year and was complete by 1919. The high school was located in the south-central part of town known as Hi-Bug. The class of 1920 saw Joe Soulsby and Marian Ferry become the first two alumni of 31 classes to graduate under the black-and-orange Bearcat banner. Bearcreek teacher Mina Sievert reported to her alumni association in 1918 that she was "having the interesting experience of organizing a high school in a small coal mining camp" and was instructing 20 students of a "largely foreign element" in French, English, and History. The last graduating class consisted of Thelma Bookout, Raymond Reid, Eileen Smith, and Jessie Cameron. With the school's closure in 1950, valley students attended high school in nearby Belfry. The white building behind the school is the gymnasium. (Murfitt.)

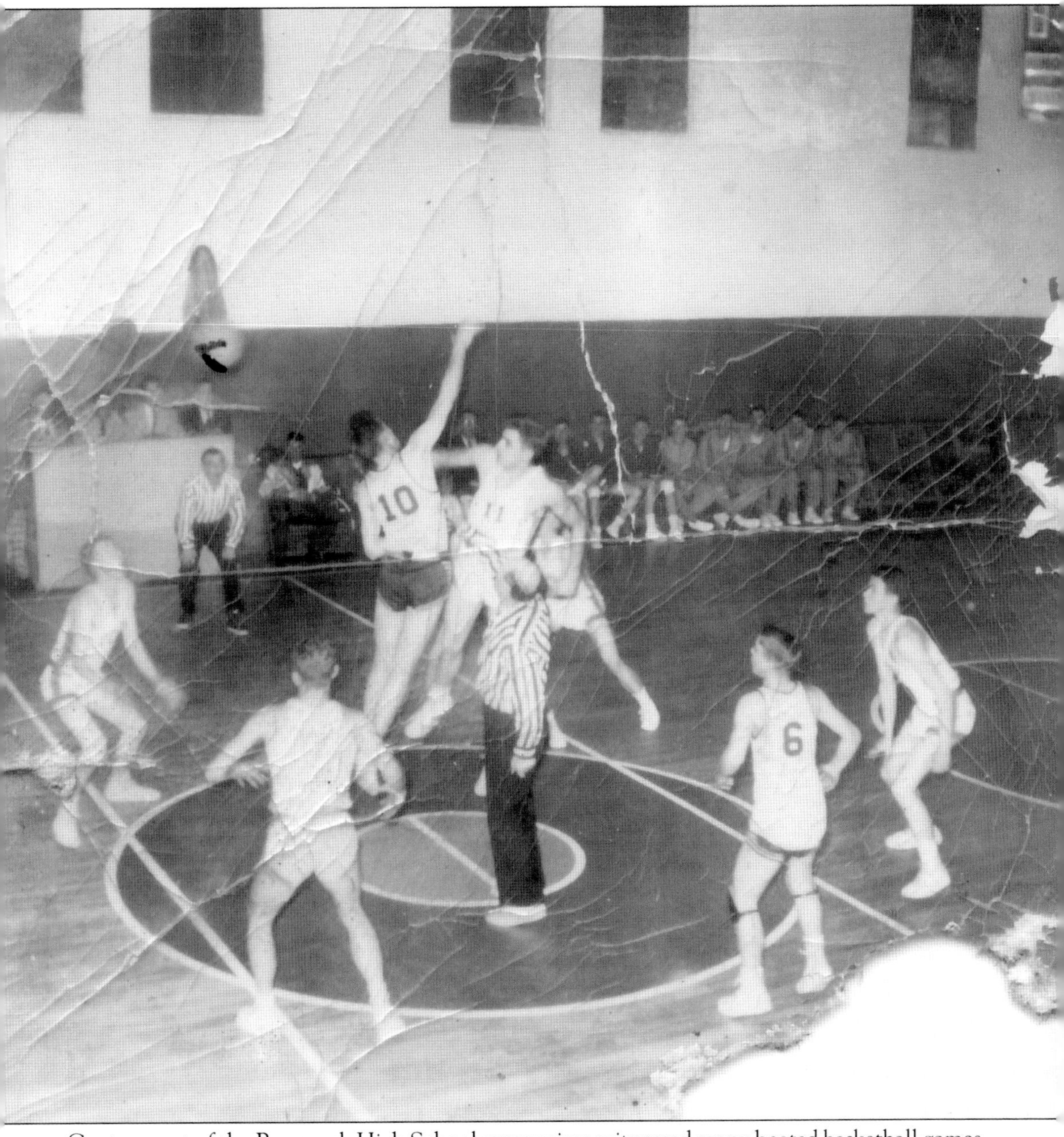

Center court of the Bearcreek High School gymnasium witnessed many heated basketball games. Due to the school district's inability to fully fund the project, the gymnasium opened two years after the high school, after valley residents contributed money and labor to finish its construction. Benches for both home and visiting teams lined the south side of the gymnasium. Spectators entered the building through the school to the north or through an outside portal on the west side of the gymnasium. The high school gymnasium was also used for community gatherings, including church services and early Smith Mine disaster memorials. Younger children used an elementary school classroom as a makeshift gymnasium: the classroom was cleared of all furniture, heavy screens were placed over the windows, and hoops were erected at either end. (Planichek.)

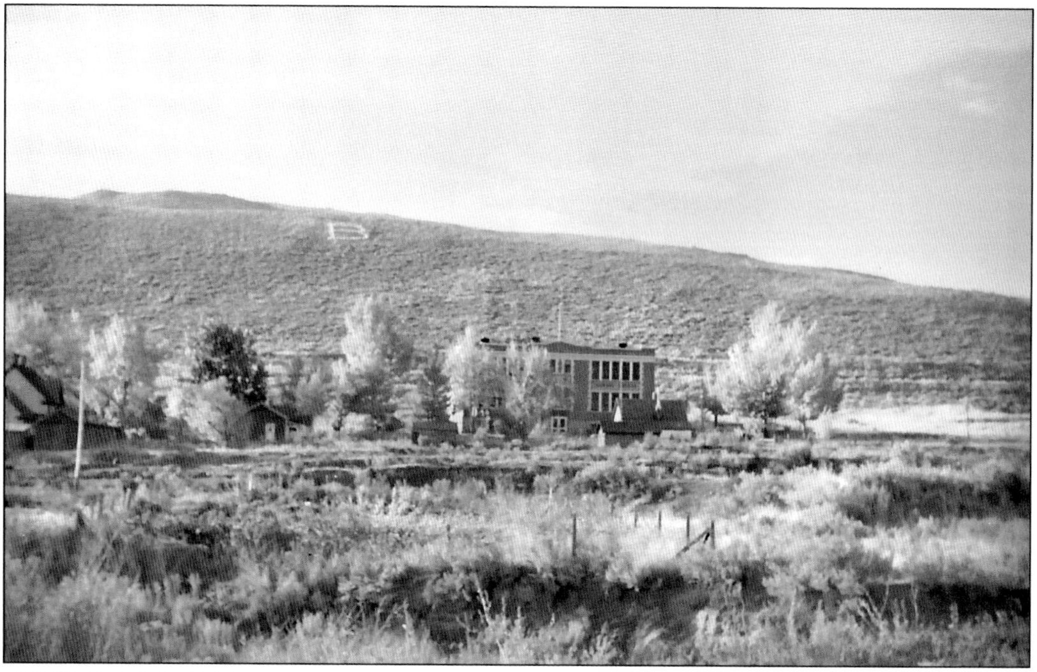

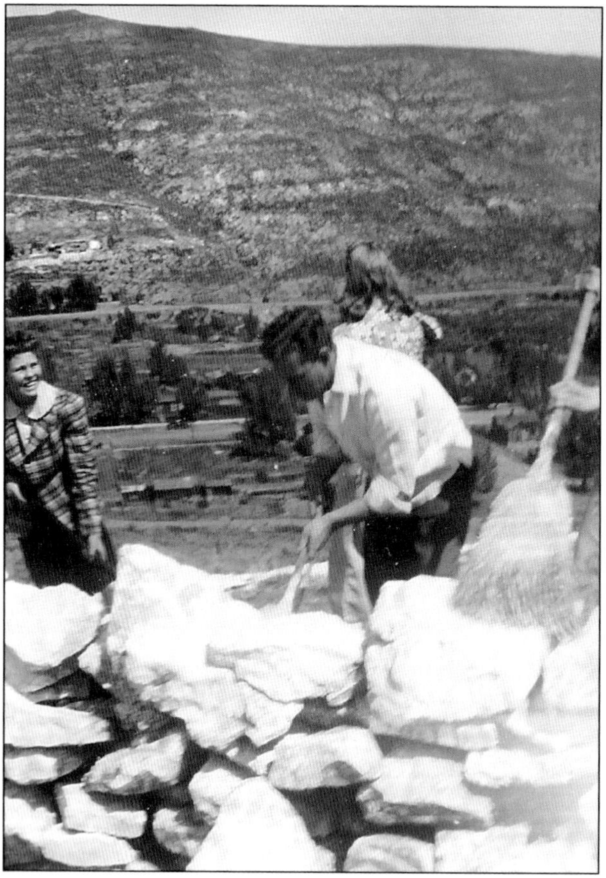

The photograph above, taken from Third Avenue South, shows Bearcreek High School below a whitewashed "B" on the hillside. Tradition dictated that incoming freshmen whitewash the stone "B" each fall as an initiation. Accompanied by teachers and sophomores, the freshmen hiked up the hill carrying buckets of whitewash and, using brooms as paintbrushes, would dutifully prepare the "B" for each new school year. Mr. Moordale is shown hard at work surrounded by his students (left). Eight principals guided Bearcreek High School through its 30-year history: Martin Kane (1916–1918), B. P. Wilcox (1918–1924), J. H. Varner (1924–1926), F. H. Bolton (1926–1929), T. E. McDonald (1929–1930), C. L. Baldwin (1930–1948), Louis H. Stahl (1948–1949), and John S. McLellan (1949–1950). (Above, Mourich; left, Wakenshaw.)

Six

Sports

Sports provided a conduit through which pride in children and community poured from the valley's residents. They also supplied a necessary and inexpensive distraction from the day-to-day stresses of difficult economic times and dangerous work.

Roger Davis, a *Billings Gazette* reporter, described the devotion the valley residents had for their teams: "From the cradle to the rocking chair, they were all fans. They would bet on their boys at the drop of a hat. They hosted, toasted and followed their athletes en masse to every contest and tournament in the state. Those whose teams played against them found to their dismay that on occasion trouble would break loose if one word was said against the Bearcreek boys."

William A. Romek elaborated on this latter assertion with a story from a late-1920s district boys' basketball tournament held in Fromberg. Bearcreek and its archrival, Red Lodge, met in the championship game. Residents who had seen sparse work that year managed to collect $130 to wager on their team. Bearcreek defeated Red Lodge, and the residents saw a nice return on their bets. A disgruntled Red Lodge fan challenged any willing Bearcreek supporter to a fight. As Romek described the event, "Alex Laird accommodated him and gave him a thorough thrashing. There were no more challenges."

The adult population played sports as well. Washoe, Bearcreek, and the larger corporate mines fielded baseball and soccer teams. Foot races highlighted each Labor Day celebration. Trout fishing in the summer, whitefish fishing in the winter, and bird and big-game hunting in the fall provided both recreation and food for the family table.

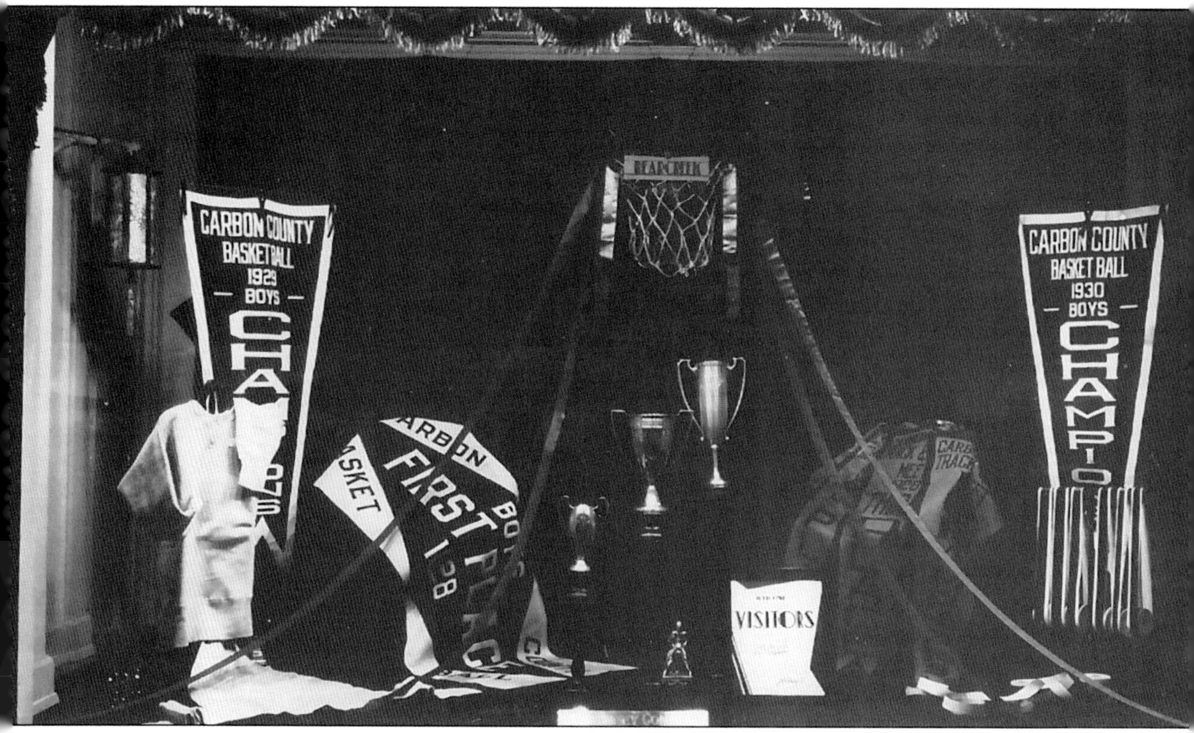

William C. Rowe paid tribute to the Bearcreek High School boys' basketball team with this 1930 J. C. Penney's window display. Under a succession of coaches, the Bearcats consistently advanced to the finals or semifinals of state and local tournaments. In 1939, the team won the Montana State Class B championship. Former coach Thorson H. Bennett paid tribute to the caliber of player the valley produced when he remarked, "It's not the coaches that make Bearcreek; it's Bearcreek that makes the coaches." The first Bearcreek High School boys' basketball team was formed in 1921 and was coached by Joe Garvey. The squad practiced in Bearcreek's LaBrun Building and played no home games. Principal J. H. Varner replaced Garvey from 1922 to 1923 and saw games moved into the new gymnasium Subsequent coaches were F. H. Bolton (1924–1929), T. E. McDonald (1929–1930), Thorson H. Bennett (1931–1933), A. Burke (1934–1935), Al Himsl (1936–1939), Dick Moordale (1939–1941), Robert Conn (1941), Bill Derr (1942–1943), Joe Naglich (1944–1946), Bob Rae (1947), Sherman B. Hubley (1948), William L. Zupan; (1949), and John S. McLellan (1950). (CCHS.)

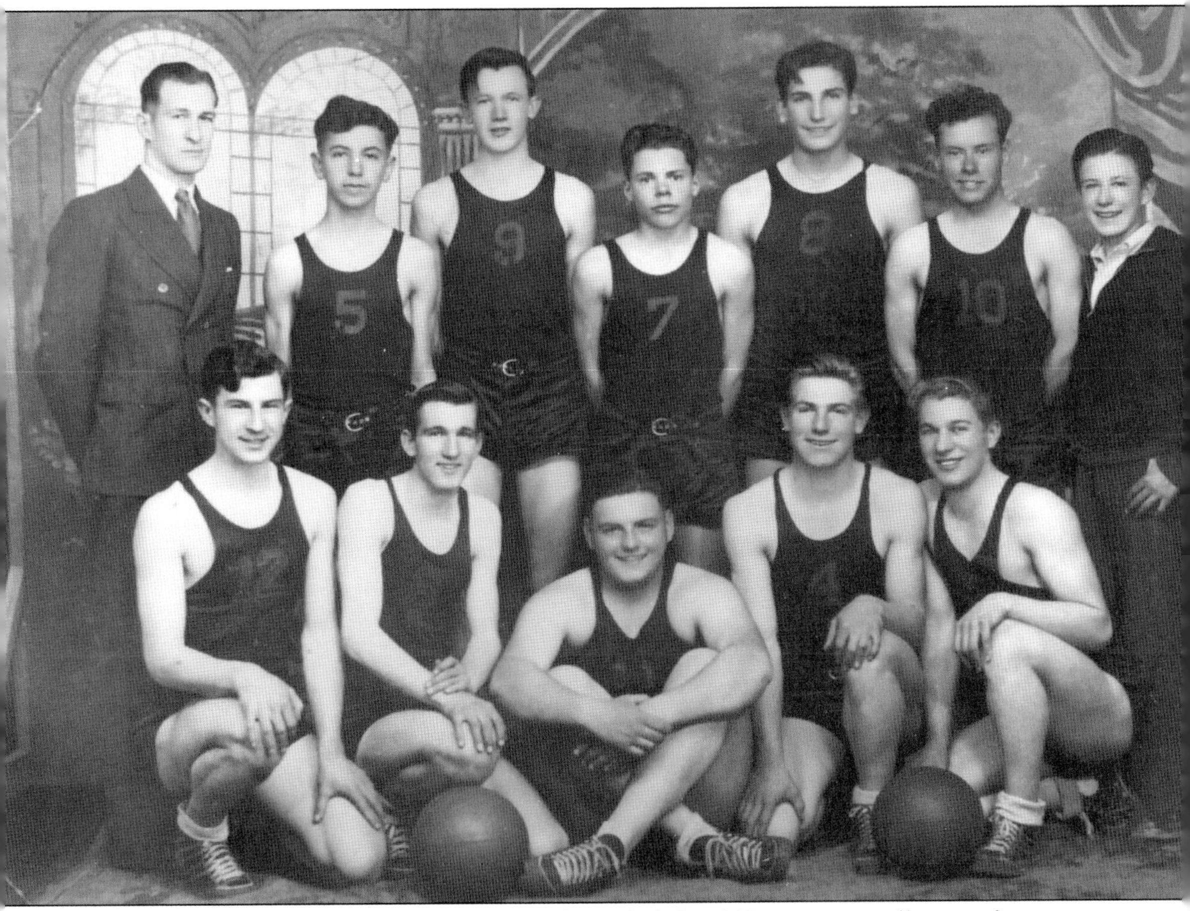

The 1939 State Class B champion Bearcreek High School Bearcats proudly pose for a team photograph. Pictured are, from left to right, (first row) Mike Sankovich, Bill Rae, Dan Pekich, Edmund Crtalic, and Walter Fatur; (second row) coach A. V. Himsl, Mike Naglich, Bill Anderson, Emmett Madding, Bill Crtalic, Allen Madding, and trainer Felix Brezar. Theirs was truly a team victory: no member of the squad was selected to the all-state team. Bill Crtalic went on to play for Rocky Mountain College, where he was a member of the 33-1 team of 1947–1948 and was later inducted into the Montana High School Association's Athletes Hall of Fame. Bill Rae's brother Bob coached the Bearcats for one season before moving to Belfry High School, where he led a squad of Bear Creek Valley and Clarks Fork Valley boys to three consecutive State Class C championships in the early 1950s. (Mourich.)

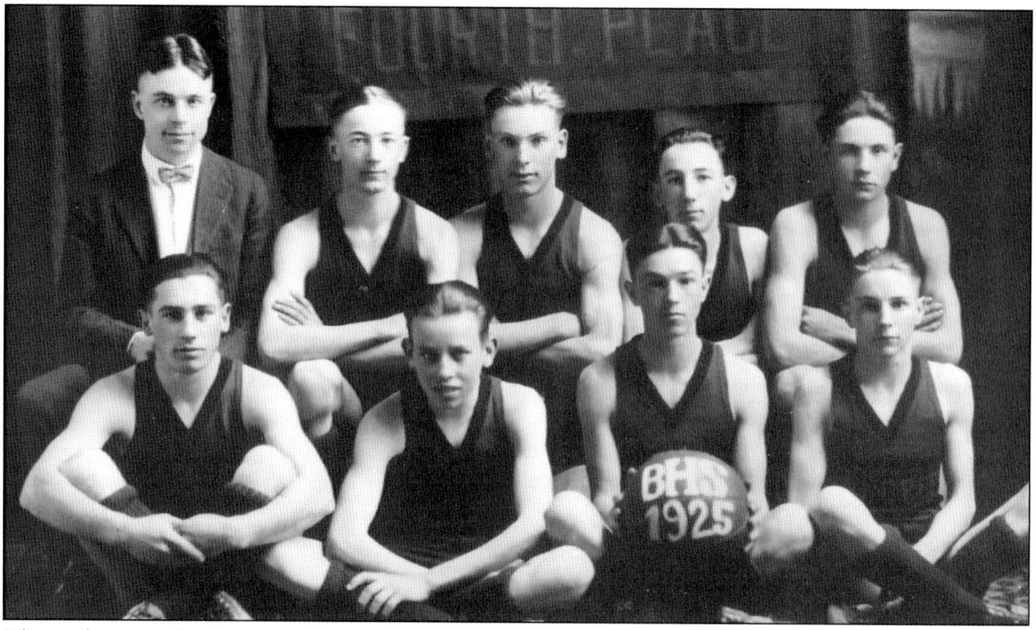

These photographs show two Bearcreek High School basketball squads from the 1920s. Both groups wear dark jerseys, orange on black, and early versions of today's high-top shoes. The members of the 1925 boys team are, from left to right, (first row) David Murray, Godfrey Sumicek, Harvey Graham, and Phil Noble; (second row) coach F. H. Bolton, Willard Reid, Howard Freeman, Hollis Johnson, and Joe Kucera. The members of the 1928 county champion girls' team are, from left to right, Mary Kastelitz, Mildred Chesarek, ? Steinmetz, Janet Murray, Betty McNeil, Nell Kane, ? Babcock, and Jean Alexander. (Mourich.)

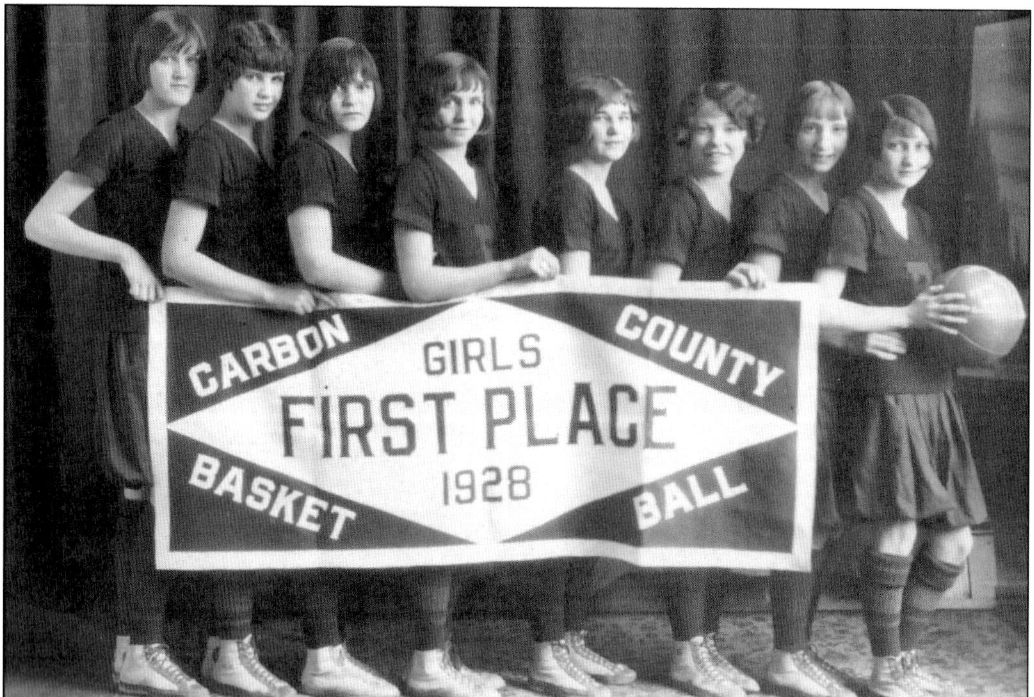

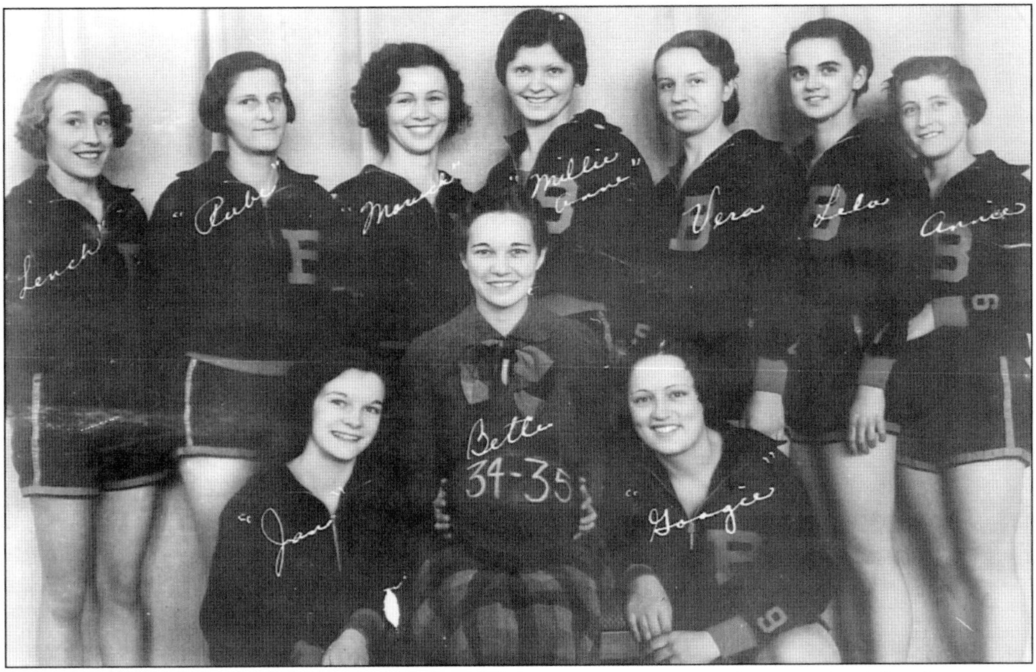

Bearcreek's star athletes of the mid-1930s are well represented in these photographs. The photograph above shows the girls' 1934–1935 basketball team. Note the dramatic change in uniform style from those worn by the 1928 team shown previously. The Bearcreek High School lettermen are shown below on May 19, 1933. The members are, from left to right, (first row) Art Santinica, William Beeney, Joe Naglich, Mike Barovich, Frank Tastavorsnik, Alex Young, Matt Danichek, and Orville Williams; (second row) coach Thorson H. Bennett, Clarence Jackson, Earl Hynds, Bill Marshall, George Bentby, Edward Kastelitz, and Clarence McLuskie. (Above, CCHS; below, Mourich.)

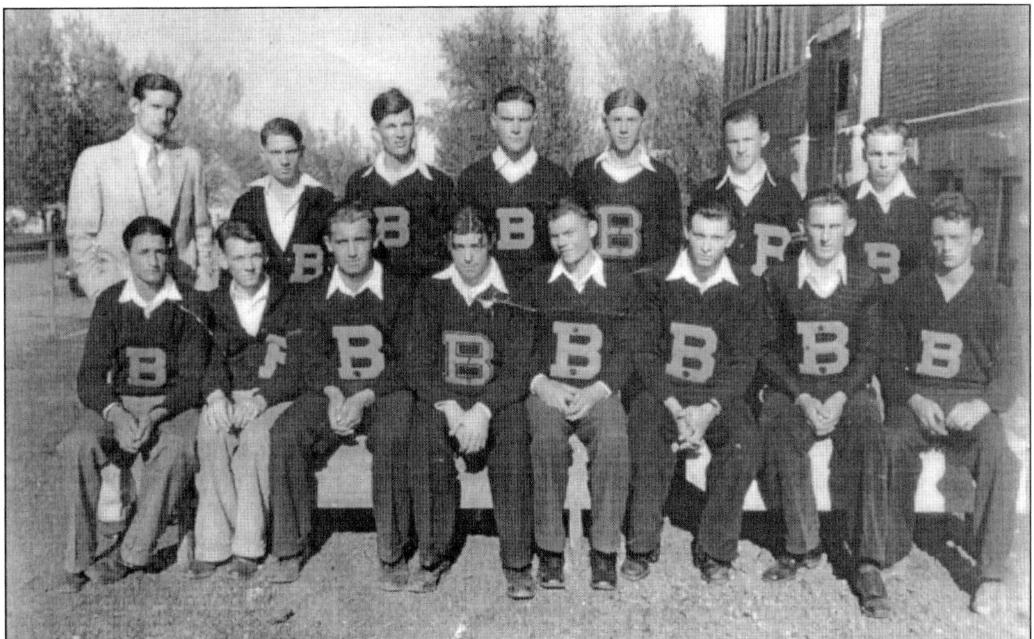

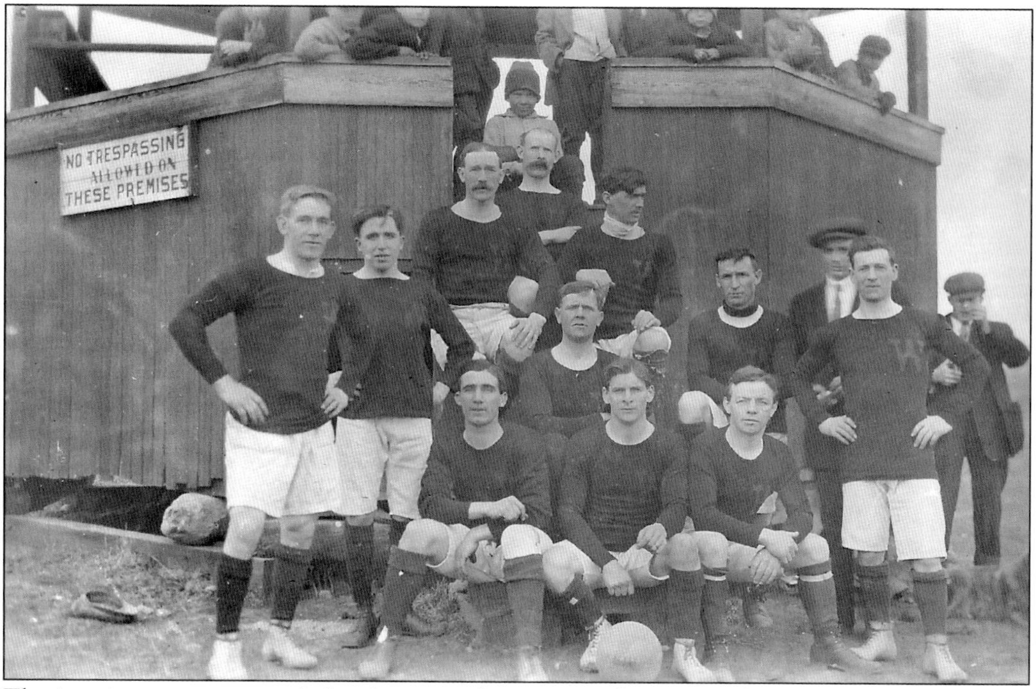

The immigrant community's familiarity with soccer made it a popular valley sport during the early days. The early-1910s photograph above shows a Washoe soccer team called the Scots, comprised primarily of Washoe coal miners. Baseball, track, and fistfighting (considered more sport than violence), soon replaced soccer as the adult sports of choice. In the photograph below, participants of a Labor Day foot race approach the finish line on Bearcreek's Main Street. Track and fistfighting merged dramatically during one Labor Day when a spectator from southern Europe tripped a Scottish participant in a foot race. The ensuing riot ended the day's celebration. (Above, CCHS; below, Mourich.)

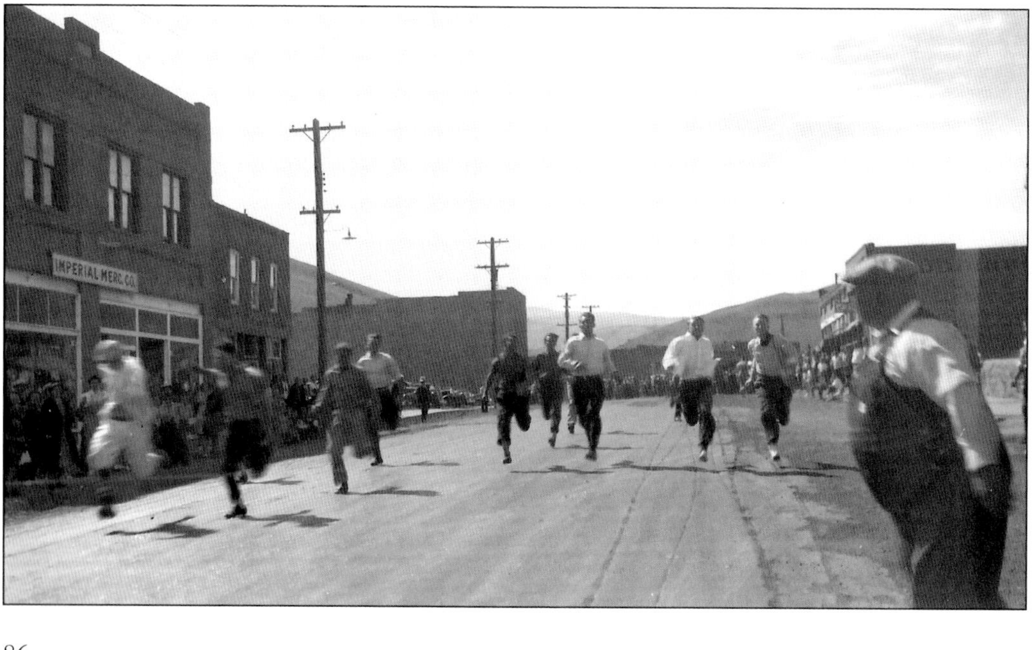

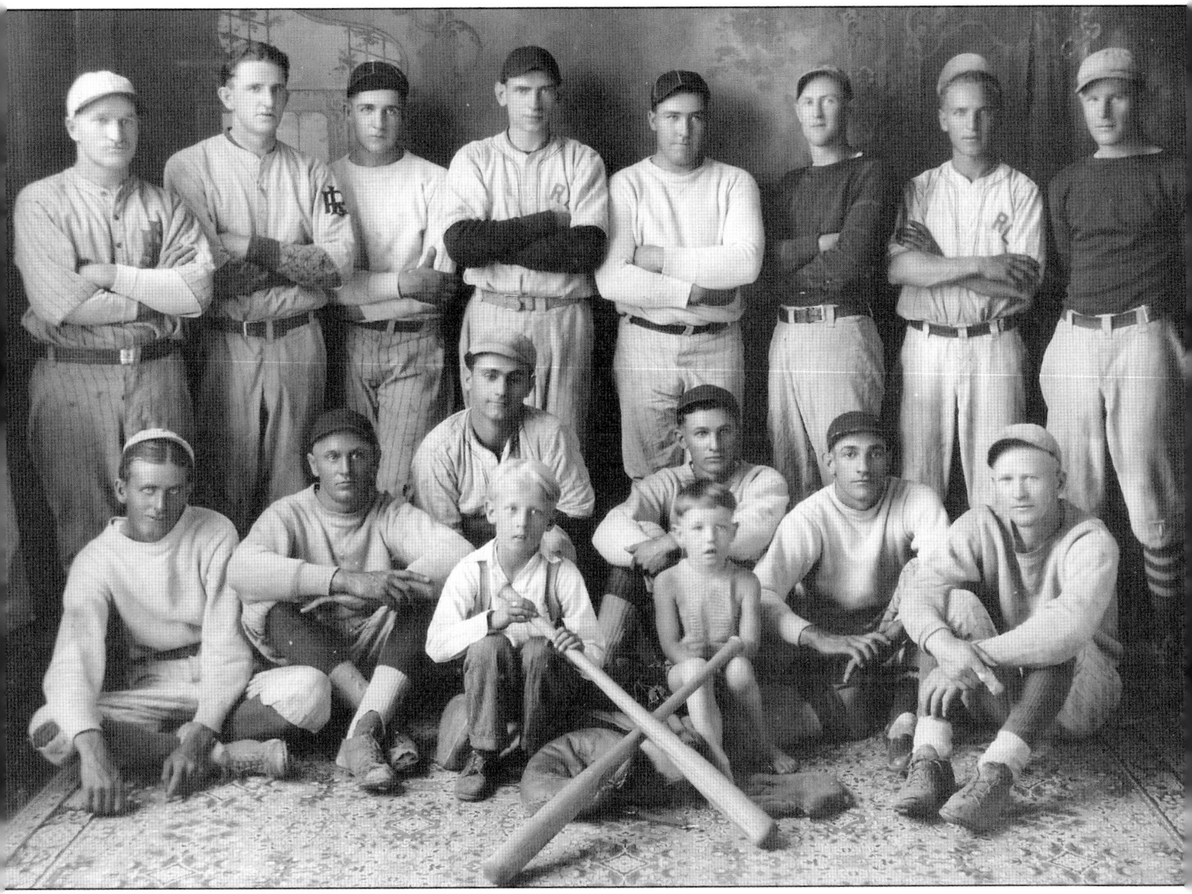

Bearcreek, Washoe, and neighboring Red Lodge all fielded baseball teams. The proximity of these teams produced intense rivalries. An early-1930s Red Lodge baseball team is shown above. Its members are, from left to right, (first row) two unidentified bat boys; (second row) Ello Heitala, Eli Houtonen, ? Marrow, Arne Wertanen, unidentified, and Elmer Toffer; (third row) Ray Hautou, unidentified, "Butch" Wadsworth, John Salono, Clarence Wadsworth, Bill Toffer, Joe Yanchisin, and Eli Turi. The valley's adult baseball diamonds sat at the western end of Washoe and at the eastern end of Bearcreek near today's water treatment ponds. A third diamond, used primarily by children, sat at the western end of Bearcreek near the elementary school. Players came from all walks of life. Bearcreek's town marshal in the 1920s, Bill Simmons, using the now-illegal quick pitch, became a star pitcher for the Bearcreek team. (CCHS.)

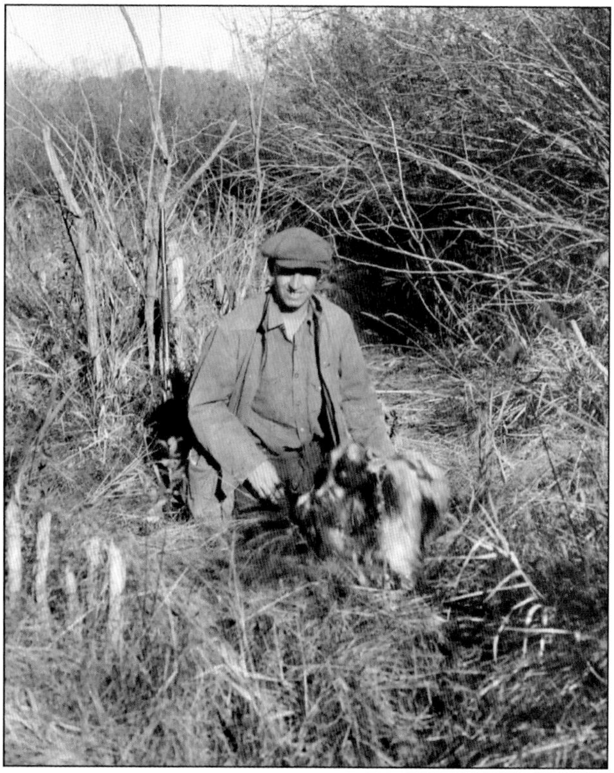

A bird-hunting trip for Jake McNeish and Thomas Bailey's (Jake's father-in-law) family spaniel, Bonnie, meant hours of relaxation, while success meant food on the table. Jake and Bonnie proudly pose with a duck Bonnie has just retrieved. Duck was a particular favorite of Jake's. Geese, pheasants, partridges, and grouse were also hunted during bird season. Big-game season included whitetail and mule deer, elk, and moose. (Author's collection.)

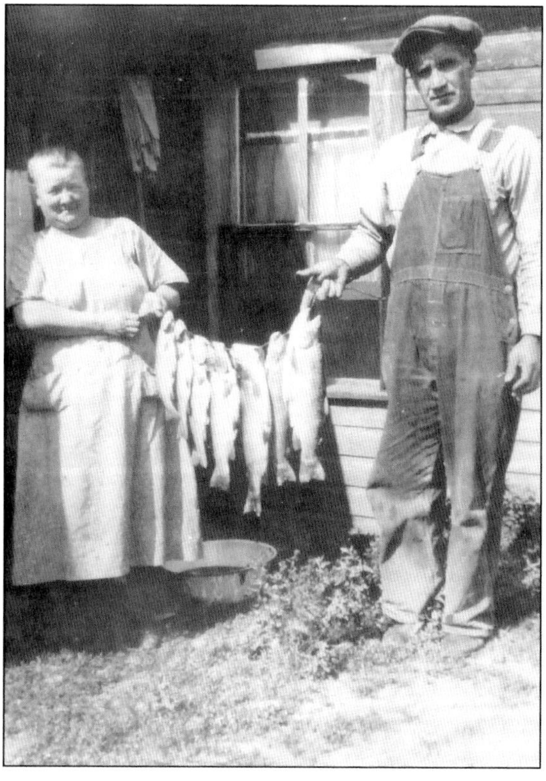

Holding a string of trout, Agnes and Samuel Alexander stand in front of their Bearcreek home. Rainbow, cutthroat, brown, and lake trout were harvested from the stream, rivers, and mountain lakes of Carbon County. During the late winter, the Clark's Fork River provided an abundance of whitefish, which were soaked in brine and cured in private smokehouses prior to eating. (Mourich.)

Seven

ENTERTAINMENT

Residents of Bear Creek Valley worked hard and played harder. Music and dancing topped the list of popular activities, followed closely by holiday celebrations, sports, fishing, and hunting.

Carbon County is known for the quality of its musicians, and Bear Creek Valley was no exception. With so many musically talented residents available, it was easy for an event organizer to assemble a fine dance band or even a complete brass marching unit.

When the holidays approached, local unions and businesses assured that every child in the valley received a Christmas package filled with apples, oranges, and a variety of hard candies. The immigrant roots of its citizenry allowed many different holidays to become standard fare for all to celebrate. Non-Slavic people joined their neighbors in celebrating the Montenegro/Serbian Christmas two weeks after the American Christmas, and the valley adopted the Scottish practice of first-footing on New Years Eve. First-footing involved calling on neighbors to offer them a toast of strong drink, receiving a drink and some holiday sweets in return, and then gathering up those neighbors and moving as a group to the next home to repeat the whole process.

Picnics, hunting, fishing, and travel to the mountains filled the brief months of the Montana summer and autumn. Picnics allowed time to gather with family and friends over a dinner of pan-fried trout, homemade salads, and wine, and a rousing game of cards.

For the people of the valley, work could even be made into entertainment if done correctly. Home and road building were often social affairs. Construction projects were completed over the course of a weekend or during times of unemployment. A popular Bear Creek Valley expression reveals the community spirit shown in such projects: "The only thing you need to build a house is a keg of beer and a Saturday."

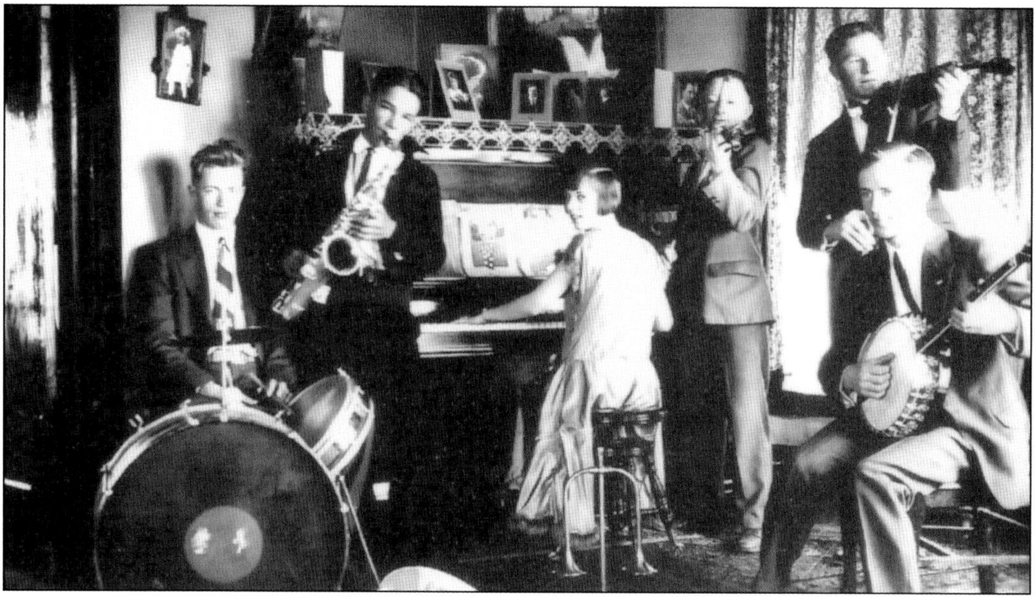

Bear Creek Valley produced many outstanding musicians and bands. One Bearcreek band, the Novelty Six (above), played during the 1920s. Posing here in the home of Isabelle Romek are, from left to right, William Cameron (drums), Louis Mourich (saxophone), Gladys Rue (piano), Smox Thompson and Jack Mourich (violins), and Alexander Cameron Sr. (banjo). The Novelty Six played modern dance music, while the Scotch Coulee Band (below) played traditional Yugoslavian music for marriages and parties. Members of this band are, from left to right, Jack Mourich, Louie Crtalic, Louis Mourich, and George Wereholtz. (Mourich.)

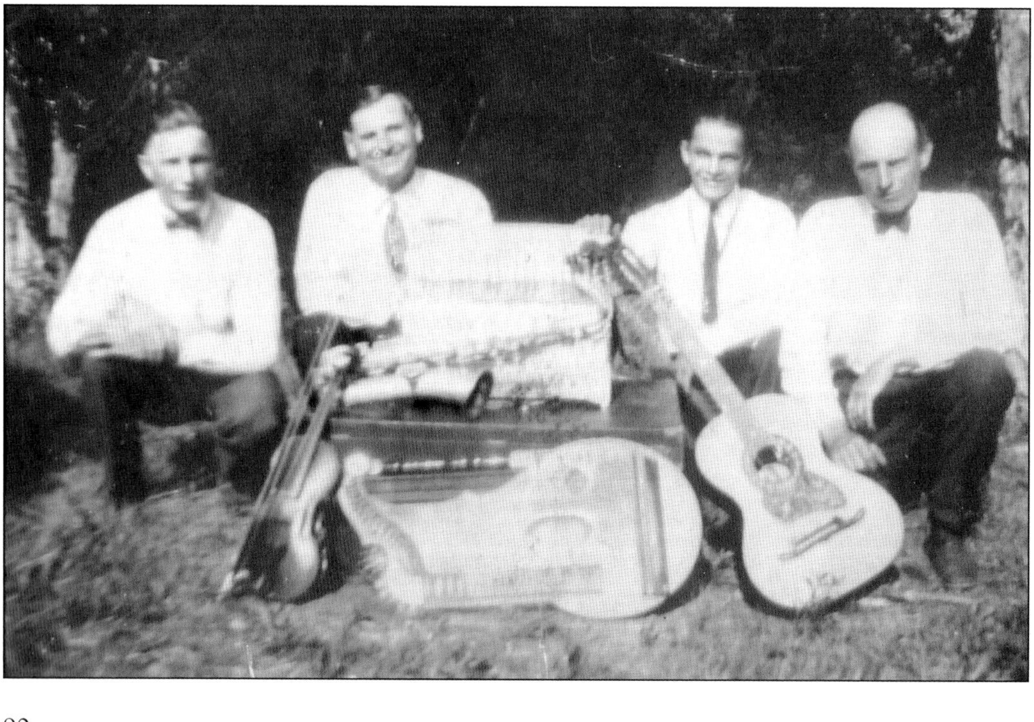

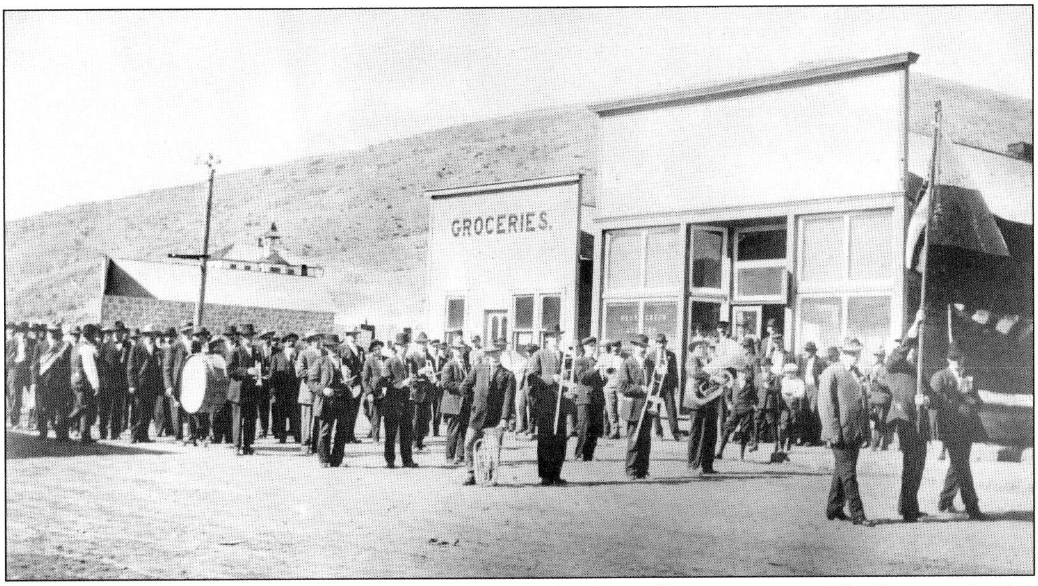

Marching bands provided additional opportunities for the valley's musicians. The Bearcreek City Band (above) leads a 1920s Labor Day parade down Main Street. Buildings in this photograph are, from left to right, the Bearcreek Elementary School, unidentified, a grocery store, and the Bearcreek Saloon. In the photograph below, of either the Bearcreek or Joilet city band, Adam Wakenshaw is the mustache-wearing trombone player in the back row. Adam played for both the Bearcreek and Joliet city bands. A 1909 edition of the *Carbon County News* illustrates the importance of music to Carbon County in reporting Wakenshaw's move to Joliet. The article read, "Mr. Wakenshaw is an expert slide trombone player, and his presence here [Joliet] will add materially to the strength of Joliet's musical population." (Above, CCHS; below, Wakenshaw.)

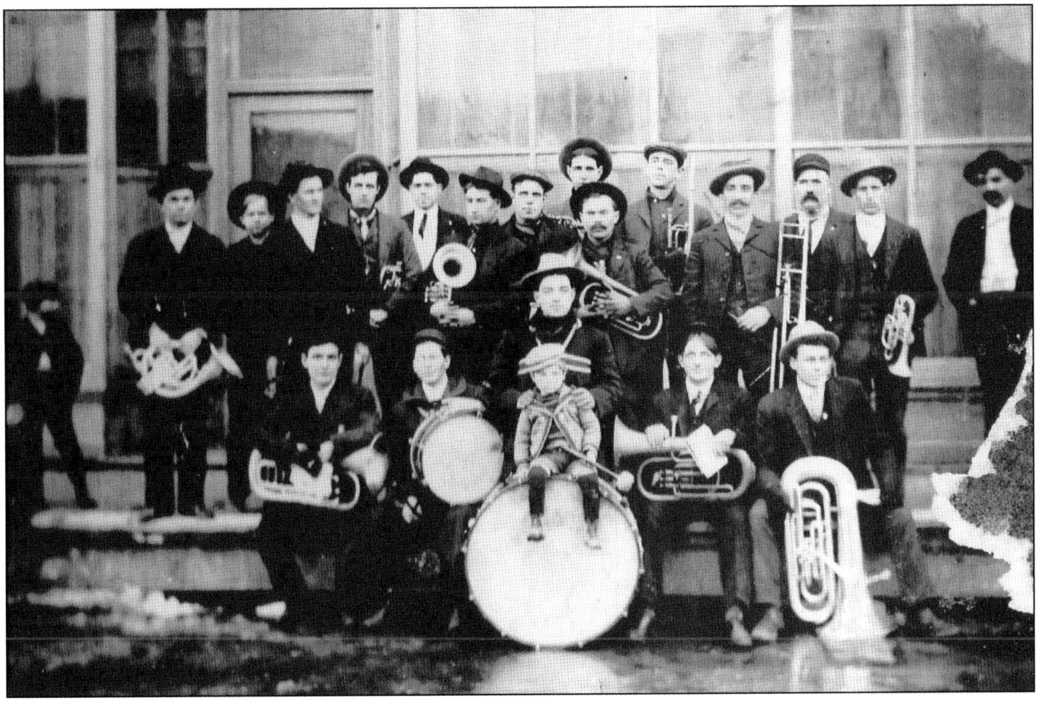

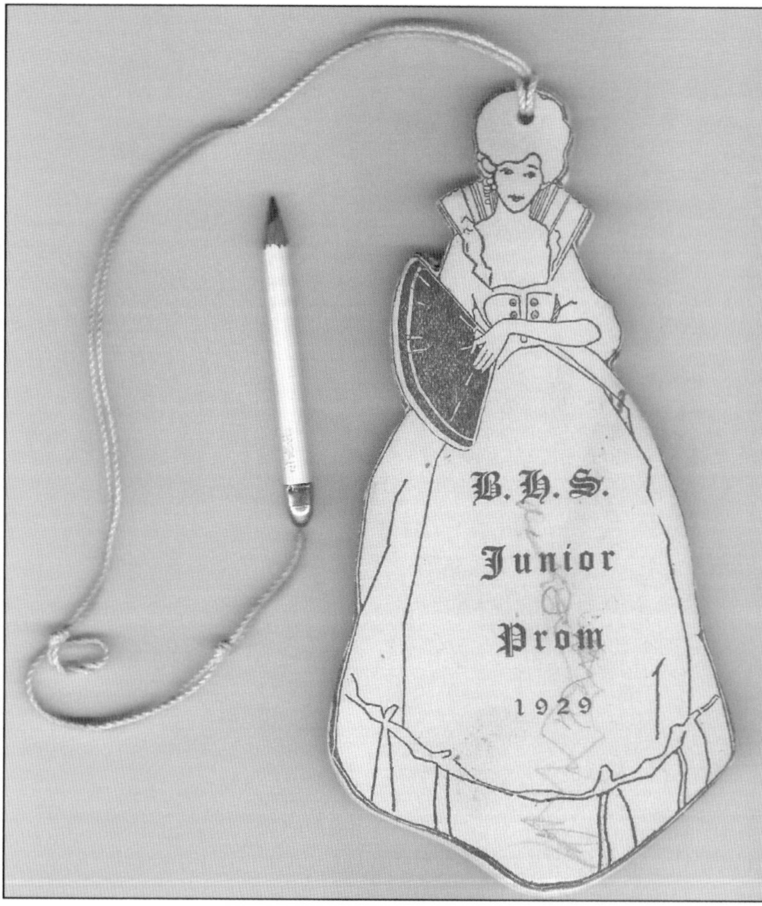

A dance card from the 1929 Bearcreek High School junior prom illustrates a more formal valley event. The valley offered many locations in which to hold a dance. Bearcreek venues included the Lamport Hotel and the second stories of the People's Co-Op store and Louis Sasich's General Store. The Scotch Coulee Hall and the Washoe Community Hall offered additional location possibilities. (Murfitt.)

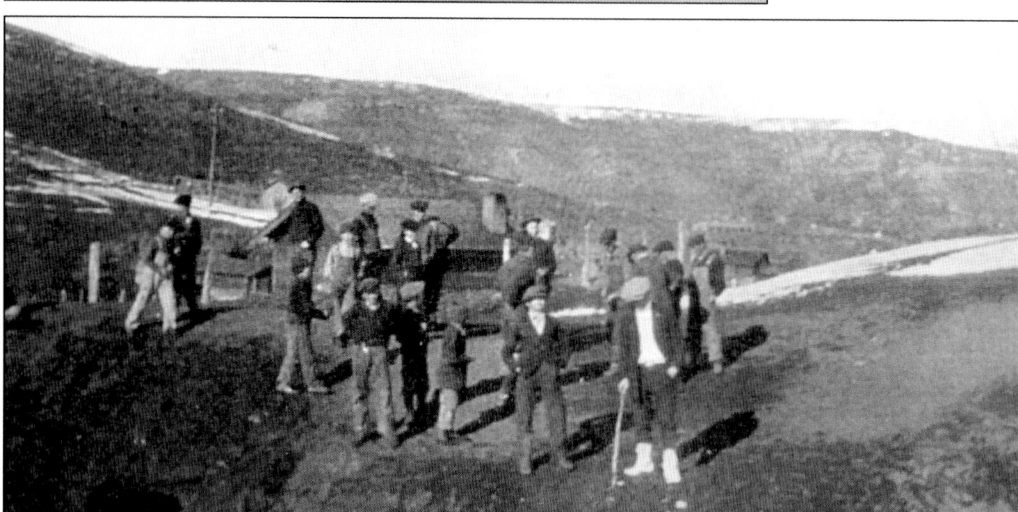

Undeterred by less-than-ideal terrain, early Scotch Coulee residents managed to play a game of golf from time to time. This photograph was taken on the eastern side of the coulee. Immediately behind this optimistic group sit two Scotch Coulee homes. In the far distance is the Scotch Coulee Mine. (Planichek.)

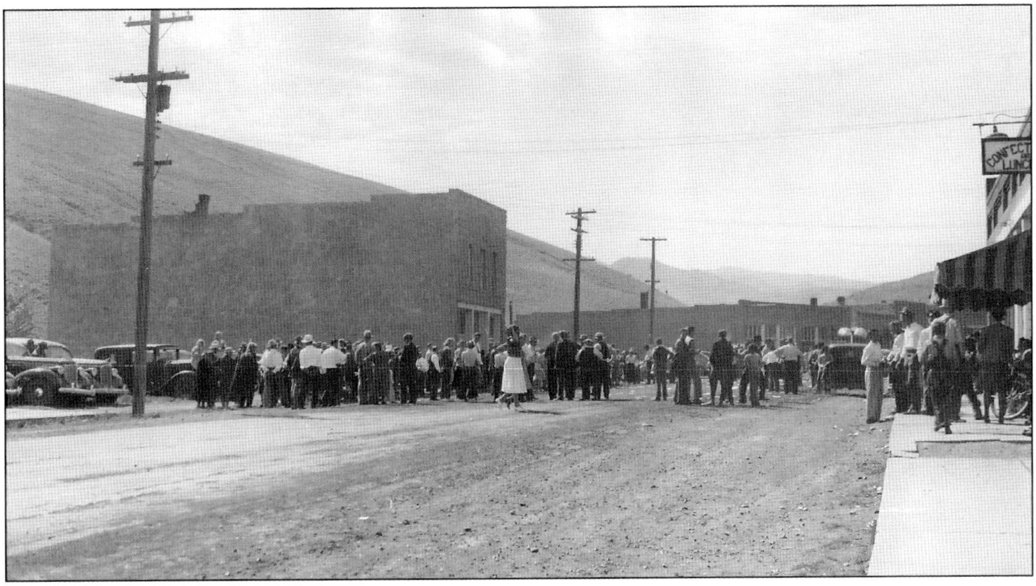

In the 1930s photograph above, a crowd gathers near the finish line for foot and wheelbarrow races at Bearcreek's western end. Buildings visible above are the Labor Temple (left), Marchello's Market (center), the Bearcreek Bar (next to Marchello's), and Little Joe's Confectionery (far right). The Bearcreek and Washoe chapters of the United Mine Workers of America organized and funded Labor Day celebrations. Initially the Labor Day venue alternated between Washoe and Bearcreek. In later years, Bearcreek became the primary location. Labor Day events included speeches, races for adults and children, and a parade. Prizes were given for races and a variety of parade entry categories. The Rado Jovanovich family consistently took home the ham awarded to the winner of the "Largest Family" category. Wheelbarrow race contestants approach the finish line in the 1930s photograph below. (Both, Mourich.)

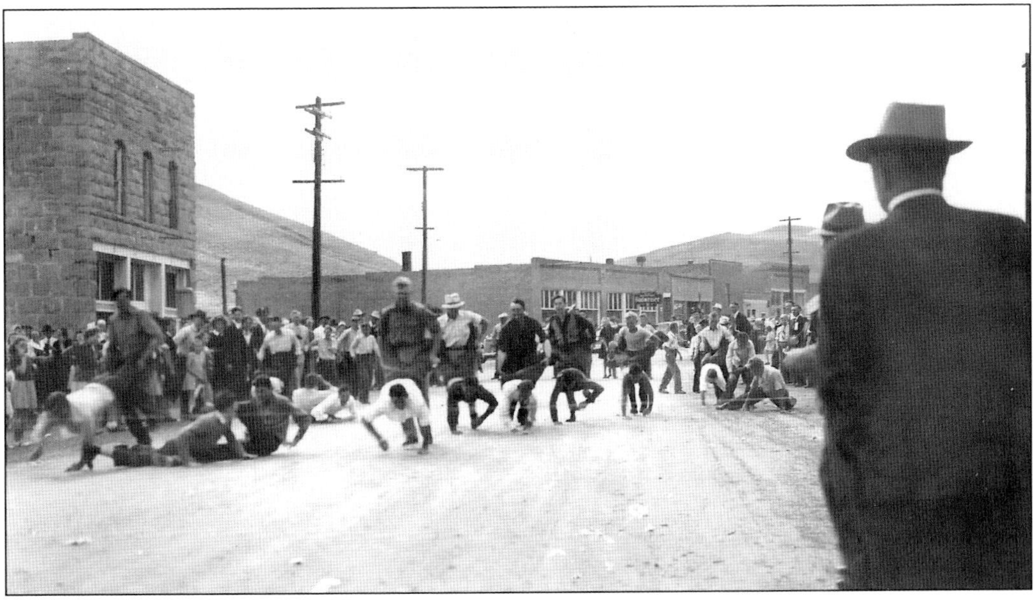

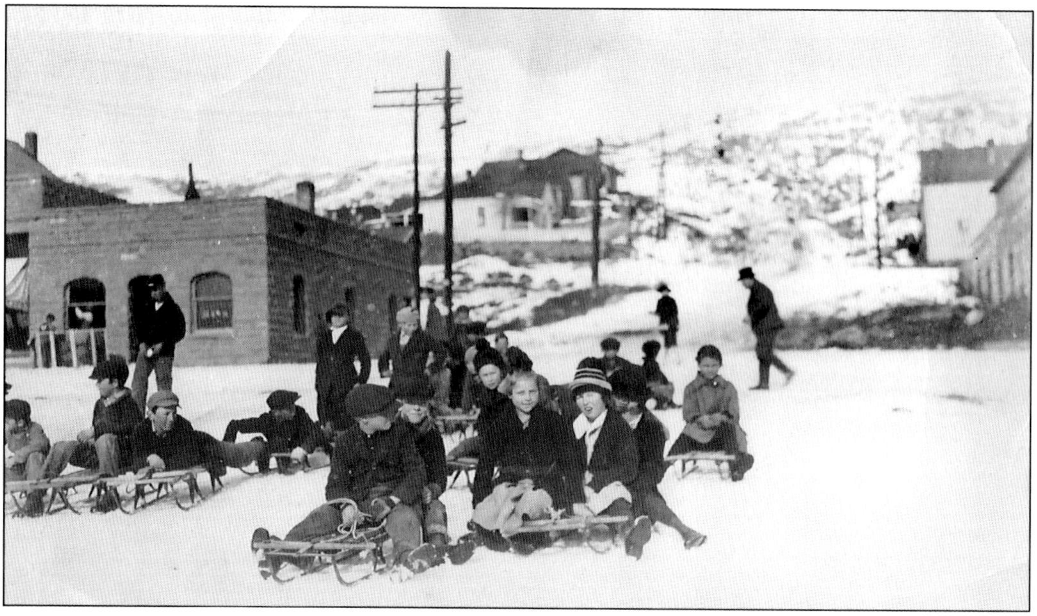

The children of Bear Creek Valley used every inch of the valley as their playground. In these photographs, a group of them sled through the intersection of Second and Main Streets. The photograph above provides a good view of the northern side of Second Street flanked by the Clark-Wright Bank and the F. and S. Garage. During the winter, children occupied themselves with sledding and snowball fights, basketball games, dances, and frequenting Little Joe's Confectionery. During the summer, a number of swimming holes became available, and the Bearcreek pool was filled from a nearby fire hydrant. Children also explored the hills and played crack the whip, kick the can, capture the flag, baseball, and basketball until dark. (Above, Mourich; below, Planichek.)

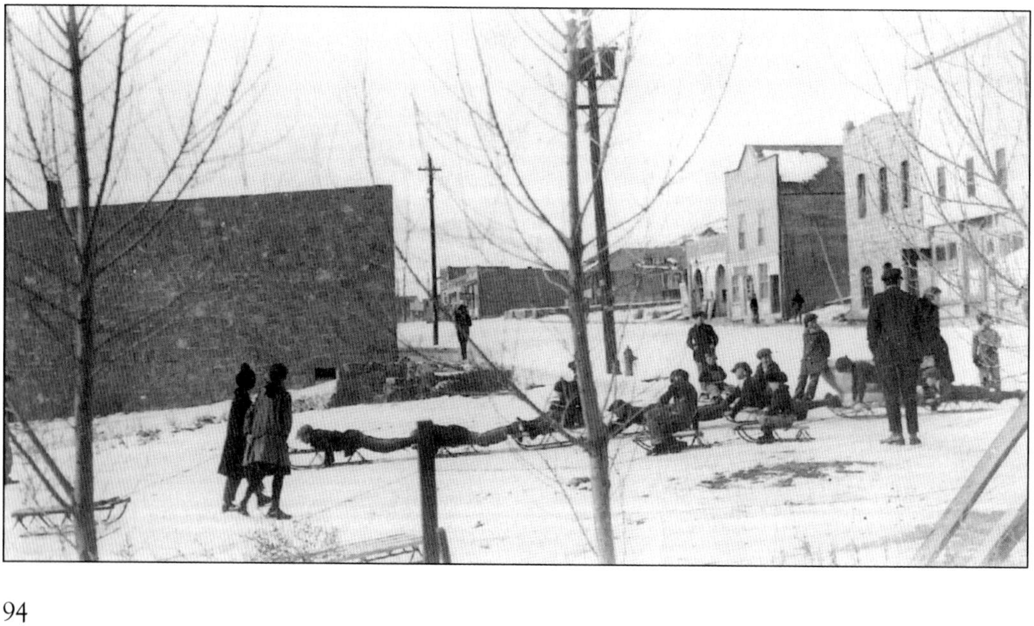

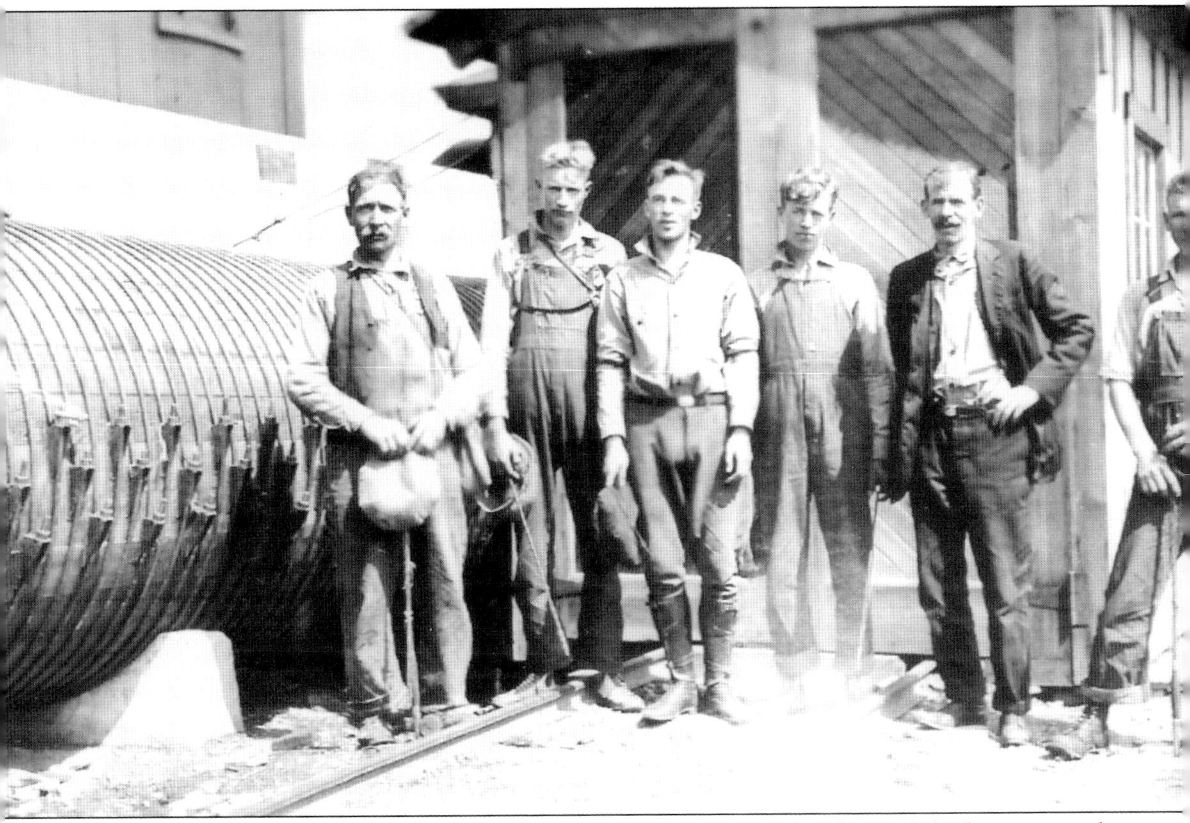

Unemployment increased dramatically during the summer as the demand for heating coal decreased. Families depended on garden plots, fishing, hunting, and credit accounts at local stores to survive these lean times. Valley residents made the most of their downtime by gathering in the neighboring mountains to camp for weeks at a time. The mountains provided a cooler climate, plentiful fishing, and wild mushrooms and berries for the taking. The men of these groups took turns staying in town to tend the gardens and watch for temporary mine work. If such an opportunity appeared, the watchman would head up to the mountains to gather the other men. Pictured above is a group of Scottish immigrant miners on a fishing trip to Mystic Lake high in the Beartooth Mountains. They are, from left to right, David Sommerville, Jacob Cameron Jr., Alexander Cameron, William Cameron, Jacob Cameron Sr., and John Sommerville. (Garcia.)

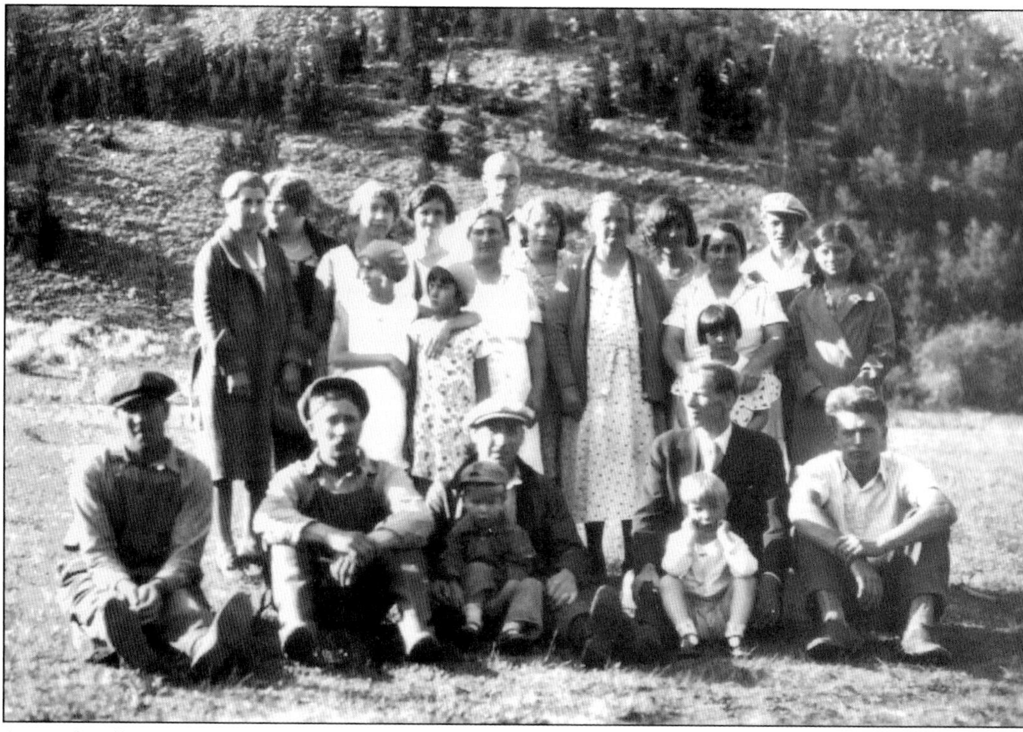

Several valley families are represented in this 1930s photograph, taken during a mountain picnic. They are the Cameron, Freeman, McDonald, McNeish, and Sommerville families. The three men seated on the left are, from left to right, James McNeish, David Sommerville, and Abraham McDonald, brothers-in-law who would soon die in the Smith Mine disaster. (Garcia.)

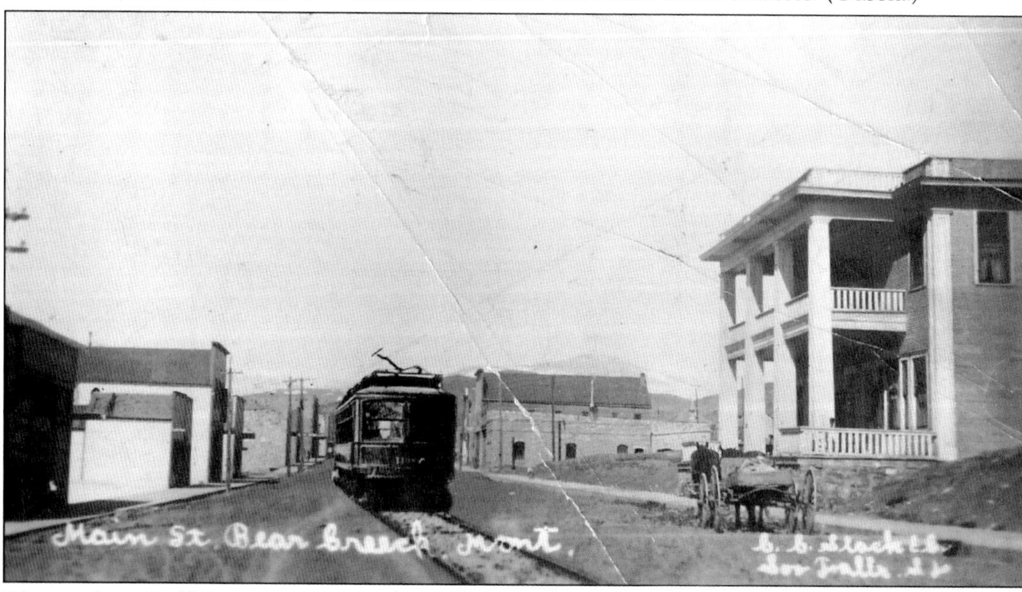

The good sense of humor permeating the valley is evidenced by this doctored postcard of Bearcreek's Main Street—no streetcars existed in the valley. Practical joking ran rampant through the valley and was considered an art form. New miners often found their lunch pails nailed to a bench during their first lunch break. (Wakenshaw.)

Eight

People

From community leaders to everyday citizens, the people of Bear Creek Valley displayed a zest for life and community, an indomitable spirit in the face of adversity, and an innate sense of humor rarely seen today. After suffering economic hardships in their native lands, the area's European immigrants had the strength of body and character required to leave behind family, friends, and homeland to start a new life in a raw new country

Their labor contributed to America's industrial expansion, and they defended their adopted country through two world wars. They endured the 1918 Spanish flu pandemic and Montana's worst coal-mining disaster. They lived through and, arguably, managed to thrive during America's Great Depression.

These people transformed Bear Creek Valley from two small coal camps into a thriving community. They built homes, roads, community halls, and schools. They established businesses and formed unions, fraternal lodges, and service organizations. They raised children and grandchildren and instilled in them a deep devotion to community and pride in their heritage.

These values can be found in Carbon County today, as evidenced by the Festival of Nations celebration held in neighboring Red Lodge every summer and the widespread community support shown for recent efforts to restore original valley buildings and place the Smith Mine on the National Register of Historic Places.

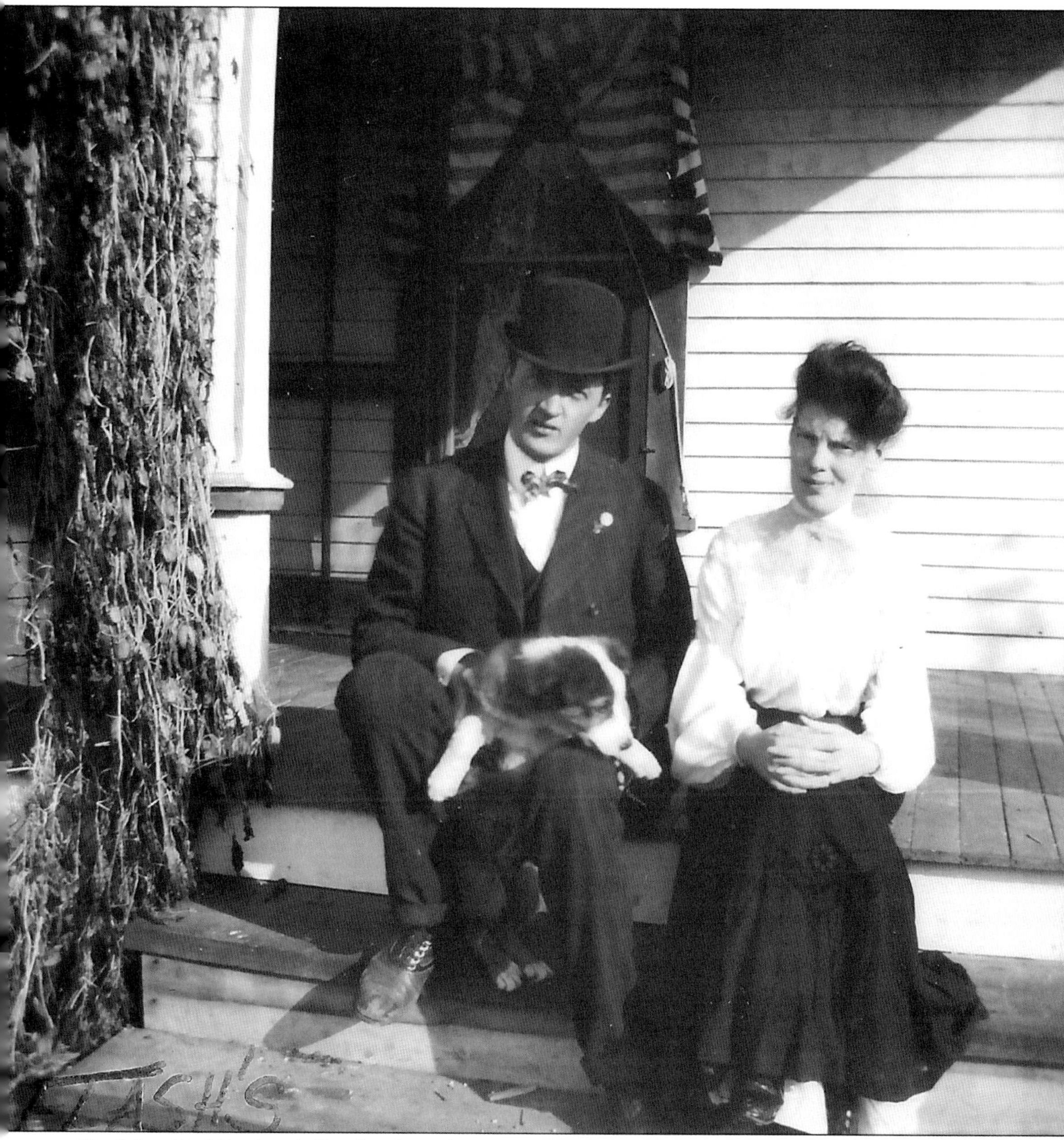

Dr. John Carl Frederick Siegfriedt enthusiastically accepted the tacit role of community leader that came with his position as a coal camp physician. From his home and hospital in Bearcreek, he served the eastern end of Bear Creek Valley from 1906 to 1930. During this time, Dr. Siegfriedt acted as town mayor for several terms, was elected to one term in the Montana Senate, and organized, financed, and led the Black and White Trail Association. This association made the first attempt at constructing a highway from western Carbon County over the Beartooth Mountains to Cooke City. Born in Davenport, Iowa, in 1879, Dr. Siegfriedt attended the University of Iowa and then the University of Illinois, receiving his medical degree in 1902. He married Lily Fort in Chicago, Illinois, in 1903. This photograph shows John and Lily Siegfriedt on the porch of their Bearcreek home. (Flash's Photography.)

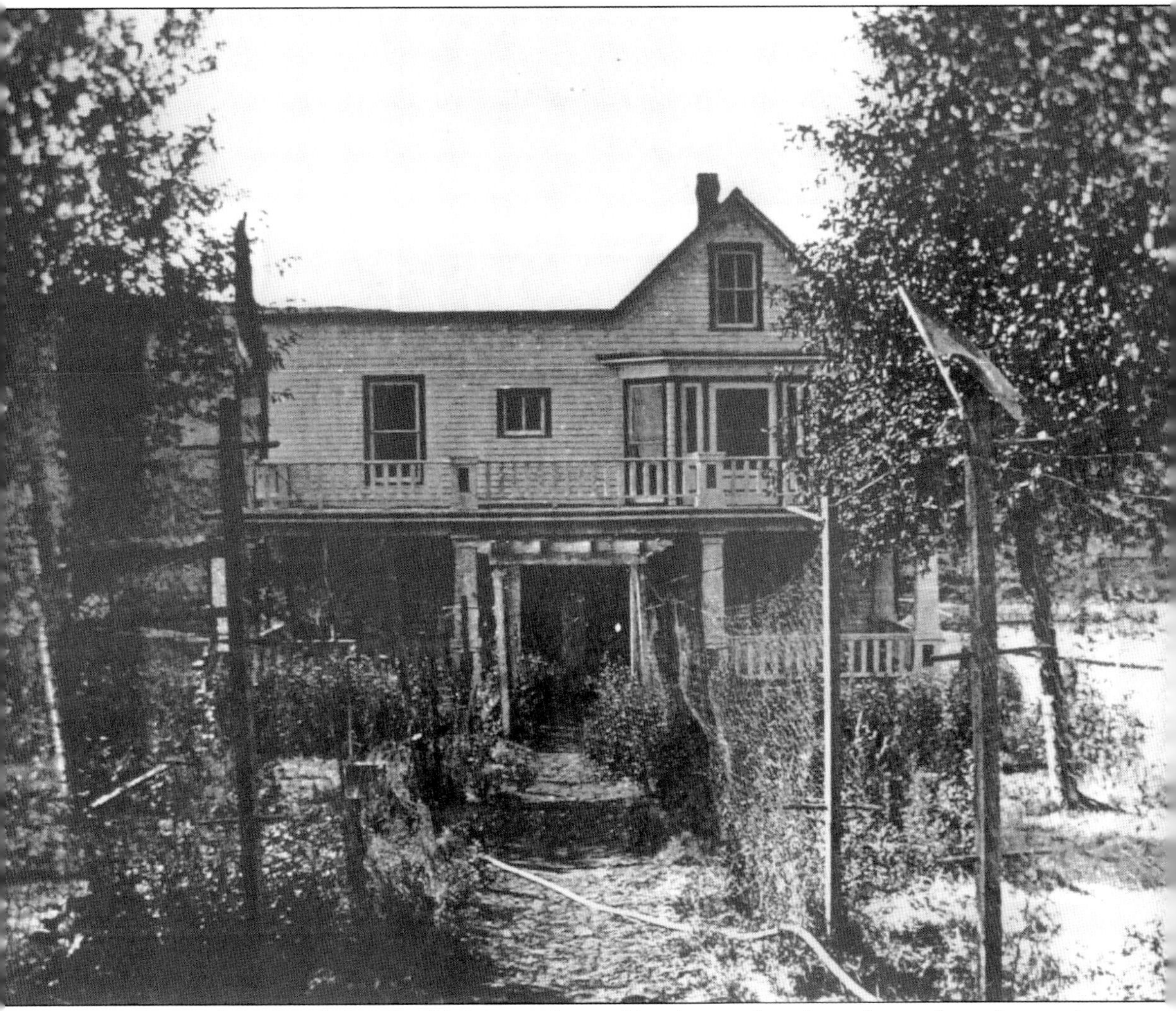

Dr. John Carl Frederick Siegfriedt's home adjoined his hospital and was located on the south side of Main Street between Third and Fourth Avenues, across from the Lamport Hotel. Dr. Siegfriedt saw the valley through mining-related illnesses and accidents, childhood diseases, and an outbreak of typhoid fever. During the late-1910s flu pandemic, Dr. Siegfriedt served as a lieutenant in the Army Medical Corps. In 1918, he was stationed at the Yale Army Laboratory School in New Haven, Connecticut. The pandemic hit the valley particularly hard that year, and by 1919, he had returned to Bearcreek. Siegfriedt approached his role as physician with dedication and compassion. He did not keep formal track of fees due him, nor did he refuse service to anyone based on ability to pay. Dr. Siegfriedt's interests extended beyond medicine and civics, including paleontology, photography, hunting, fishing, and playing the zither. (Planichek.)

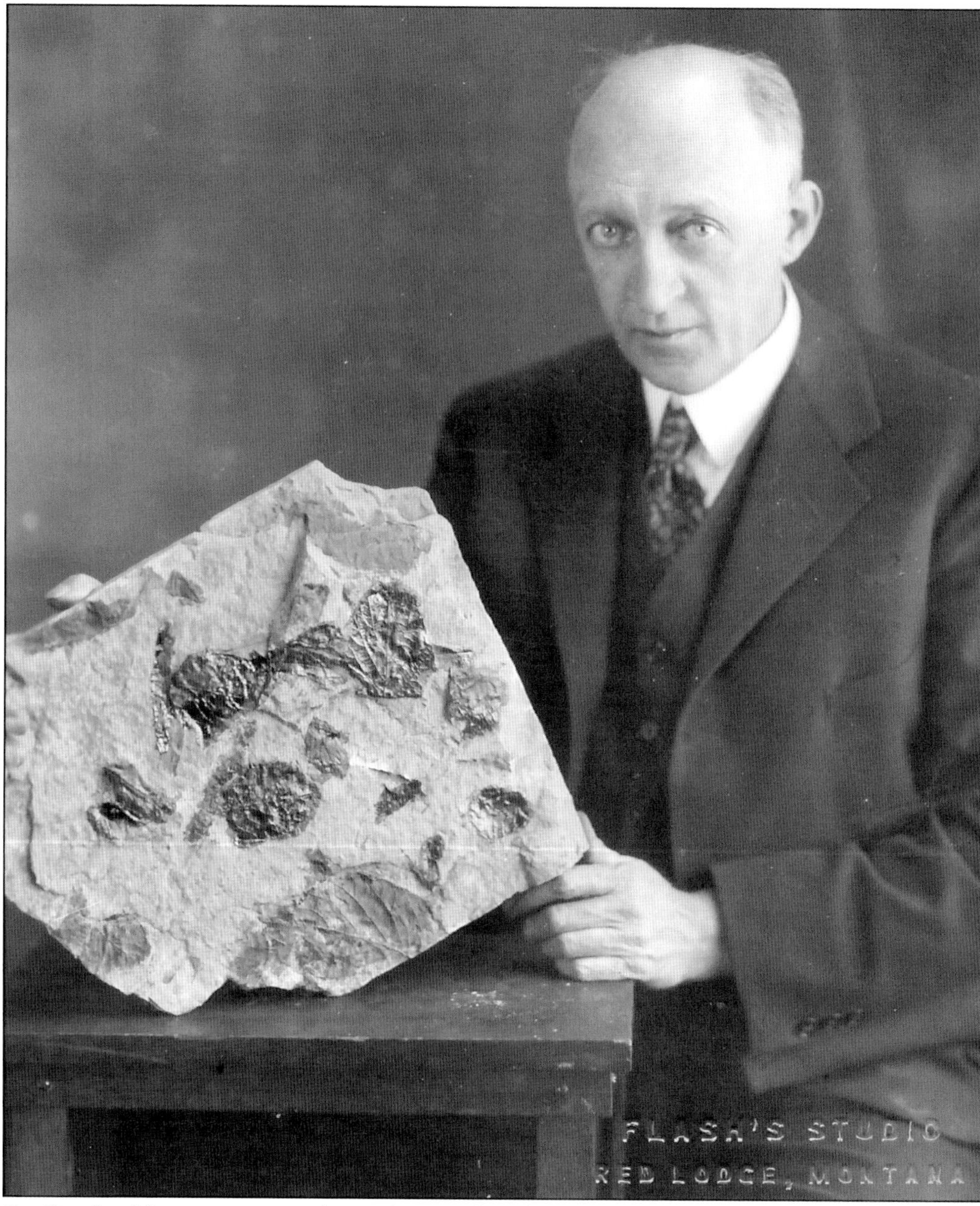

Dr. Siegfriedt's interests in paleontology and geology earned him acclaim and controversy. Working from fossils found in the valley's numerous coal mines (above), Siegfriedt initiated the first scientific analysis of the valley. Dr. Siegfriedt sent his collection to the American Museum of Natural History in 1927, prompting an influx of researchers to the area. This resulted in the classification of a new mammalian family, several new genera, and five new species. One new insect species was given the name *Entomolestes siegfriedti* in Siegfriedt's honor. The scientific interest sparked by Dr. Siegfriedt resulted in the first discovery of dinosaur eggs in North America. An expedition from Princeton University found these eggs on Dry Creek, north of Bearcreek. Siegfriedt went on to play a key role in establishing the Yellowstone Bighorn Research Association. (Flash's Photography.)

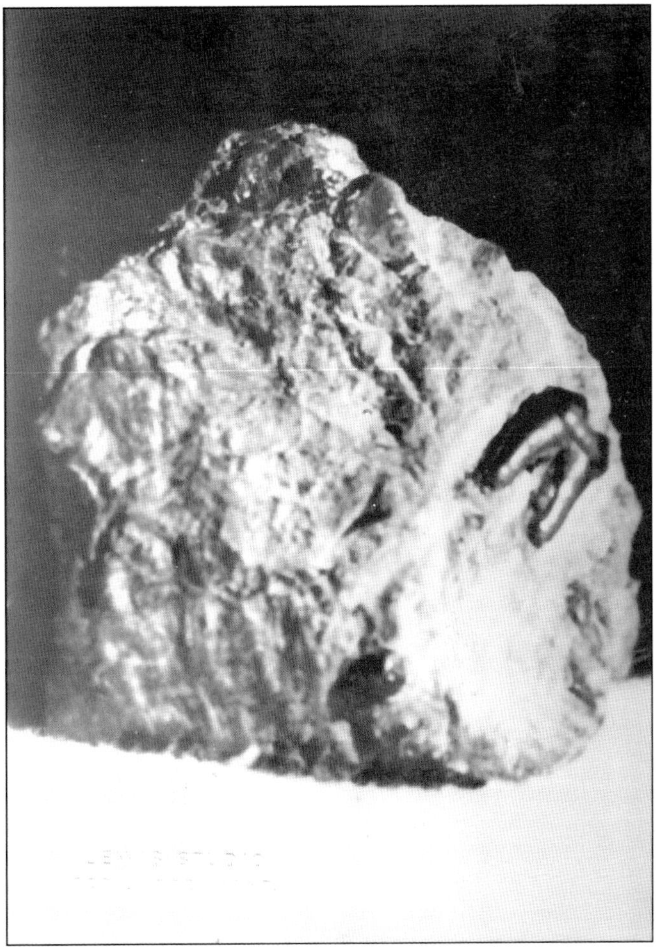

In 1926, Dr. Siegfriedt reported finding the fossil pictured at right, which he believed to be a human tooth predating all other evidence of human life. Local papers quickly announced that this find would "rearrange theories of geologic evolution," but many academics just as quickly dismissed the possibility that the fossil was a human tooth. The debate raged for several months and is still debated in some circles. Siegfriedt expressed his consternation with his critics when, in early 1927, he wrote, "I was simply bringing my discovery to the public notice and from the attitude that was hurled at me, one would think I was trying to hold up a bank." Siegfriedt discovered the fossil in the Eagle Coal Company Mine in Foster Gulch, seen below. (Both, CCHS.)

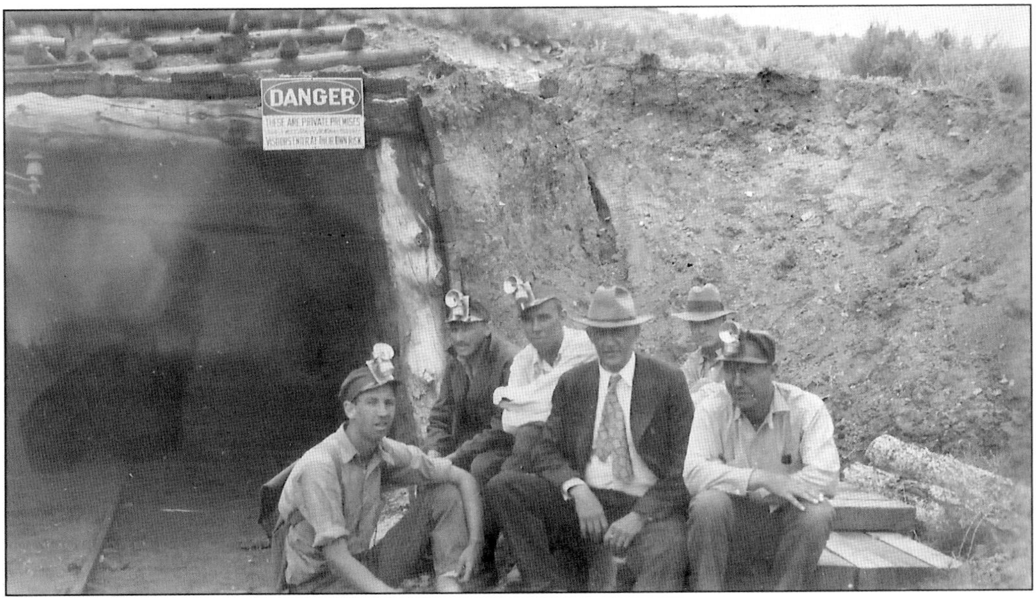

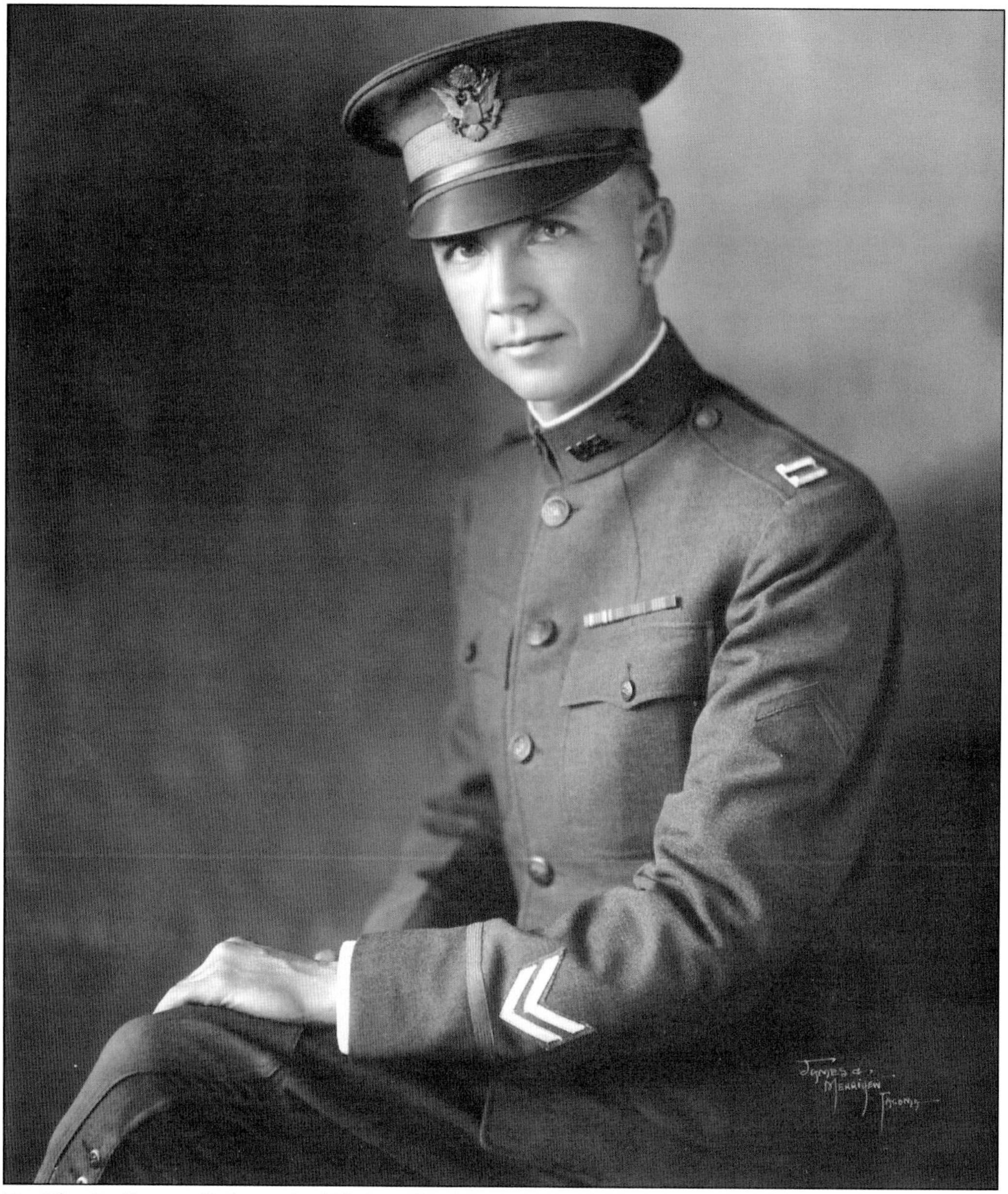

Dr. Charles Eugene Beltzer, the Washoe Coal Company physician, treated patients on the western end of Bear Creek Valley. Beltzer was born in Nebraska in 1880. Like Dr. Siegfriedt, he attended the University of Illinois, receiving his medical degree in 1909. That same year, he came to Bearcreek to work with a Dr. Souders, who also practiced with Dr. Siegfriedt in Bearcreek for a time. He soon became the Washoe Coal Company physician and continued practicing from Washoe until his death in 1951. Military service played a key role in Beltzer's life: he served with the Nebraska National Guard in high school and then enlisted for service in the Spanish-American War. In 1898, he was wounded in the capture of Manila and wounded again eight months later. He was honorably discharged in 1899. Dr. Beltzer volunteered for duty during World War I, was commissioned as first lieutenant in the reserves in 1917, promoted to captain in the regular army in 1918, honorably discharged, and promoted to major in the reserves in 1919. (CCHS.)

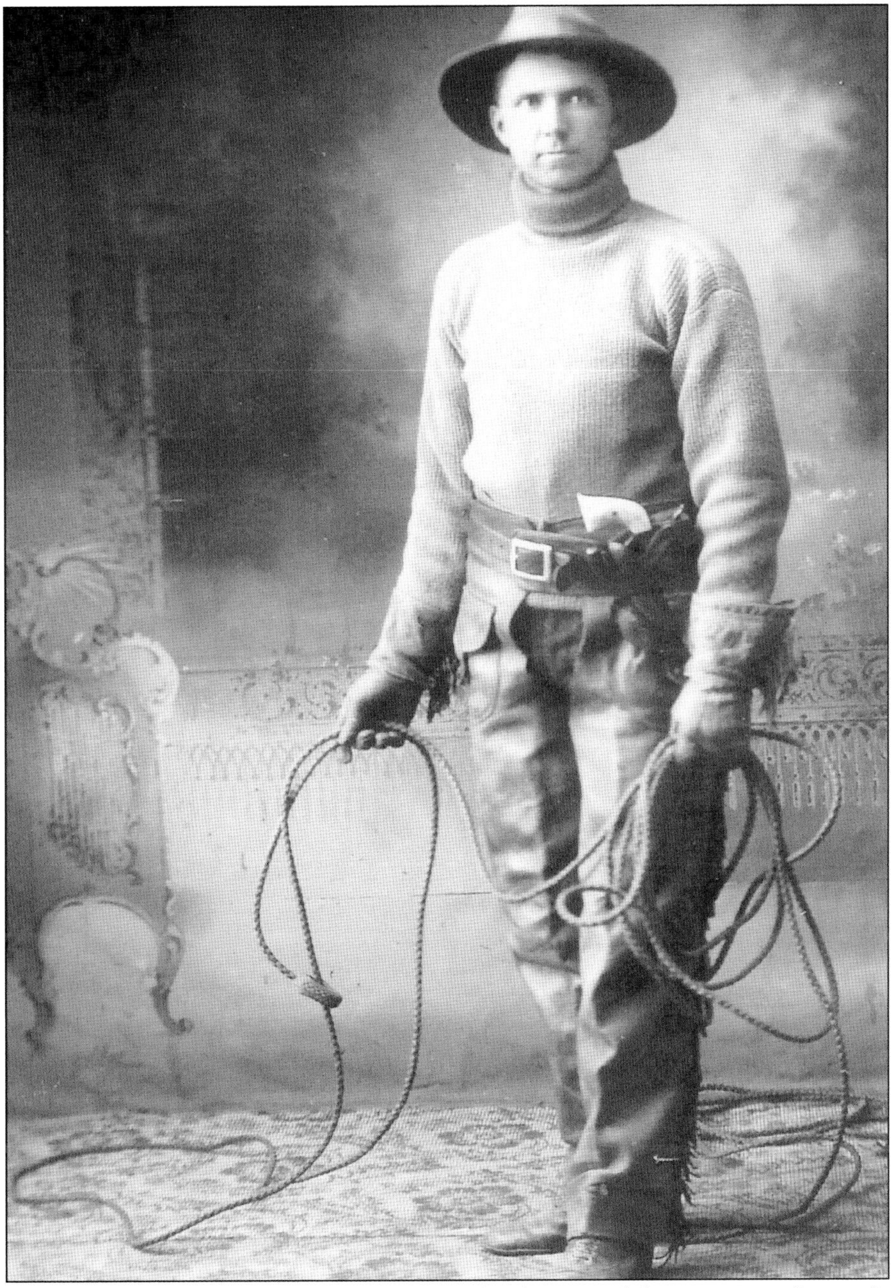

Dr. Beltzer returned from service in the Philippine Islands to spend three years as a hospital steward for the Nebraska Soldiers and Sailors Home. He left the Nebraska Soldiers and Sailors Home to spend two years as a cowboy and range rider in Canada and western Montana before enrolling in medical school. These years of western life drew him back to Montana and Bear Creek Valley upon graduating from medical school. After a three-month courtship, Beltzer married Washoe schoolteacher Marta Emalee McNeill on New Year's Eve 1925 in Cheyenne, Wyoming. In an interview with Mary Fages in 1974, Marta Beltzer recalled that their marriage was kept secret for six months so she could complete the spring semester. At the time, only unmarried women were permitted to teach. (Lodge.)

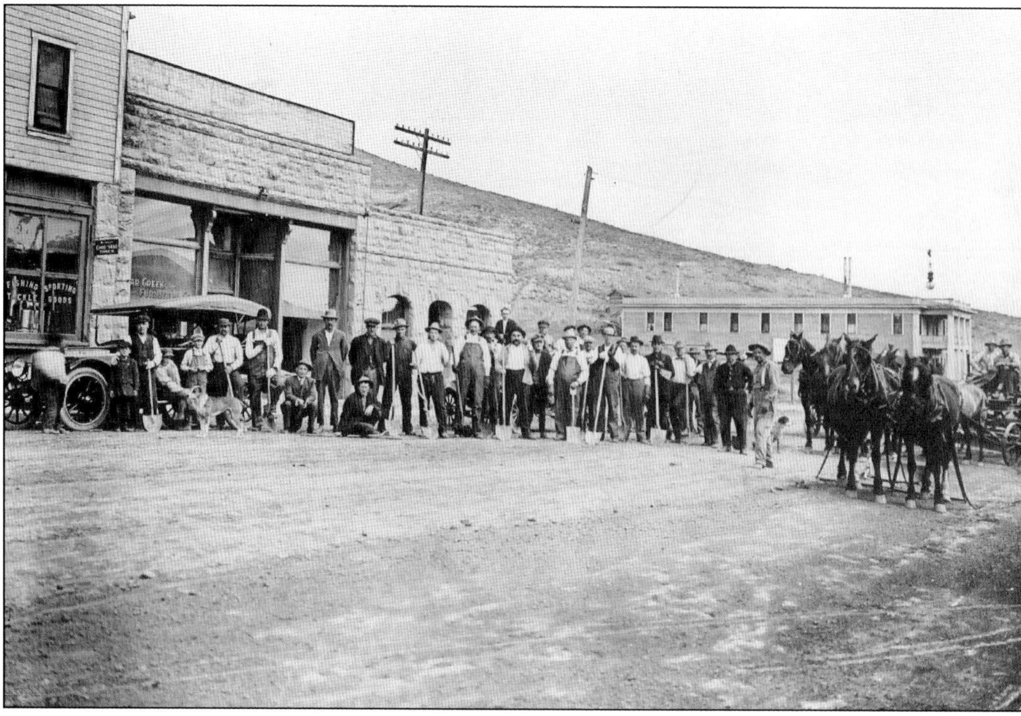

These photographs illustrate the commitment and respect for community held by Bear Creek Valley citizens. During a miner's strike in 1922, Dr. Siegfriedt, as mayor, organized improvements to Bearcreek's Main Street (above). Out-of-work miners volunteered their time and equipment to the project. Siegfriedt stands in the center of this photograph, holding a shovel in his right hand and wearing bib overalls. The buildings in this photograph are, from left to right, a fishing tackle and sporting goods store, the Bear Creek Furniture Company, the Clark-Wright Bank, and the Lamport Hotel. In the photograph below, a black-clad procession marches east through Bearcreek toward the valley's cemetery on Memorial Day. (Above, CCHS; below, Planichek.)

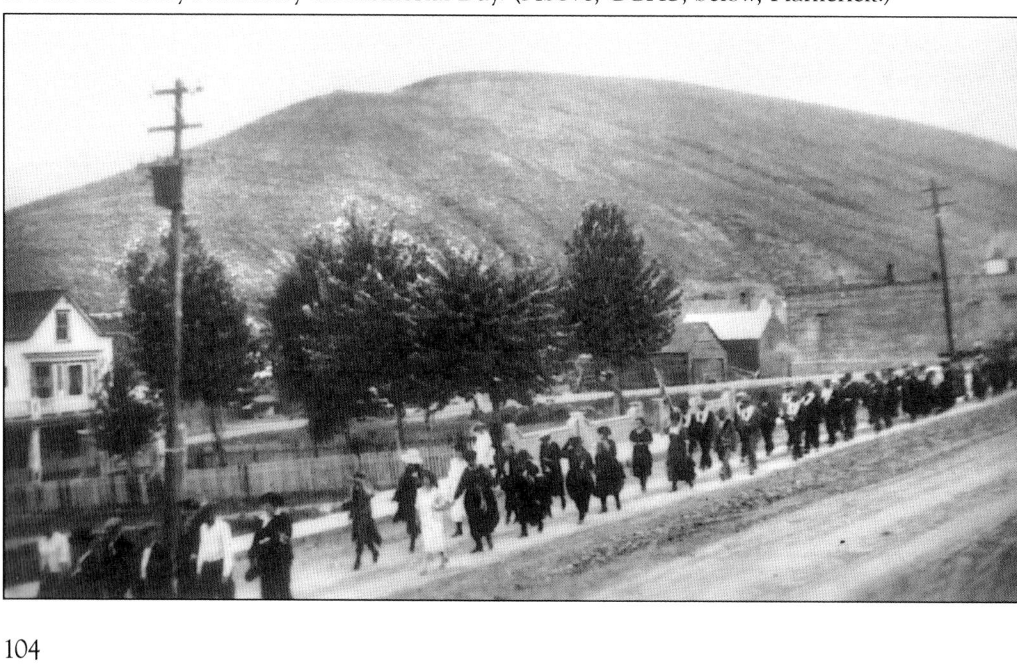

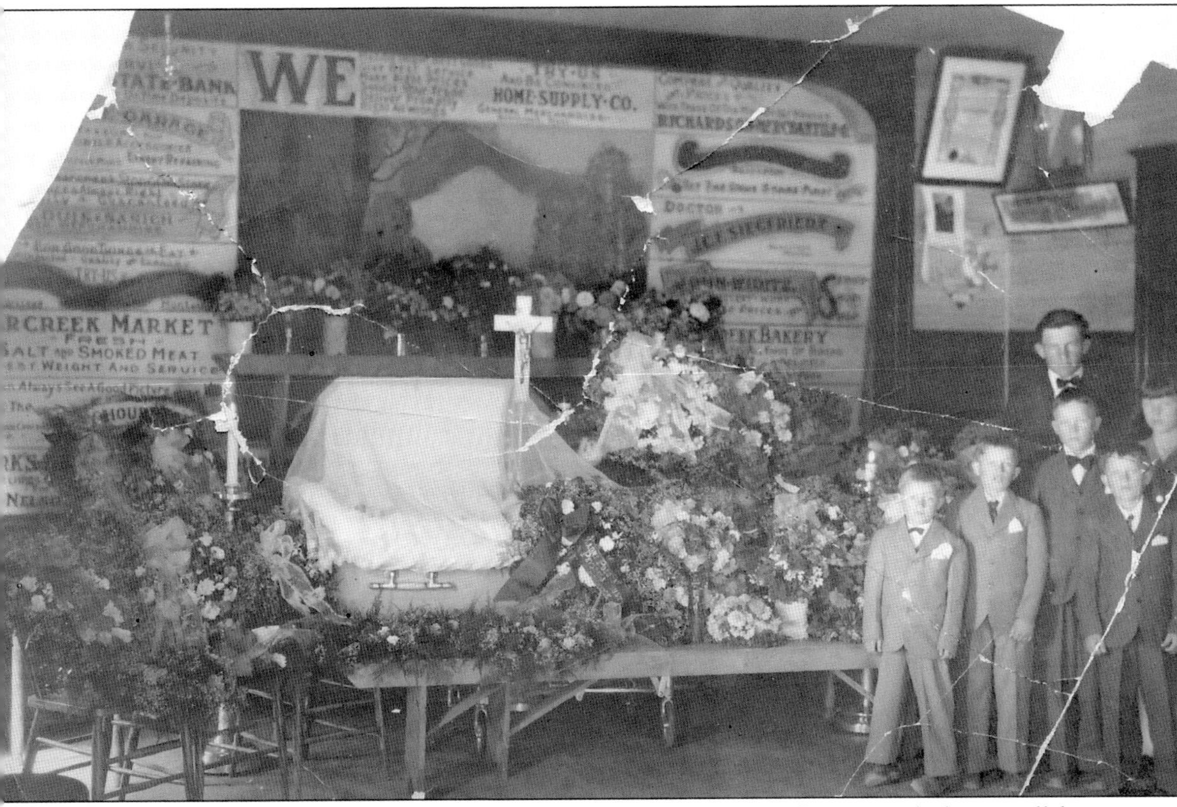

The dangers of coal mining and difficulties of life in Bear Creek Valley exacted a heavy toll from its families. Blaz and Anna Mourich Planichek's children knew this all too well. Their mother became lost in a snowstorm while returning to her home in Scotch Coulee late one evening in January 1924. A party of local miners and law enforcement searched for three days before finding Anna's body near the Scotch Coulee Reservoir. For the funeral, Anna's casket was placed on the stage at the western end of Scotch Coulee Hall. This photograph shows Anna's children gathered near her casket on that day. They are, from left to right, (first row) Henry (age three), Dave (age five), Tony (age seven), Eddie (age five), and Annie (age 10); (second row) Frank (age 11). Four years later, the children lost their father, Blaz, to an accident in the Washoe Coal Company Mine. (Planichek.)

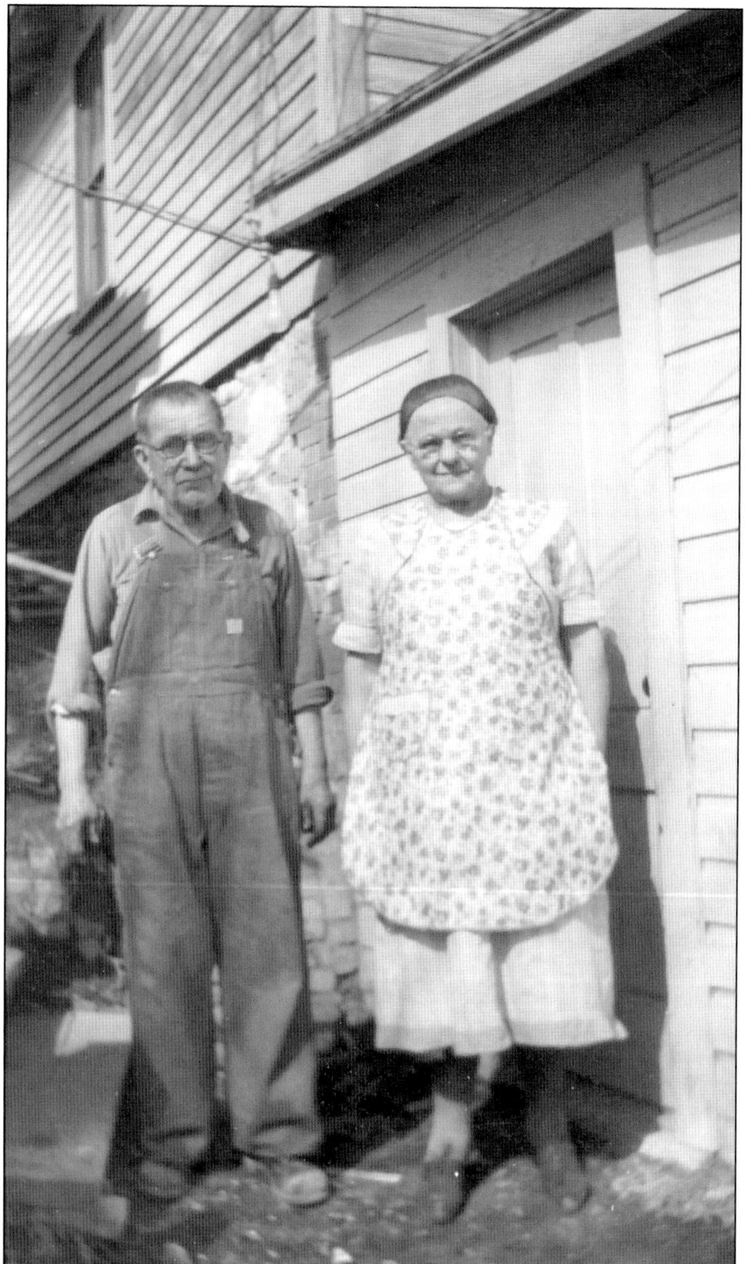

Jacob and Ursula Sens Mourich were well-known and respected members of the Scotch Coulee community. Jacob was a cabinetmaker, and Ursula was a midwife who delivered many of the Scotch Coulee children. They were the maternal grandparents of Blaz and Anna Planicheks' children, who were orphaned by two tragic accidents in the 1920s. These Austrian immigrants took their grandchildren into their home and raised them to adulthood. Many years later, Henry, the youngest Planichek child, wrote that they were, "real jewels," and admitted, "us kids were sure lucky to have them." The loss of their daughter, Anna Planichek, and son-in-law, Blaz, was not the only tragedy to befall Jacob and Ursula. Two of their three remaining children, Frank and Jack, died in the Smith Mine disaster, leaving them only one son, Louis. (Planichek.)

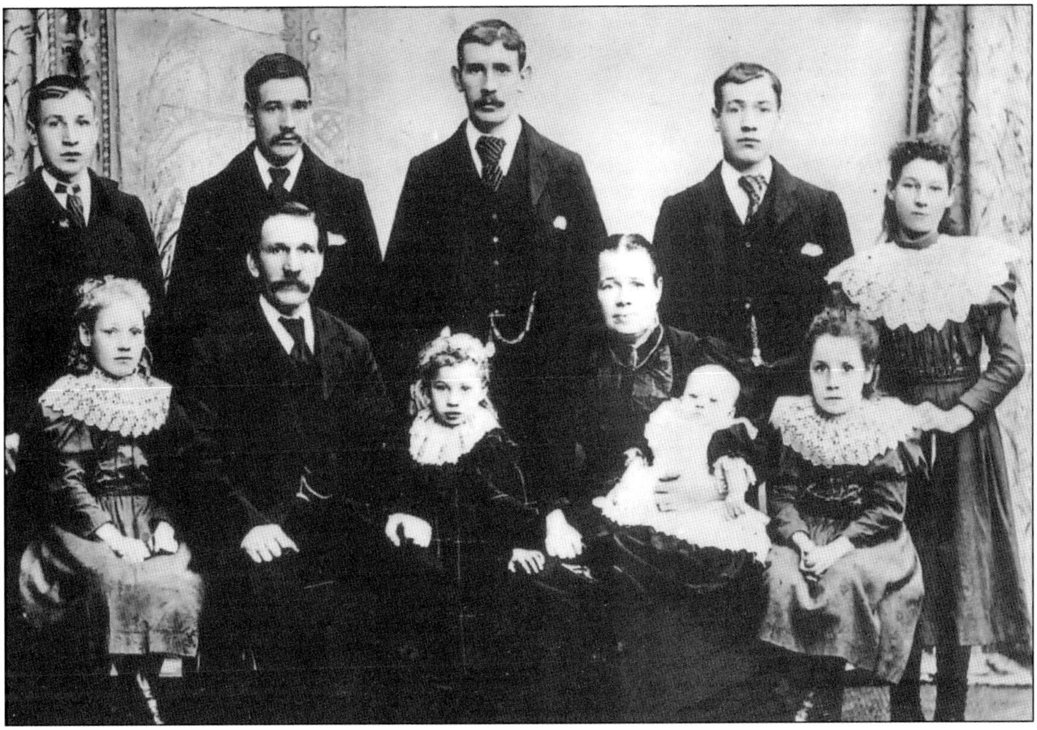

The Scottish immigrant family of John and Mary Cameron McDonald (above) arrived in Bear Creek Valley in the early 1910s. Members of this family are, from left to right, (first row) Jean, John, Mary, Mary C., Gilbert, and Euphemia; (second row) Abraham, Daniel, John R., Alexander, and Catherine. As with so many immigrant families, the valley became the McDonalds' permanent home in America. They lived, worked, married, had children, and died here. Decades after the family's arrival, three of the four McDonald sisters posed for the photograph below. Shown in this photograph are, from left to right, Janet Cameron, also a Scottish immigrant; Jean Sommerville; Euphemia McNeish; and Mary McNeish. (Above, author's collection; below, Mourich.)

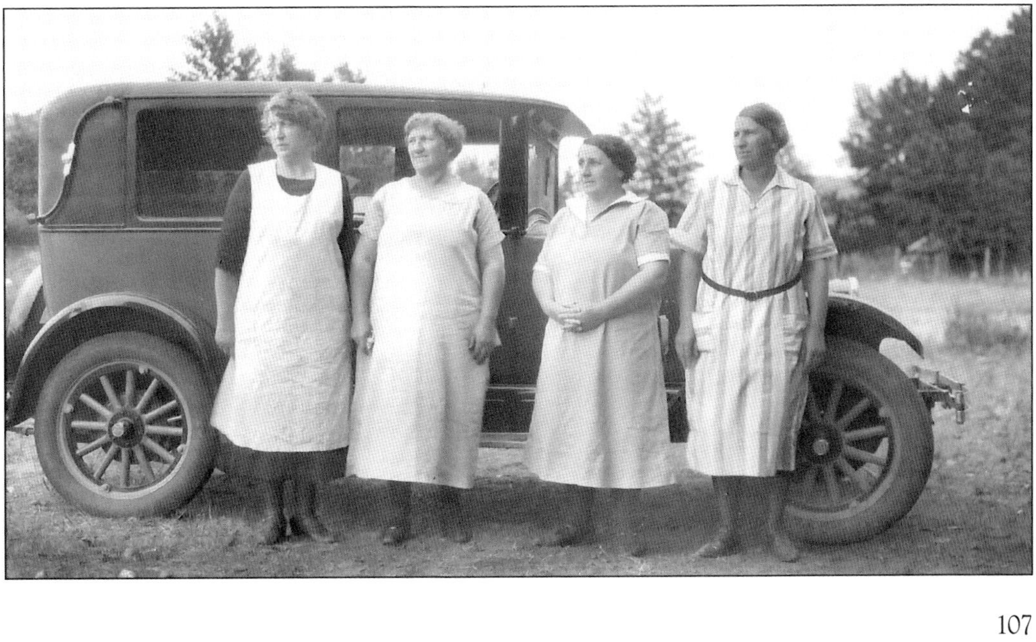

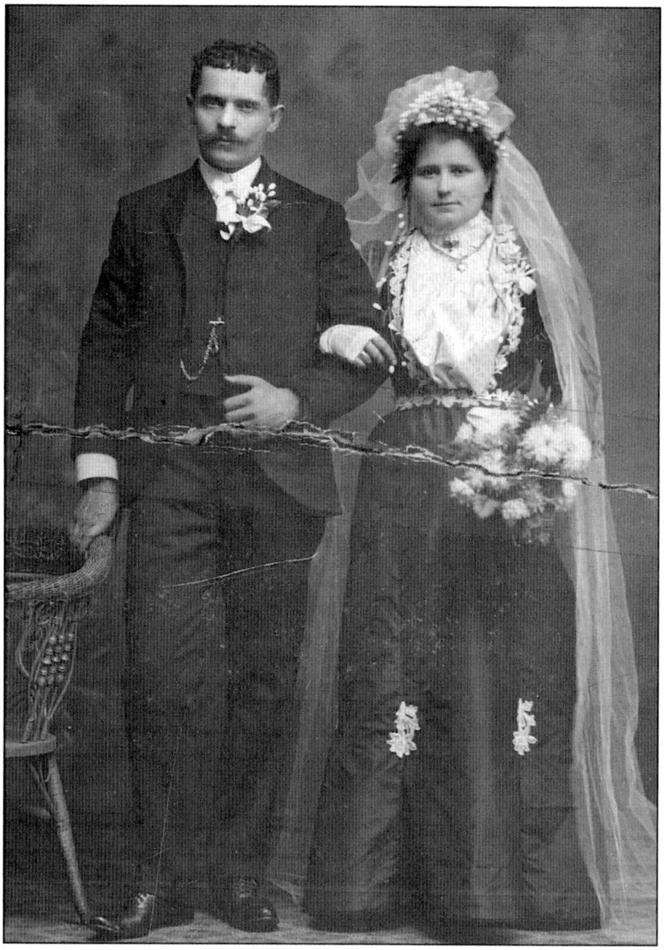

The 1903 wedding photograph of immigrants John and Frances Chesarek (left) shows them dressed in traditional Slovenian wedding garments. John and Frances arrived early in Bear Creek Valley, purchasing a two-story saloon and boardinghouse and a family residence next door. The bar, named the First and Last Chance Saloon, occupied the bottom floor of the business, with the boarders housed upstairs. In 1925, seven of John and Frances's nine children posed outside their Bearcreek home on the southwest side of Main Street (below). The children are, from left to right, Bill, Josephine, Mary, Henry, Mildred, John, and Frances. Not pictured are Joe and Frank "Shorty" Chesarek. The children's distinctive, 1920s American–style clothing contrasts sharply from that worn by their parents in 1903. (Both, Vorachek.)

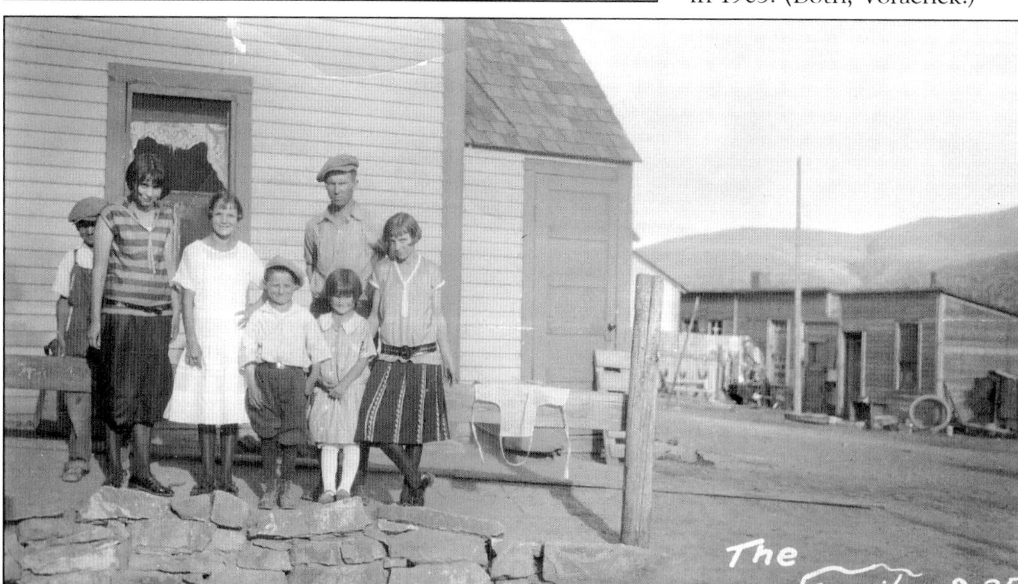

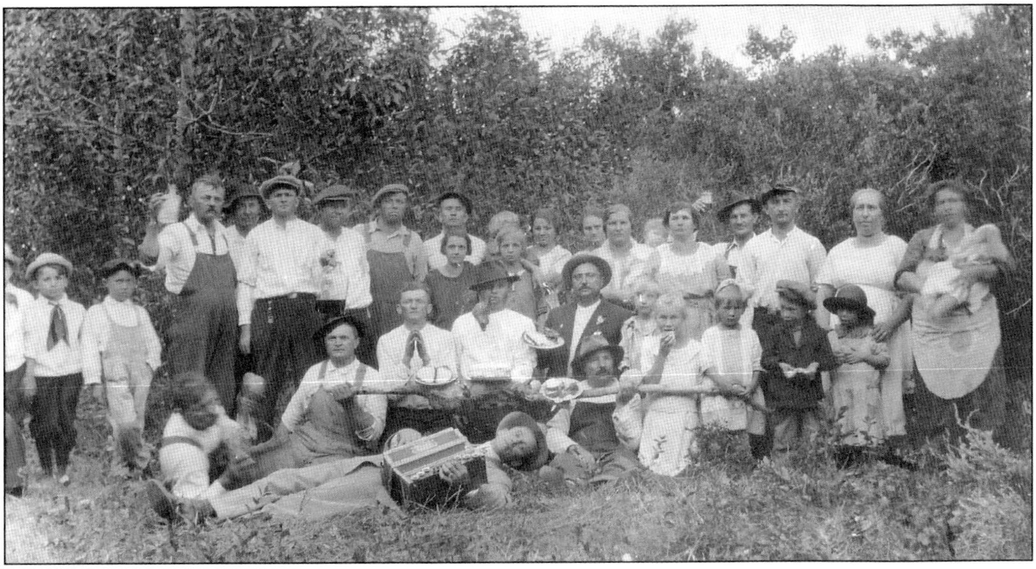

Summertime picnics and celebrations provided residents of Bear Creek Valley with more than entertainment. This was particularly true with the Slavic immigrants, where these festive events served to keep similar communities throughout south-central Montana connected. Mary Mourich, a local historian, described one Slavic wedding (above) as follows: "The bride and groom were of Eastern Orthodox religion and Serbian descent. A priest was summoned from Butte to perform the wedding in a hall. The lively wedding celebration lasted for three days with the Tamboritza orchestra furnishing music, singing, toasting, and feasting. Wedding guests were from Red Lodge, Scotch Coulee, Bridger, and Roundup. Celebrations were used as a vehicle for young people from the various towns to meet and marry. In earlier years, arranged marriages were not uncommon." (Both, Planichek.)

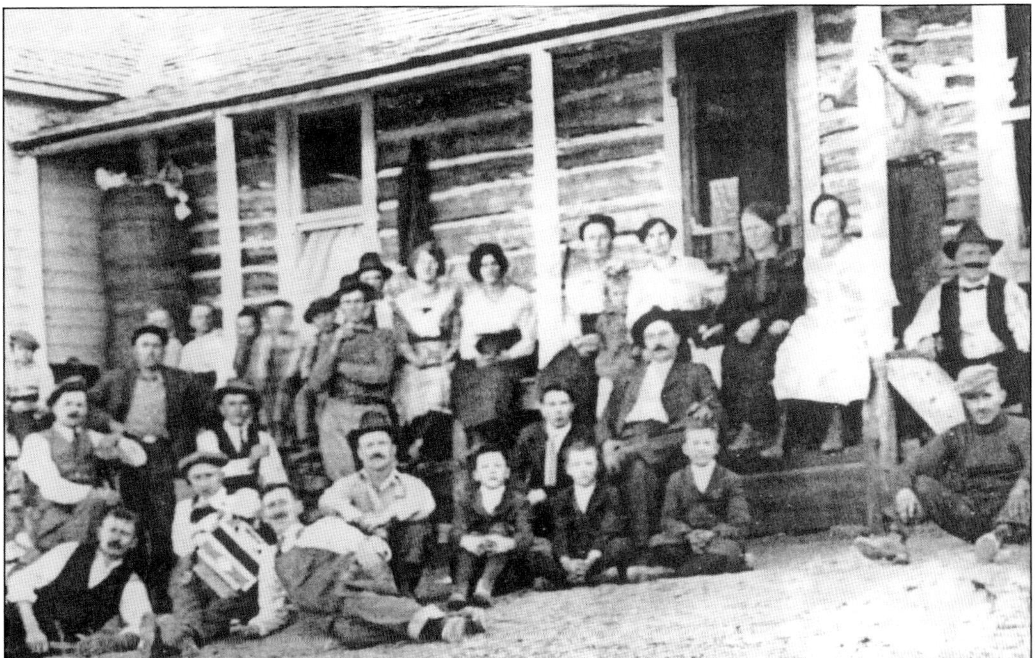

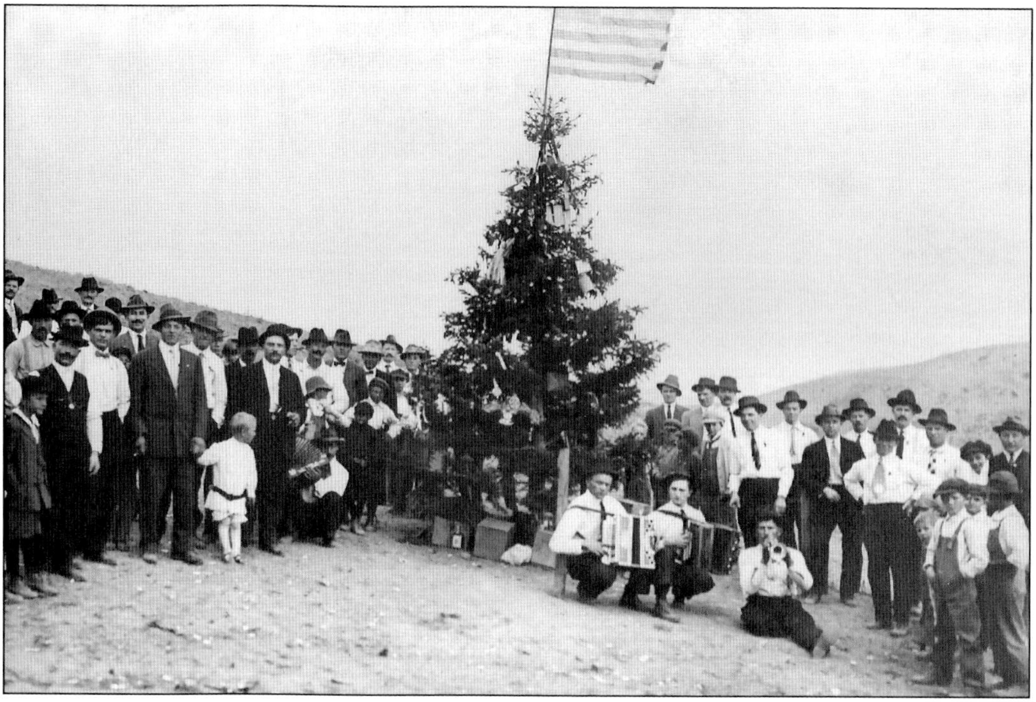

Immigrant citizens of Bear Creek Valley established fraternal lodges to promote camaraderie, preserve ethnic traditions, and promote civic projects in their new communities. The annual Bearcreek–Scotch Coulee charity tree party (above) illustrates one such project. In an effort to continue participation in these lodges and promote cultural awareness and ethnic pride in their children, these organizations maintained junior lodges. The photograph below shows members of the Junior Montenegro Lodge giving a concert in the garden of a Scotch Coulee home. Their instruments reflect the folk music commonly played in southern European nations. (Above, Mourich; below, Planichek.)

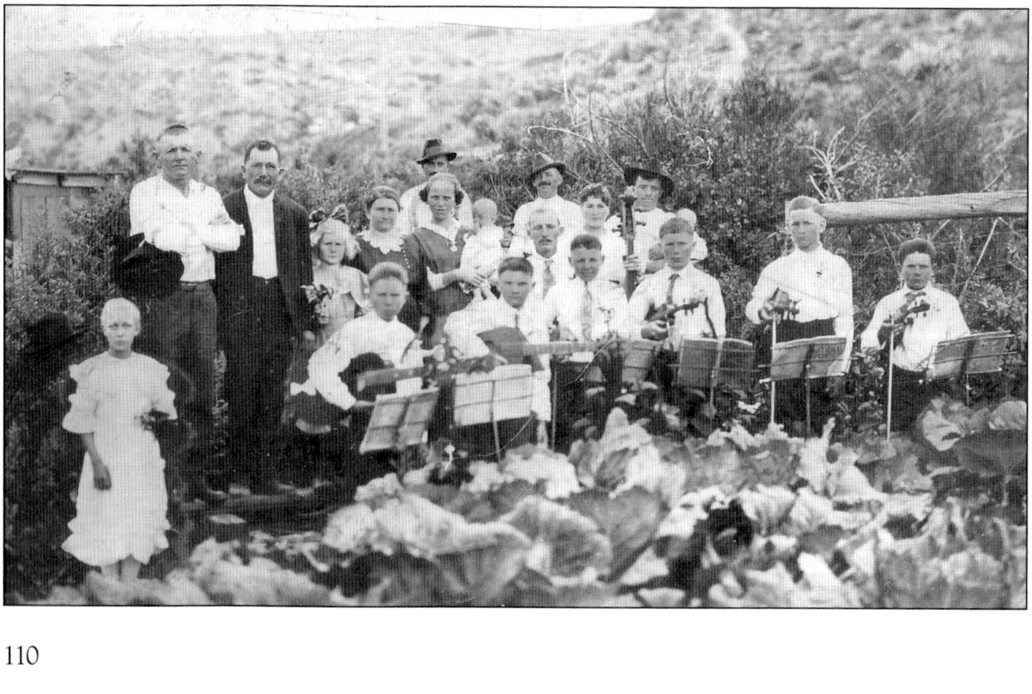

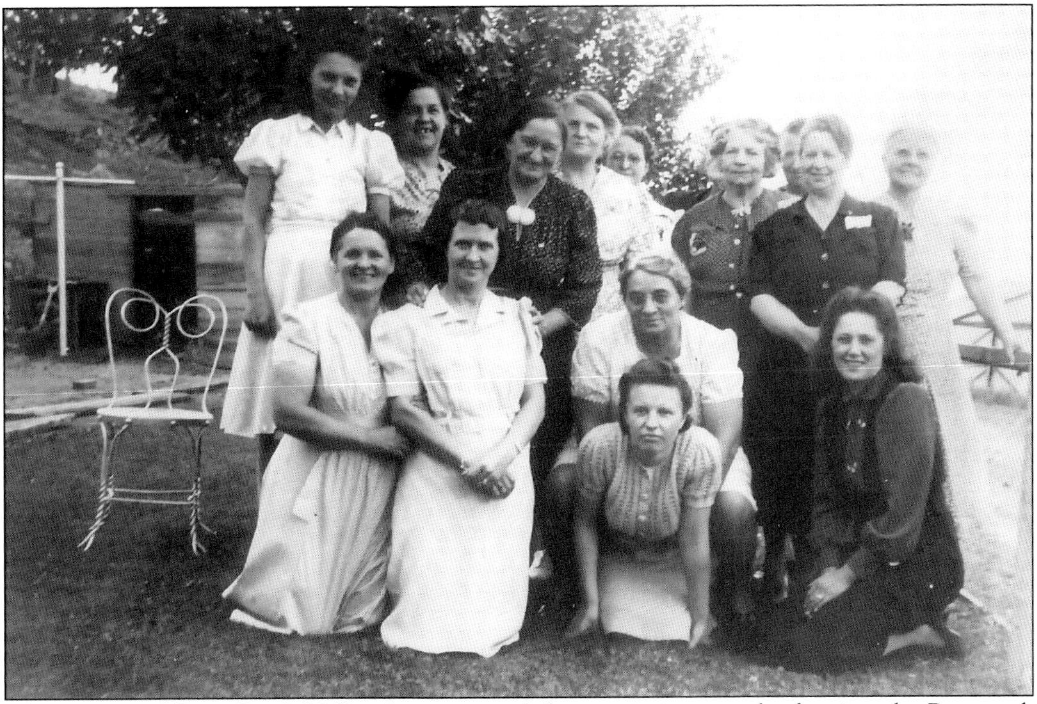

The women of Bear Creek Valley demonstrated their civic interests by forming the Bearcreek Ladies Aid Society, which promoted public works in Bearcreek and the surrounding areas. Their accomplishments included the creation of the Bearcreek City Park as well as the purchasing of a town fire bell (below). Many of the society's active members in the 1930s are shown above. These members are, from left to right, (first row) Mrs. Maxwell, Jessie Hunter, Beth Doyle, Vera Naglich, and Mary Wakenshaw; (second row) Winnie Freeman, Ruth Maxwell, Rose Rae, Mrs. Thomas Irvine, Mrs. Hawthorne, two unidentified, Marian Pryde, and Mary Irvine. (Above, Mourich; below, Murfitt.)

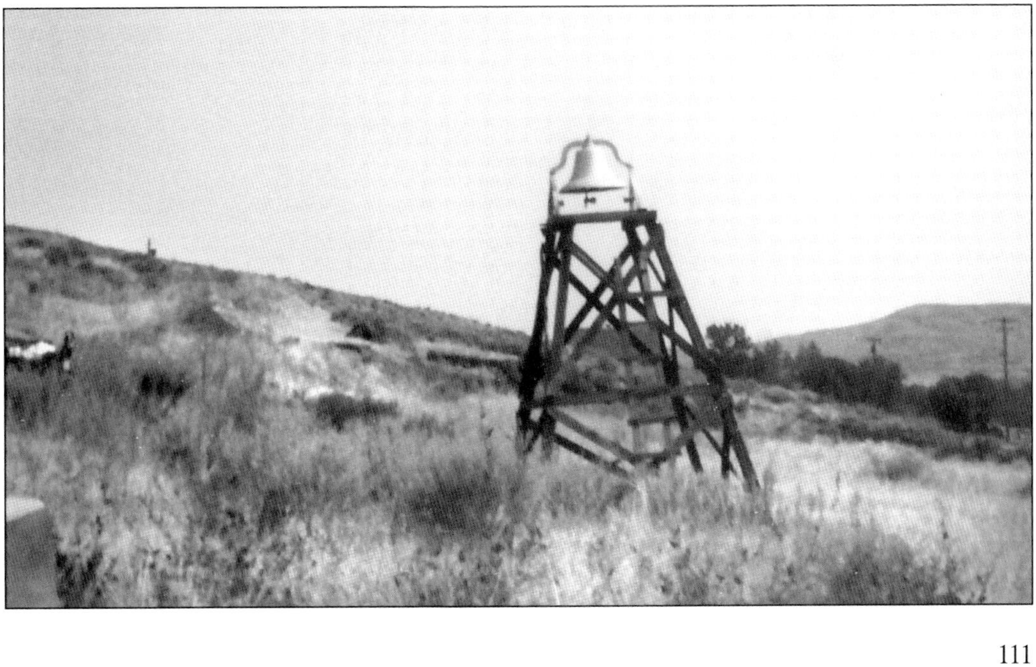

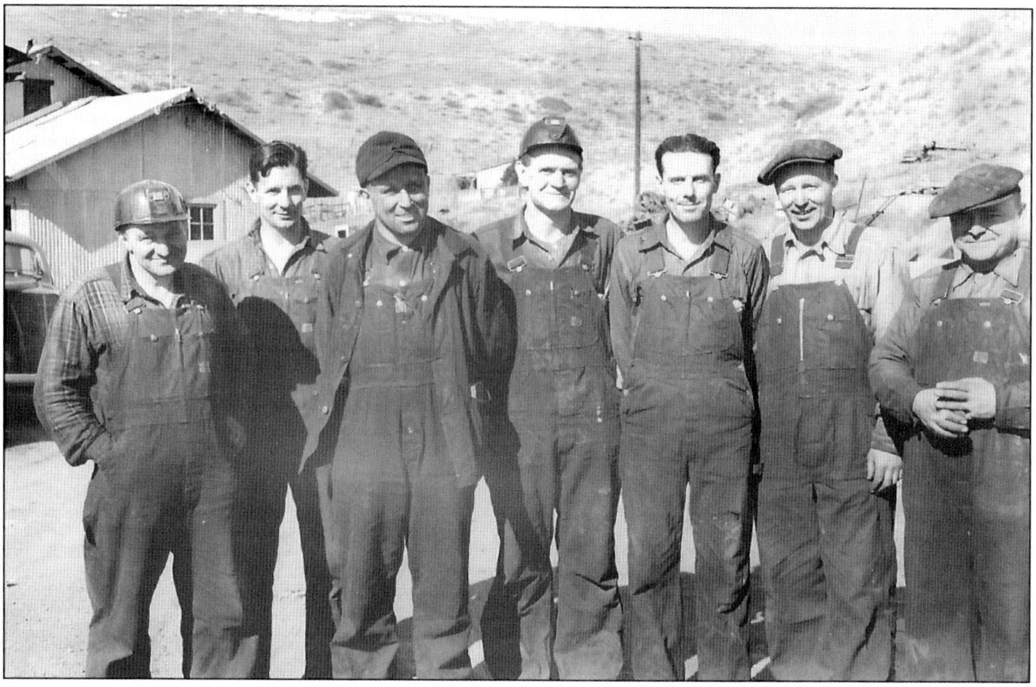

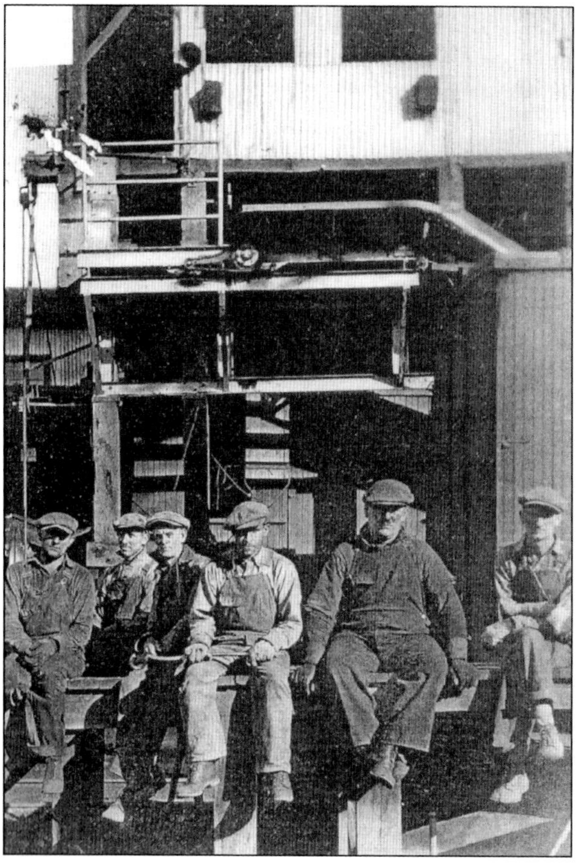

The vast majority of Bear Creek Valley men worked as coal miners, and most enjoyed their chosen occupation, despite its many dangers. It was warm in the winter and cool in the summer; the miners' primary complaint was the lack of consistent work. These photographs show groups of Smith Mine workers from the 1930s. Members of the group pictured above are, from left to right, Adolph Steinmasel (master mechanic), Howard Freeman (electrician), Sam Carpenter (foreman), Bill Freeman (head electrician), Henry Freeman (electrician), Alex Cameron (mechanic), and Earl Gregory (machinist). The miners pictured at left are, from left to right, two unidentified, Tom Freeman, Earl Gregory, Rado Jovanovich, and possibly Les Thom. (Both, Mourich.)

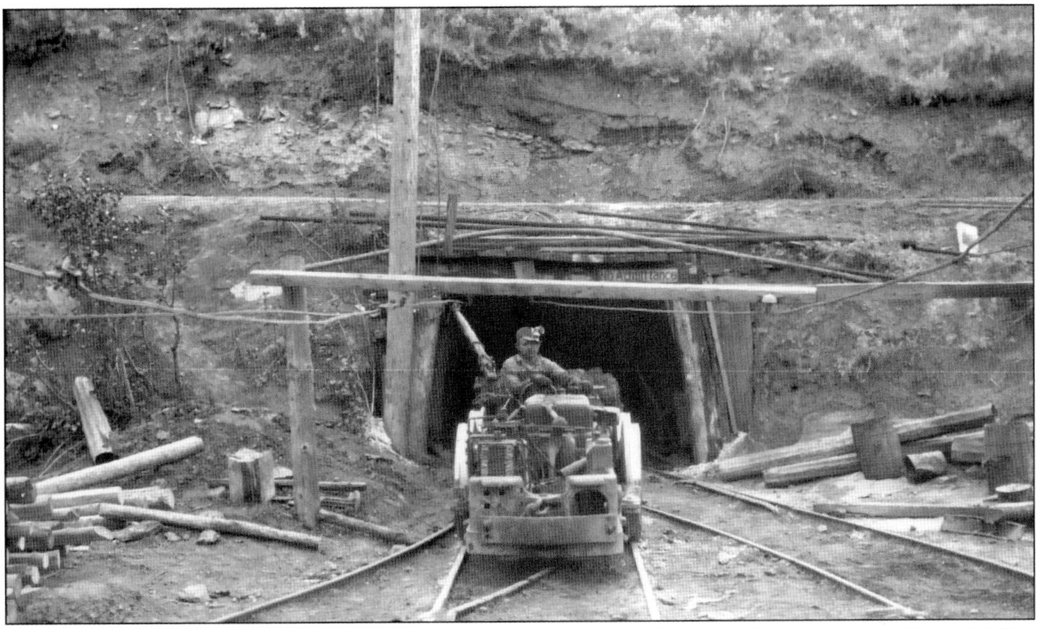

These 1920s Smith Mine photographs illustrate the day-to-day work life of a Bear Creek Valley coal miner. Above, a motorman pulls fully loaded coal cars out of the mine using his electric engine. These engines weighed 20 tons and were powered by electricity (note the trolley wires above). Below, early miners wear cloth caps with open-flame carbide lamps attached. Open-flamed lamps remained in use until the early 1940s, despite the availability of battery-powered lamps, as they were cheaper and some miners felt they provided better light. Several miners carry lunch pails typical of this era. They consisted of three nested containers for drinking water, food, and coffee. (Both, Flash's Photography.)

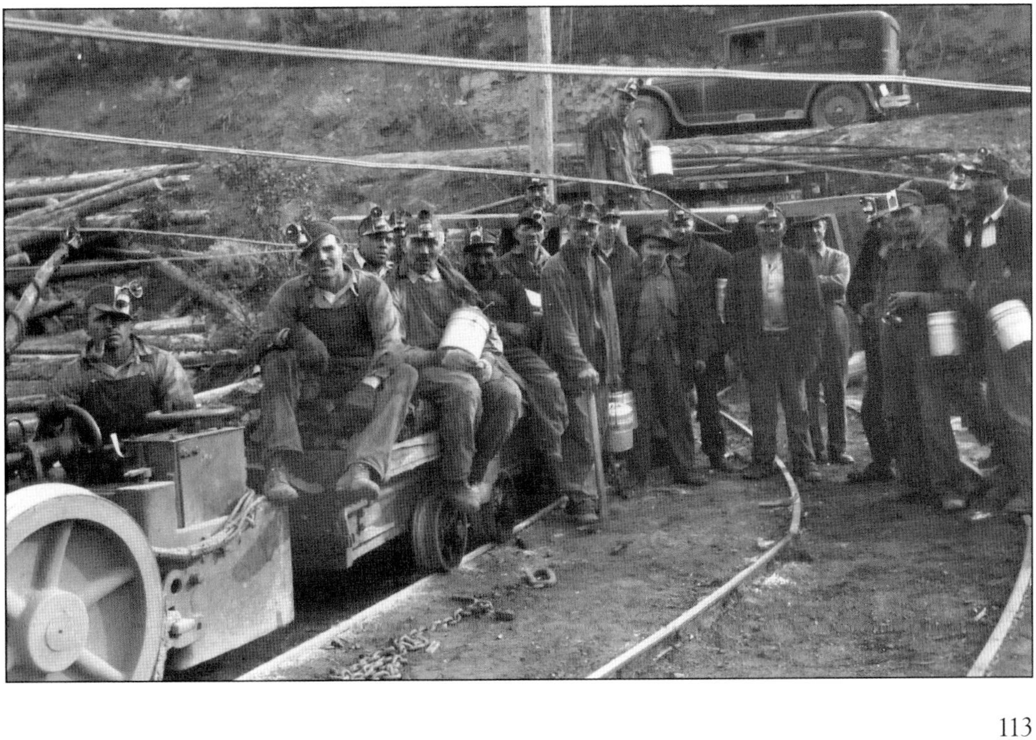

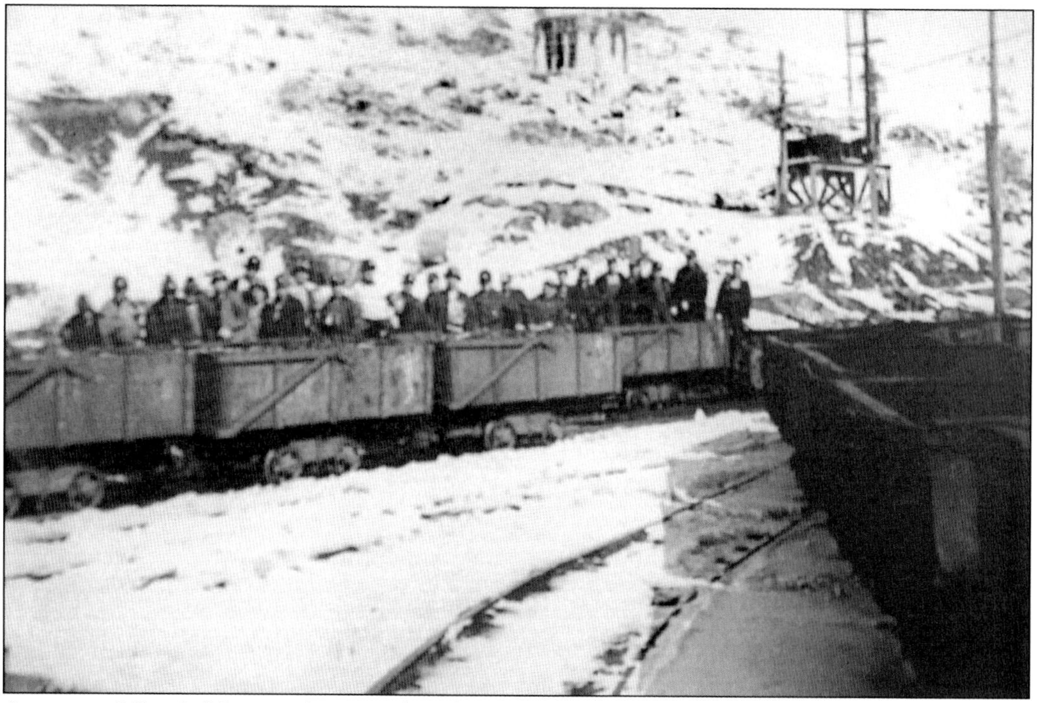

A group of Smith Mine underground workers prepare to enter the mine in these late-1930s to early-1940s photographs. The electric engine's first daily trip into the mine, and its last trip out, carried miners rather than coal. These trips were known as man-trips. In many cases, the working areas of the mine lay 1.5 to 2 miles from the entrance. The photograph above shows two water towers on the hillside above the tracks. These towers stored water pumped out of the mine for use in the Smith Mine's power plant. In the photograph below, the older cloth caps with open-flame carbide lamps have been replaced by hard hats and electric lamps. (Both, CCHS.)

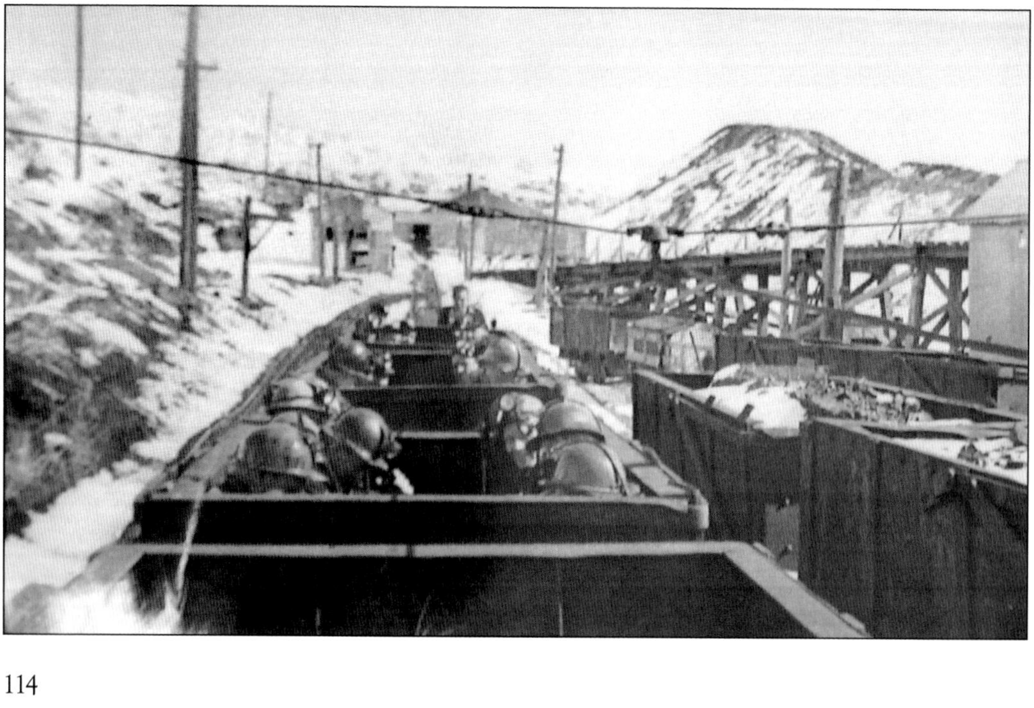

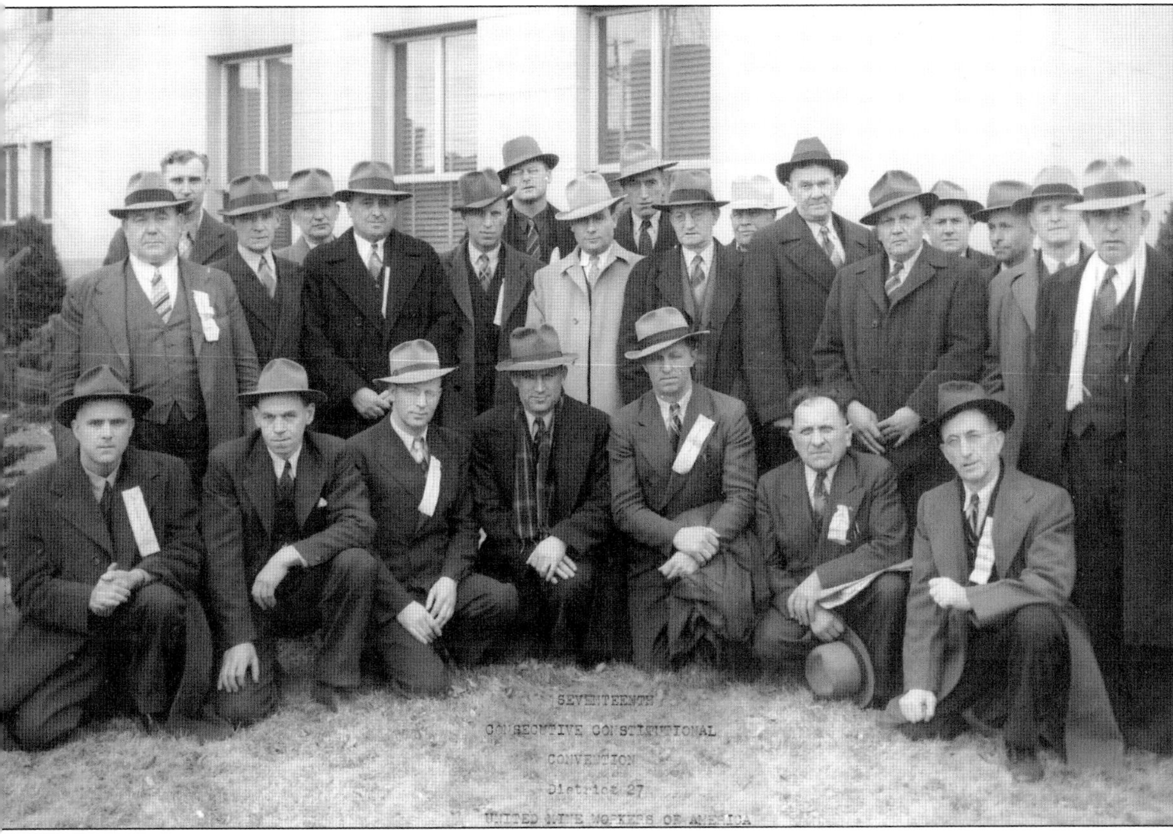

The importance of the United Mine Workers of America (UMWofA) in Bear Creek Valley cannot be overstated. This organization fought to improve the working conditions, lives, and rights of its members when the laws and support mechanisms of today did not exist. Union members worked in one of the most dangerous environments imaginable without workplace safety laws, health insurance, workers compensation insurance, disability insurance, sick time, unemployment compensation, or Social Security. Delegates to the District 27, UMWofA, 17th annual convention (shown above) are, from left to right, (first row) William. J. Pearce, David Murphy Jr., Alex Cameron, J. E. Pepos, J. F. Sanders, Joe Bosone, and James Ussin; (second row) John McPherson, Joe Hunter, Joe Masini, Joe Yanchisin, William A. "Tony" Boyle, Andrew Martin, Roy Bolin, Joe Mihalik, William Riddell, and Thomas Colton; (third row) William Godina, Edward Davies, Tony Persha, John Radosevich, Stanley Klimas, Archie Pratt, and Frank Schafer. (Mourich.)

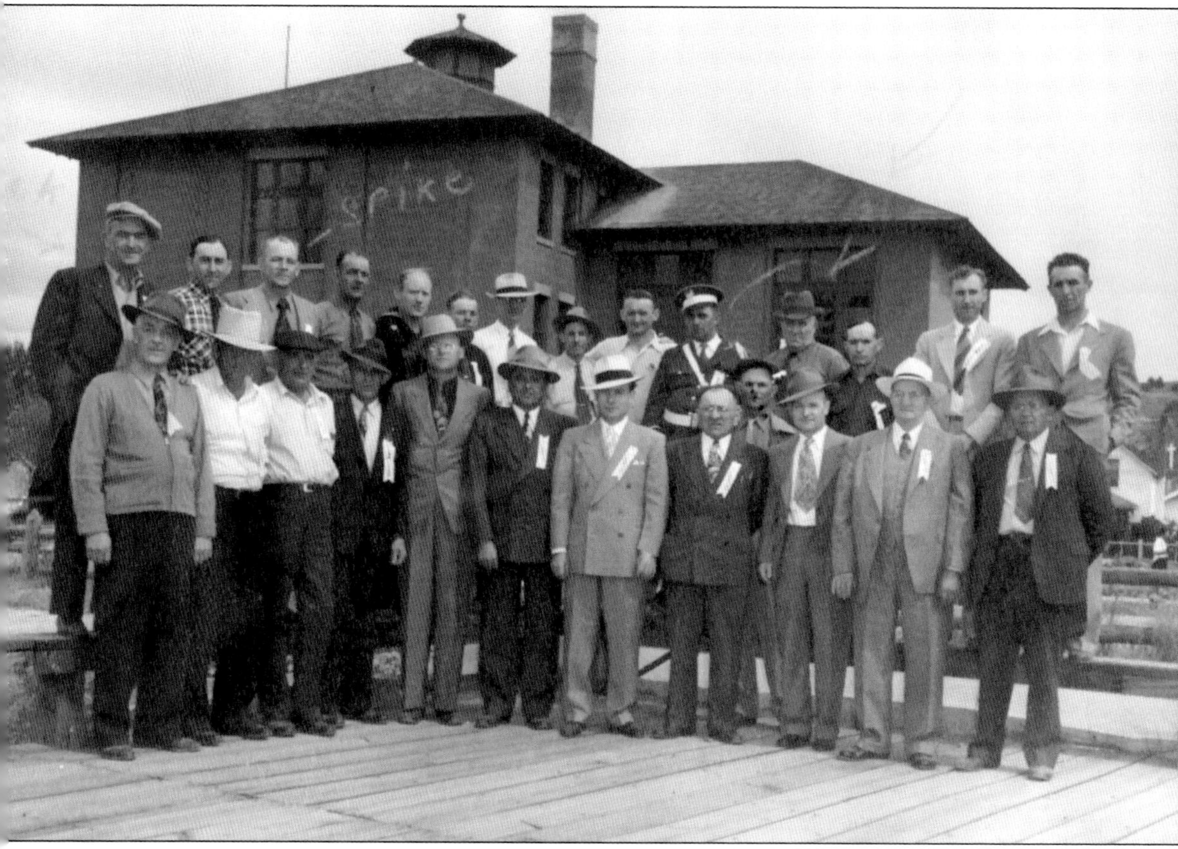

Carbon County union dignitaries stand gathered in front of the old Red Lodge High School during Labor Day celebrations on September 6, 1948. They are, from left to right, (first row) unidentified, Butch Wadsworth, Dominic Grassse, Eli Ponich, Tony Persha, unidentified, W. A. "Tony" Boyle, Joe Bosone, Jim Orser, Jack Boyle, and Andy Martin; (second row) Jack Lindsey, Celeste Roat, Waito Koski, Art Murdo, Guido Marchello, Sollie Reid, Hank Rae, unidentified, John Kastelitz, Rube Irvine, unidentified, Jerry P. Marwin, Earl Gregory, Bill Godina, and unidentified. The organizational hierarchy of the United Mine Workers of America (UMWofA) included an international level. Below that were districts, and below that were local chapters. District 27 encompassed Montana. Local chapters existed in Bearcreek, Washoe, and Red Lodge. Of particular note in this photograph is W. A. "Tony" Boyle, who became John L. Lewis's second successor to the international presidency of the UMWofA. Boyle served in this capacity from 1963 to 1969. (CCHS.)

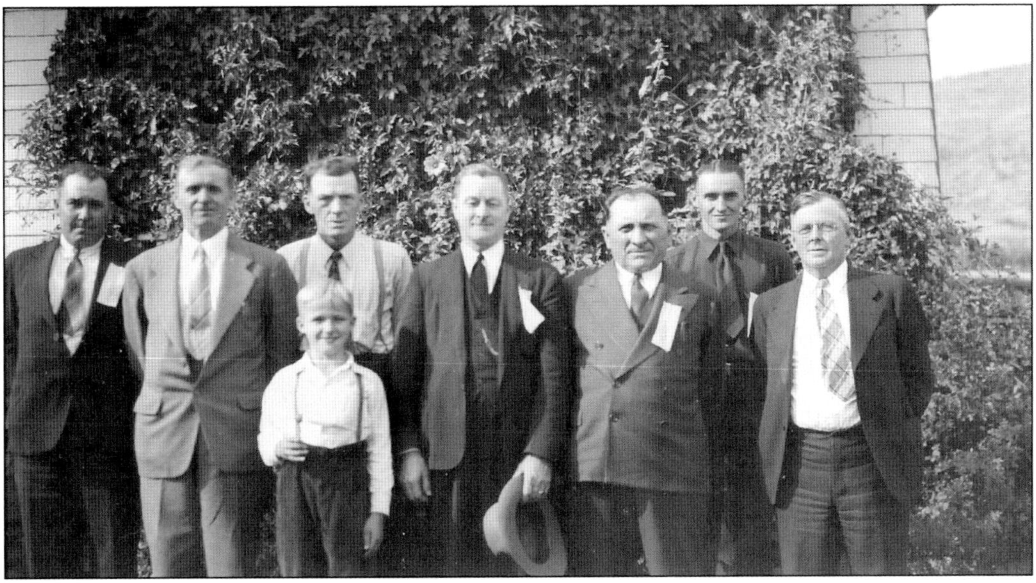

The Bearcreek Local No. 858 Labor Day committee is shown above. They are, from left to right, (first row) unidentified; (second row) Alex Hawthorne, John P. Mates (principal speaker and District 9 international board member), Joe Bosone (former District 27 president), and Jules Besinque (Bearcreek Local Union No. 858 president); (third row) two unidentified and Frank Kastelitz. (Mourich.)

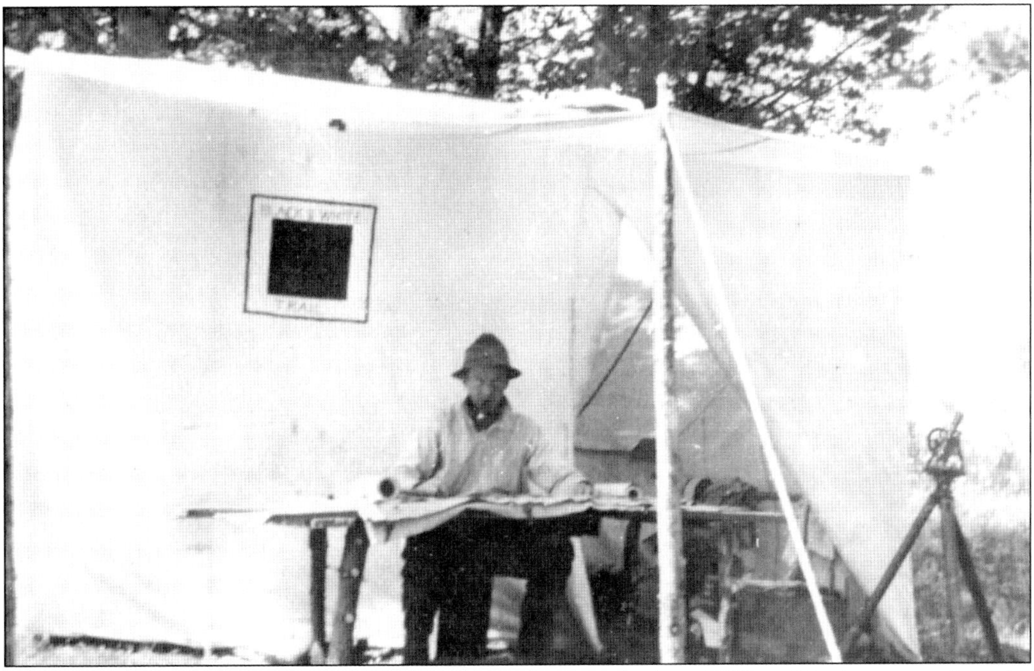

T. V. "Red" Thatcher, chief engineer for Dr. Siegfriedt's Black and White Trail project, plots the road's path in this c. 1919 photograph. Siegfriedt had high praise for Thatcher's work. In a *Billings Gazette* article, Siegfriedt remarked that Thatcher "has laid out a wonderful piece of engineering. Those who travel the road will marvel at the ingenuity necessitated in order to negotiate the grade." (CCHS.)

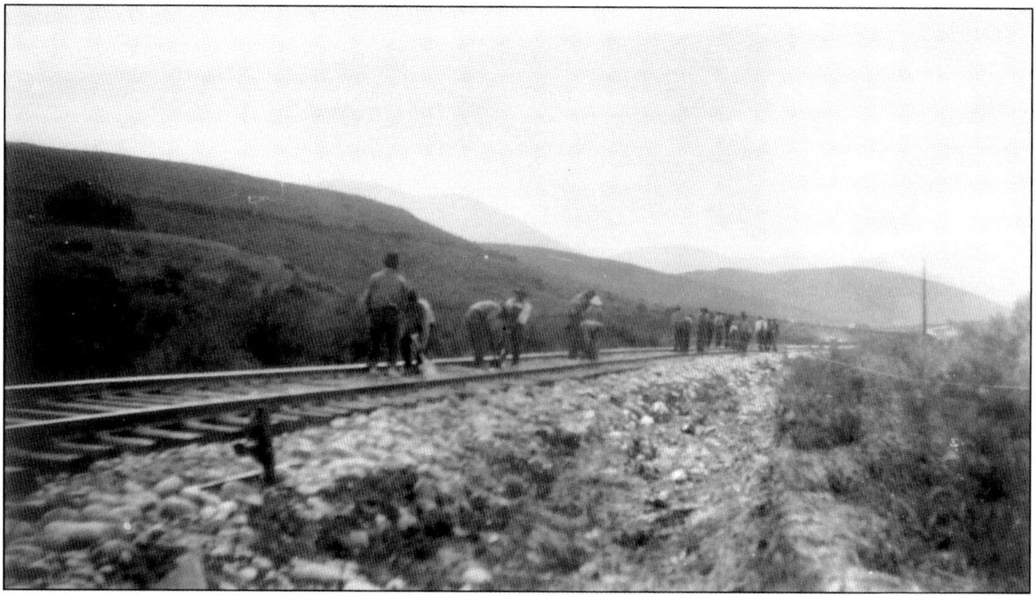

The rail industry was second only to coal mining in providing employment opportunities to Bear Creek Valley's citizens. The Montana, Wyoming, and Southern Railroad (MW&S) employed track maintenance crews (above), as well as carpenters, civil engineers, and bridge builders (below). All of these positions were permanent in nature, owing to the line's poor initial construction quality, frequent flooding and washouts, and the stress placed on the tracks by the heavily loaded boxcars. The MW&S depots in Belfry and Bearcreek required stationmasters, bookkeepers, engineers, and mechanics as well. Secondary jobs such as boxcar loader and weighman were also generated at each coal mine. (Both, Kidwell.)

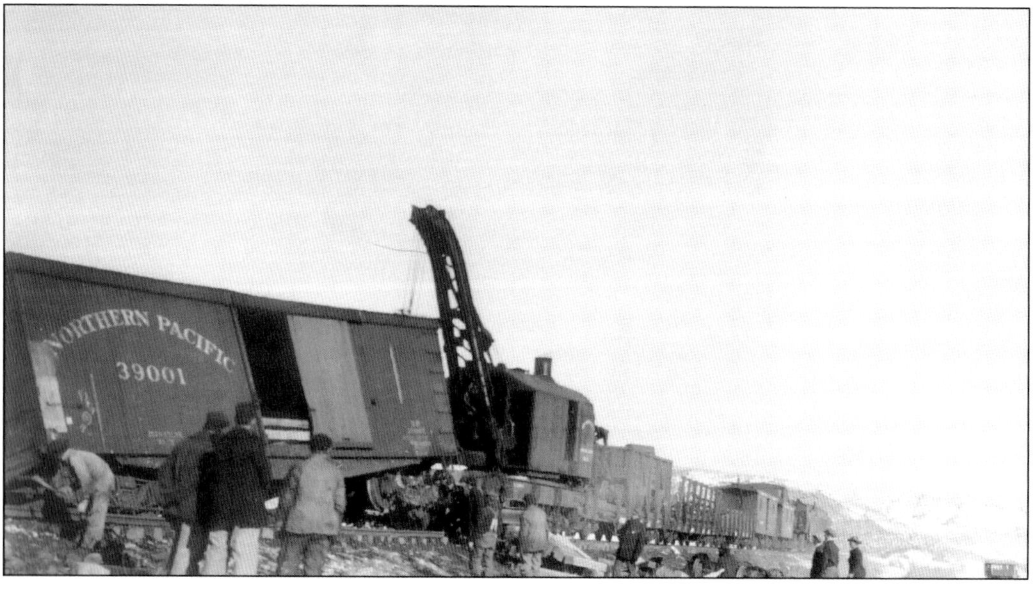

Nine

The Smith Mine Disaster

The Smith Mine disaster occurred on Saturday, February 27, 1943, at approximately 9:40 a.m. It resulted in the deaths of 74 of the 77 miners underground at the time and of one of the first rescuers to enter the mine, Matthew Woodrow. Several conflicting theories attempt to explain the exact cause of the disaster. They all agree that a small methane explosion ignited a much larger coal-dust explosion. A large portion of the mine was engulfed in the blast, and men working in these areas died instantly. Men unaffected by the blast died from exposure to poisonous gas released by the explosion.

Five men were working relatively close to the entrance of the mine. Rescuers quickly reached them and found them all unconscious as a result of exposure to noxious gases. Artificial resuscitation, performed on all five men, saved three of them. Nine days of backbreaking, round-the-clock rescue work followed. No other survivors were found, but the body of every man lost was returned to his family.

The valley's darkest days highlighted the finest qualities its inhabitants and neighbors had to offer: self-sacrifice, heroism, leadership, and love of family and community. Men worked themselves to the point of exhaustion. Women maintained round-the-clock canteens and aid stations to support the hundreds of rescuers. Older children helped wherever they could.

To this day, the Smith Mine disaster remains Montana's worst coal-mining accident in history. Coal production in Bear Creek Valley continued on a smaller scale for 25 years after the disaster, but the valley quickly faded from its past glory due to decreasing demand for coal and inability to compete with newer strip-mining endeavors.

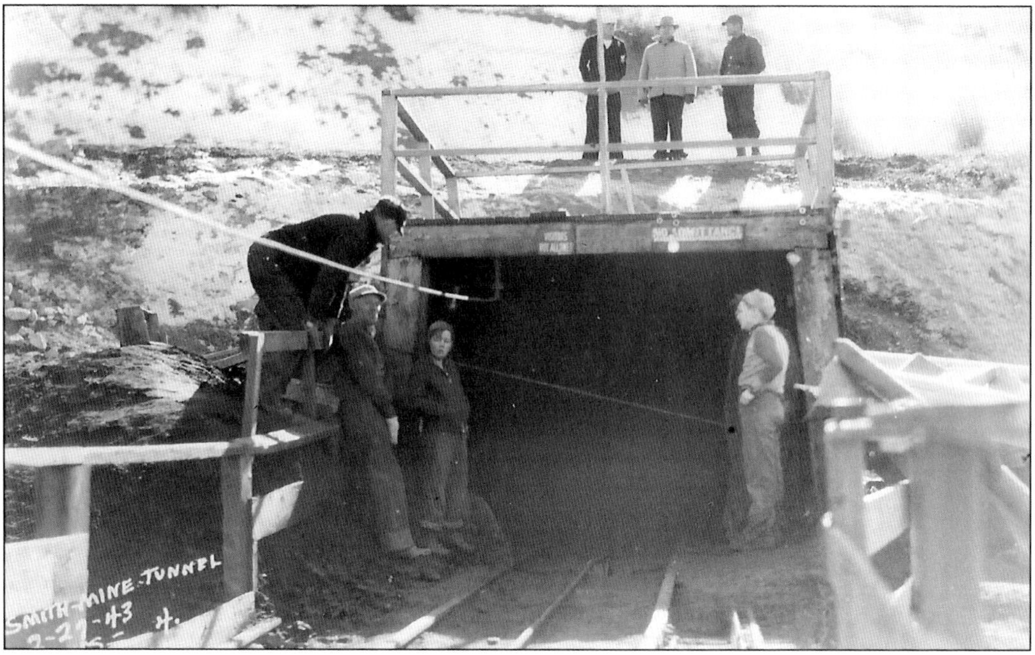

These photographs show the Smith Mine entrance soon after the explosion, possibly before the three survivors were carried out on stretchers. The boy on the left is Bob Wakenshaw, and his friend Gordon Irvine stands across from him. Melvin Anderson is third from left in the group of three people above the entrance. Bob Wakenshaw was waiting for word of his father, Bud Wakenshaw, and grandfathers, Adam Wakenshaw and Frank Sumicek. Melvin Anderson was waiting for word of his father, Emil Anderson. All four men perished in the disaster. Below, rescuers prepare to take supplies into the mine. (Both, Flash's Photography.)

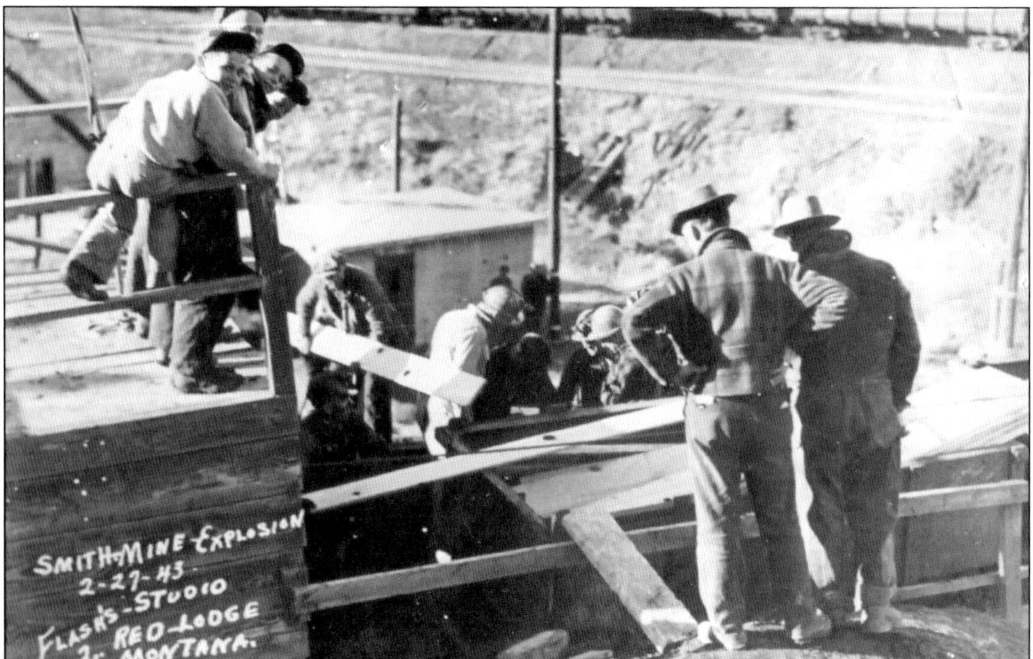

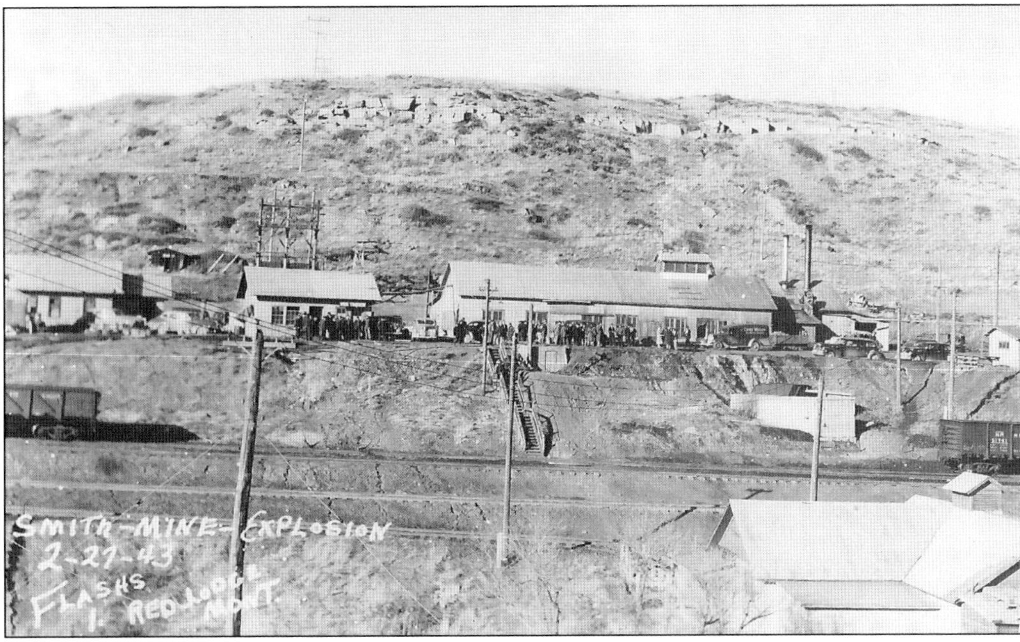

Relatives and friends gather near the mine's machine shop on the day of the explosion. The machine shop, the largest building in the center, served as a base of operations for the rescuers and support personnel who organized canteens and first-aid stations. The day of the explosion was unseasonably warm for a Montana winter, but the next day temperatures plummeted to bitter levels. Despite this, many of the wives and mothers of the trapped men waited at the mine for 72 hours or more for word of their loved ones. The Candy Wagon (below) was pressed into service as a makeshift hearse a few days later when rescuers began removing large numbers of victims from the mine. (Both, Flash's Photography.)

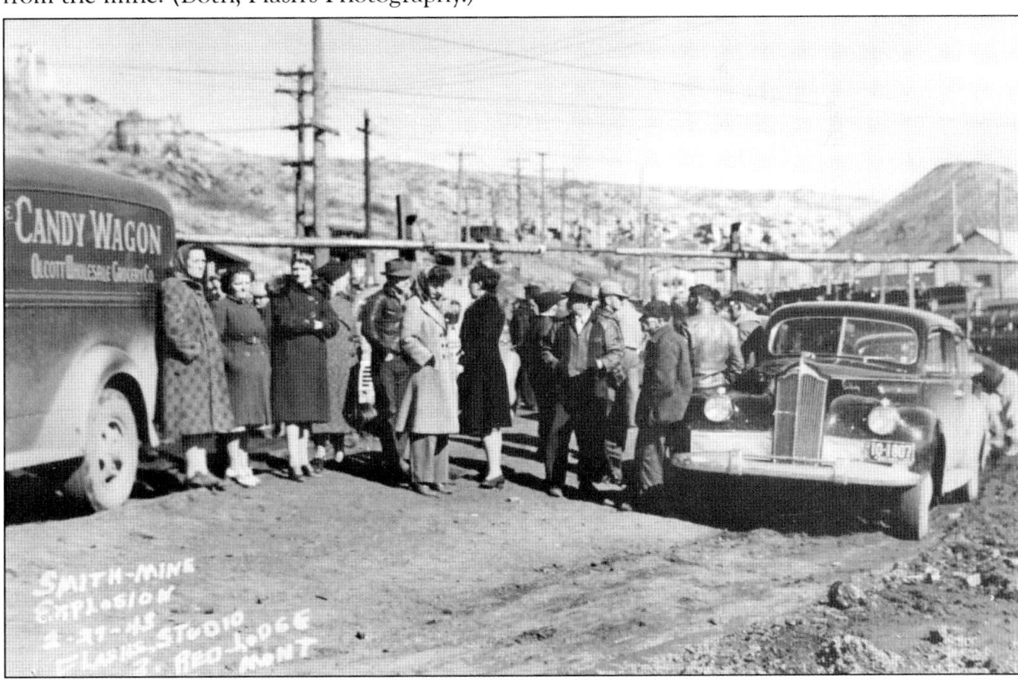

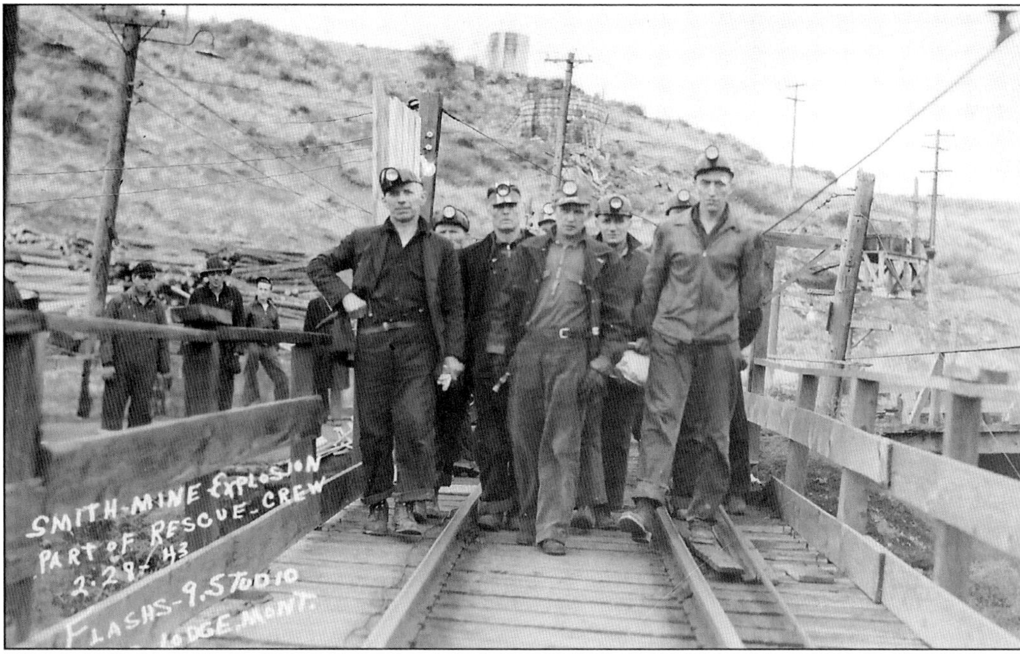

Rescue and recovery efforts lasted nine days. Rescuers worked in six-hour shifts around the clock. This was dangerous work. Local miners voluntarily exposed themselves to unsafe levels of noxious gases because self-contained breathing apparatus were only available to an elite crew of rescuers from the mines in Butte, Montana. The photograph above shows a group of grim-faced rescuers heading into the mine for their shift. The image below shows how many miners appeared as they came off shift. Exhausted and weakened by the exposure to gas, they needed assistance walking and required first aid. The local Red Cross reported treating 226 rescuers during the course of the nine days. (Both, Flash's Photography.)

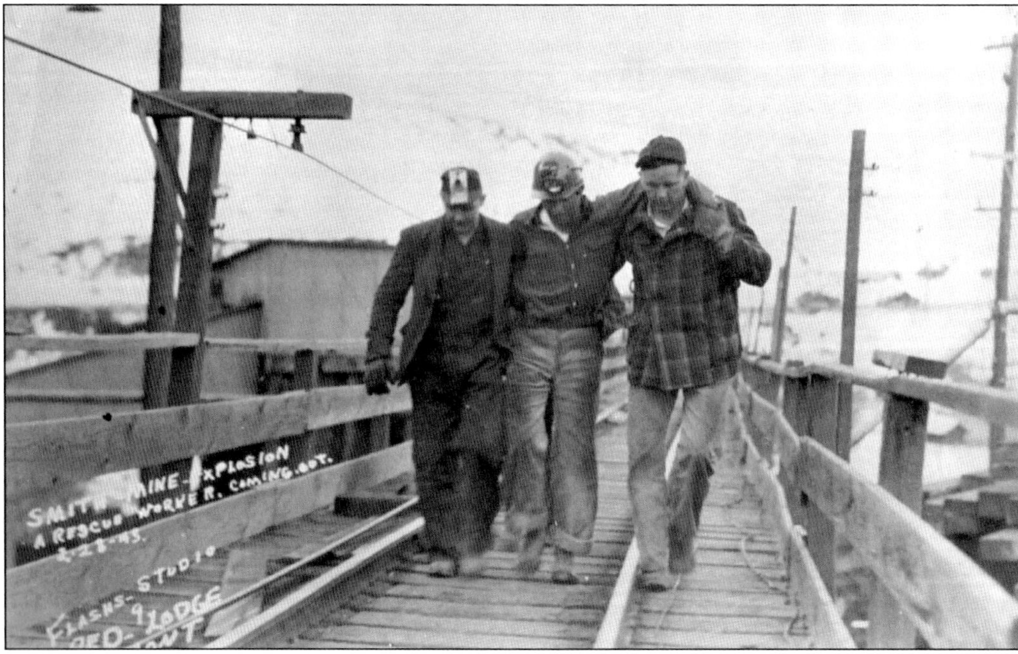

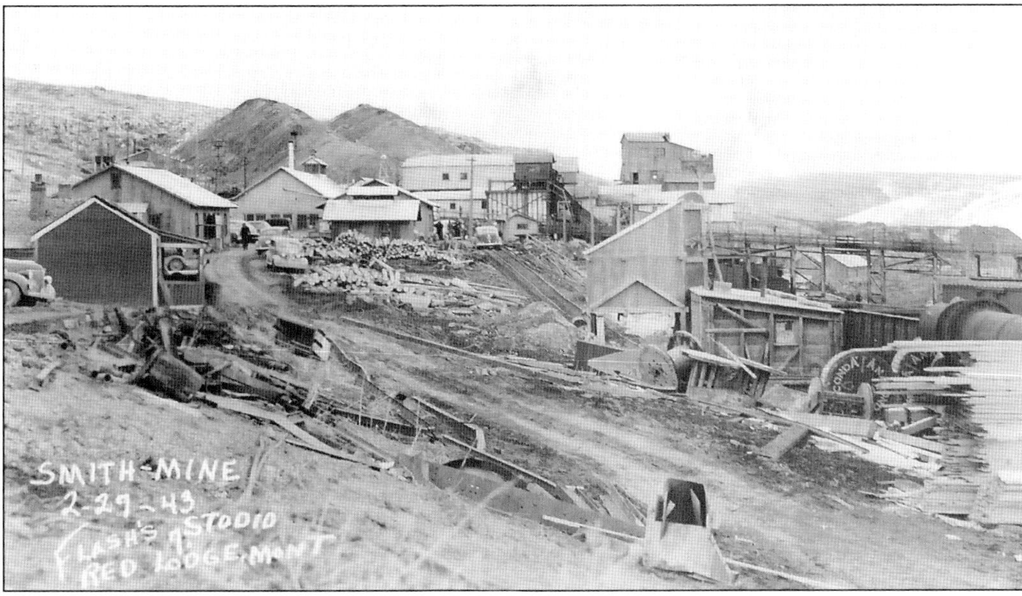

This photograph shows the Smith Mine two days after the explosion. Note the trestle across Bear Creek leading to the entrance of the mine on the south side of Kentucky Creek. Also note the stockpiles of lumber and other supplies in the foreground. These supplies were used to rebuild the ventilation system as rescue efforts advanced more than 2 miles into the mine. (Flash's Photography.)

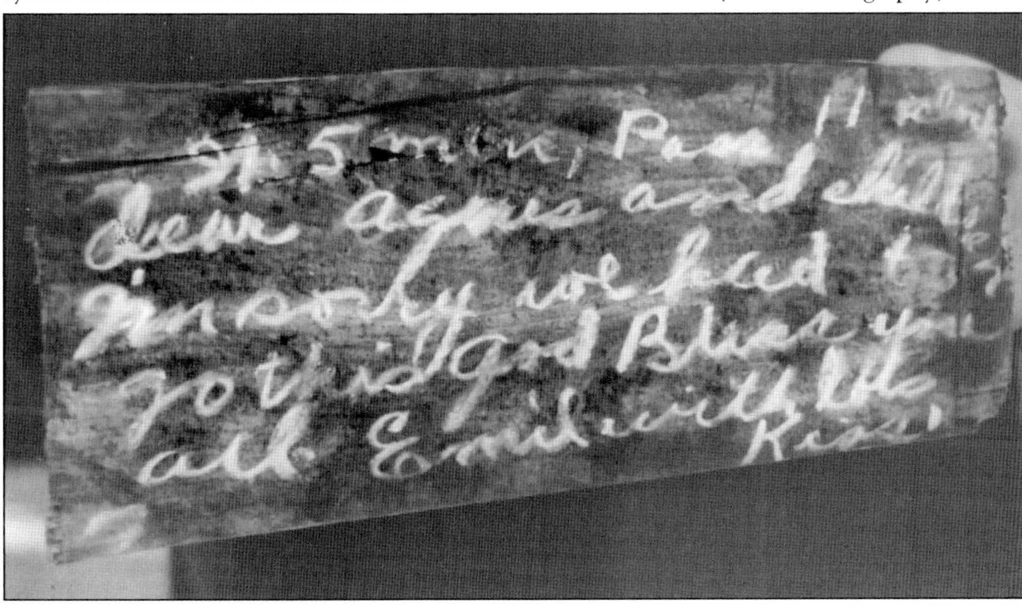

Working in an area of the mine unaffected by the blast, Emil Anderson, Walter Joki, Frank Pajnich, Fred Rasborschek, and John Sudar lived long enough to chalk three notes to their loved ones. This note, written by Emil Anderson, reads, "It 5 min. pass 11 o'clock dear Agnes and children—I'm sorry we had to go this [way]—God Bless you all. Emil with lots Kiss." These men attempted to reach the mine's entrance but were stopped by noxious gas. They returned to where they had been working in the mine and built an unsuccessful barricade against the coming gas. Because of their location in the mine in relation to the path the rescuers followed, they were one of the last groups to be discovered and removed from the mine. (CCHS.)

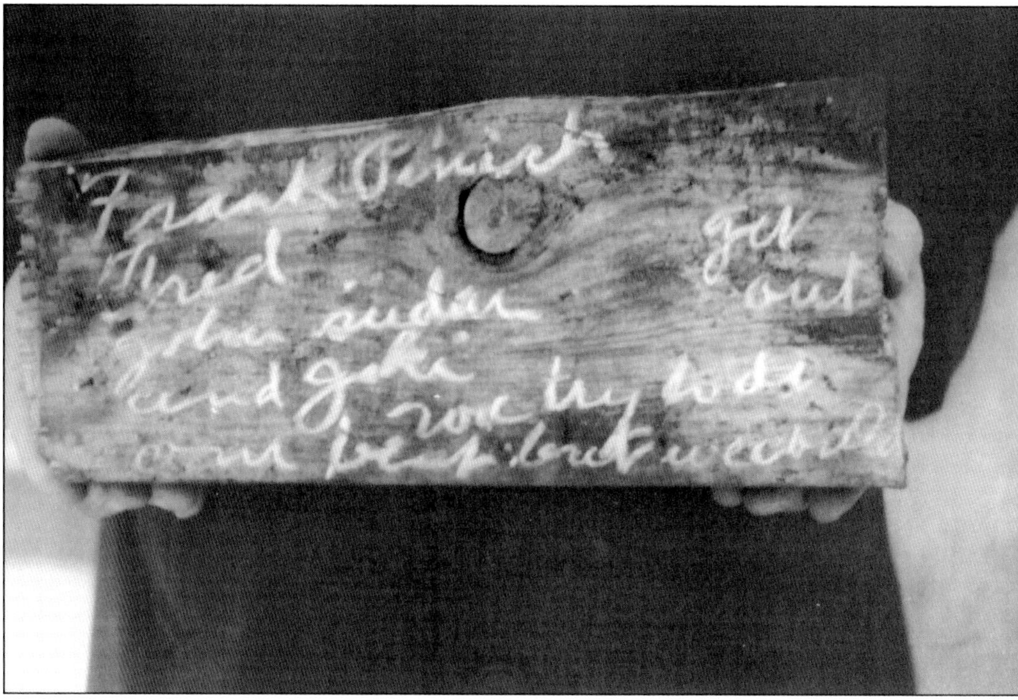

The two other notes left by Emil Anderson, Walter Joki, Frank Pajnich, Fred Rasborschek, and John Sudar are shown here. The top note, written by Frank Pajnich, Fred Rasborschek, John Sudar, and Walter Joki reads, "We try to do our best but we couldn't get out." The bottom note, written by Walter Joki and John Sudar reads, "Good bye wifes and daughters—we died an easy death—love from us both—Be good." (Above, CCHS; below, Montana Historical Society.)

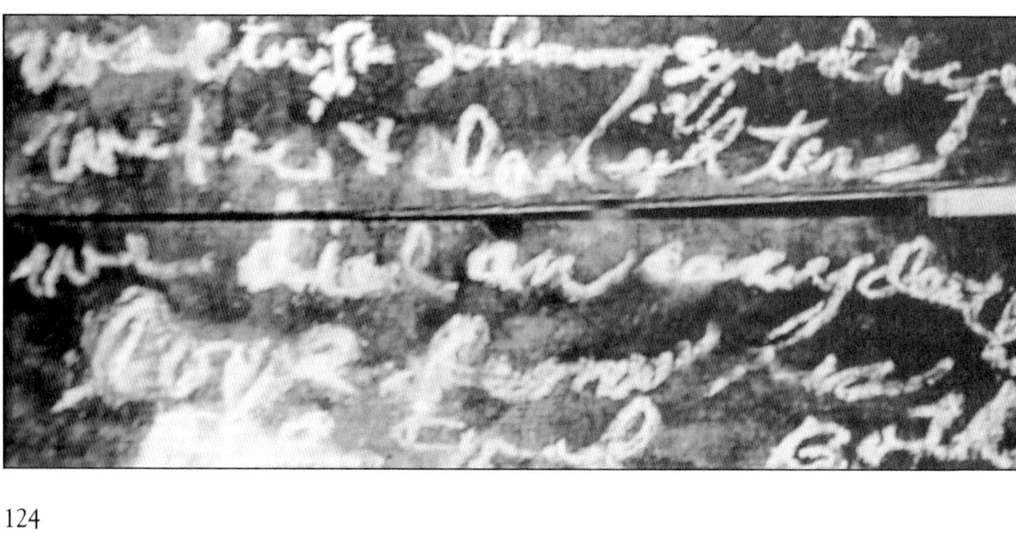

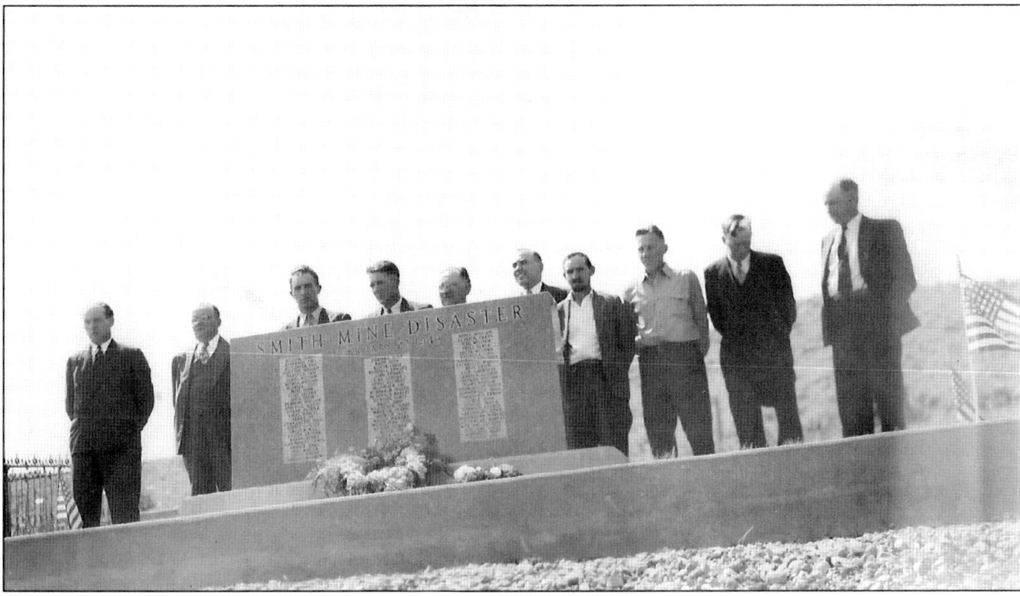

Monuments to the Smith Mine disaster victims were dedicated at the Bearcreek and Red Lodge Cemeteries on the second anniversary of the disaster. Members of the United Mine Workers of America local No. 858 (Bearcreek/Washoe), local No. 4457 (Red Lodge), and local No. 1005 (Brophy Coal Company Mine) purchased red granite memorials inscribed with each victim's name. The photograph above shows the Bearcreek Cemetery monument dedication. The dignitaries are, from left to right, Tony Boyle, unidentified, Joe Naglich, unidentified, Joe Bosone, unidentified, Earl Gregory, Alexander "Eckie" McDonald, Alexander Cameron, and unidentified. Below, Mary Wakenshaw visits the graves of her husband, Bud Wakenshaw, and father-in-law, Adam Wakenshaw, on the first anniversary of the disaster. Mary's father, Frank Sumicek, also died in the disaster. (Above, Mourich; below, Wakenshaw.)

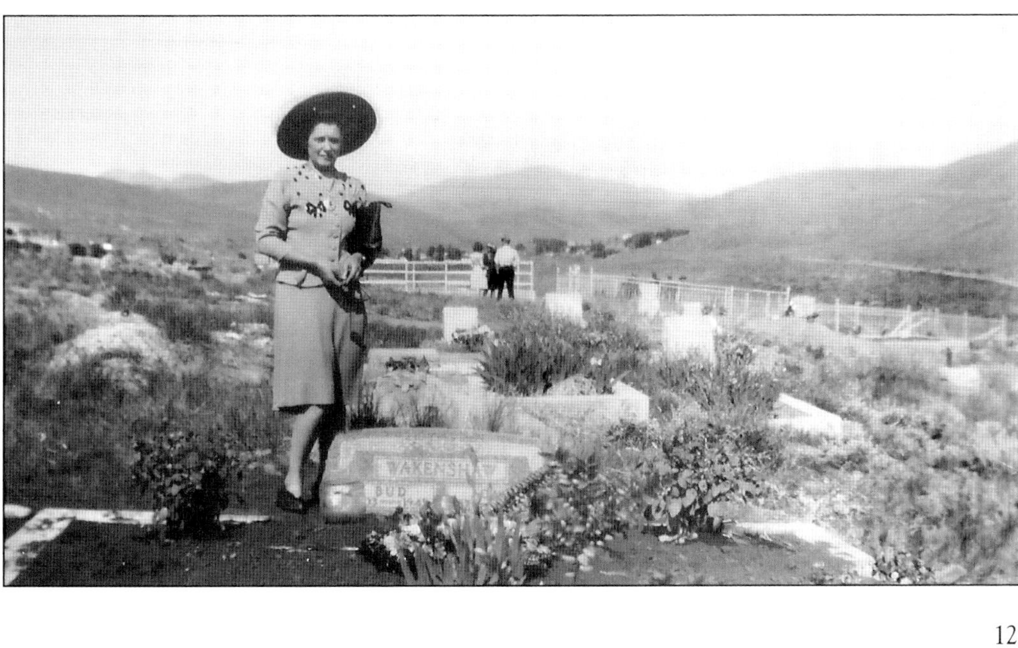

Bibliography

Much of the information in this book comes from the files of the Carbon County Historical Society. Additional and published sources include:

Anderson, Paul. *Definition and Evaluation of the Bear Creek Mining District, Carbon County, Montana.* Butte, MT: 1993.

Axline, Jon. "Bearcreek, Montana." *Montana: The Magazine of Western History*, Autumn 2004.

Axline, Jon. "Something of a Nuisance Value: The Montana, Wyoming & Southern Railroad, 1905–1953." *Montana: The Magazine of Western History*, Winter 1999.

Flaherty, Tom. "You Can Go Home Again." *The Carbon County News.* September 2, 2004.

Floerchinger, Dorothy. *To Speak of Love was not Enough: A Biography of Daniel and Panayiota McCorkle.* Conrad, MT: 1975.

Gemmill, Mel and Edward Fenlason. *Murder by the Mountains: Murder in Carbon County 1888–1929.* East Helena, MT: E & M Books, 2004.

Lewis, Thomas H. "Contributions to Paleontology by an Early Montana Physician." *Northwest Science*, Vol. 56, No. 1, 1982.

Murray, Ester. *William Romek Interview.* Billings, MT, 1976, SC1453, transcript, Montana Historical Society Archives, Helena, MT.

Robbins, Steve. *Voicing the Dead: A Poetic History of Early Day Carbon County, Montana.* Red Lodge, MT: Rocky Fork Press, Inc., 2008.

INDEX